D1179185

WORDS AND MUSIC

Philip at El Vino's in the early seventies

WORDS AND MUSIC

A selection from the criticism
and occasional pieces of

Philip Hope-Wallace

made by Jaqueline Hope-Wallace

Introduction by
C. V. WEDGWOOD O.M.

COLLINS
St James's Place, London
1981

William Collins Sons & Co Ltd
London · Glasgow · Sydney · Auckland
Toronto · Johannesburg

British Library CIP data
Hope, Wallace, Philip
Words and music.
I. Title
082   PR6058.06/

First published 1981
© Jaqueline Hope-Wallace 1981

ISBN 0 00 216309 8

Photoset in Bembo
Made and Printed in Great Britain by
William Collins Sons & Co Ltd Glasgow

This selection represents a very small part of my brother's writings on opera, theatre and other topics over more than forty years as a critic. It is inevitably a personal choice. I hope it may amuse and inform his friends and others interested in such matters, and remind them of past pleasures.

My thanks are due to the Editors of the *Guardian*, *The Times*, the *New Statesman*, *Opera*, *Punch*, the *Spectator* and *Vogue* for their ready permission to reprint many of the items included here, as also to Weidenfeld (Publishers) for permission to reprint an article from 'A Fanfare for Ernest Newman', and to the photographer, Chris Smith, for permission to reproduce as the frontispiece the photograph of Philip taken at El Vino's, Fleet Street, in the early nineteen seventies.

I am grateful also for the help I have received from Sylvia Loeb and C. V. Wedgwood.

J.H.W.

Contents

CONTENTS

DIVAS AND OTHER SINGERS

CONTENTS

9

CONTENTS

PLAYERS AND PERFORMANCES

CONTENTS

Introduction

'The best journalism is like the best talk, spontaneous, pithy and funny. The irresistible throwaway line is the work of craft. Philip Hope-Wallace was a master craftsman,' wrote John Rosselli, shortly after his death.

Philip was the best conversationalist of his generation. He was only seventeen when I first met him, but even then his spontaneous wit and deceptively casual style foreshadowed the brilliant talker whose seat at El Vino's was to be for so many years the centre of Fleet Street's liveliest conversation. On his sixtieth birthday a plaque was placed there in his honour.

Those who knew him could often hear in his writing the sound of his voice with its personal rhythms and emphases. Most of his reviews were written fast, dictated on the telephone fresh from the performance to be in time for next morning's paper. His voice is perhaps what his friends will remember longest – 'the incarnation of gregariousness and spontaneity,' as a fellow journalist described it. An invalid whose lonely hours had been solaced by his broadcasts wrote after his death, 'it was the kindness in his voice that first made him my hero.'

By nature gentle, he never intentionally wrote anything to wound or give offence. He loved and was interested in people, all kinds of people in all walks of life, and had the gift of falling naturally into the idiom of the company he was in.

He grew up in a home full of music which became his first love among the arts. But his love of drama and poetry was scarcely less.

Between school and Oxford he spent much time abroad – first he boarded in a Protestant pastor's household in Rouen – an experience which later provided him with material for some hilarious scenes of French provincial life. Here he perfected his French and slunk off to the local opera house with or without pastoral approval. Later he was with a German family where he haunted the nearest opera house – Cologne – and read voraciously. (He was one of the few English critics who really knew his Goethe.)

His taste was always personal and independent, in his undergraduate days defending Massenet and Gounod whom the highbrows at that time derided.

Coming down from Oxford in the Depression of the Thirties, he took what jobs he could get, selling gas cookers among other things. It was *The Times* which gave him his first opportunity, doing short notices mostly of Lieder recitals. But his knowledge of German led to his being sent to cover the world premiere of Hindemith's *Mathis der Maler* in Zurich and in the following year – 1939 – to report on the drama festival at Frankfurt. A copy of Gide's Diary in his luggage provoked suspicious looks from a Nazi customs officer but he got home safely. Within two weeks of his return Hitler invaded Poland.

Rejected for military service on account of his health – bad health was something that he fought stubbornly all his life – Philip worked throughout the war in the Air Ministry. In 1945 he joined Lady Rhondda's *Time and Tide* as dramatic critic, and from this beginning steadily expanded his scope and influence. He was drama and opera critic of the *Guardian* for over thirty years, but contributed also to most of the leading periodicals, the *Spectator*, the *New Statesman*, and of course *Opera*, of which he was on the board, and the *Gramophone*. He was also a popular broadcaster for many years on *Music Magazine*, the *Critics* and other programmes.

He never wrote the major book his friends hoped for – not for lack of time, for he had great concentration of purpose and would somehow have made the time had a book been in his mind. But he knew that he wrote best and most effectively when setting down or dictating an immediate impression fresh in his memory. His gift was for recording live performances, not for posthumous analytical treatment in the study.

His judgements were based on experience continually deepened and refreshed, and his enthusiasm was such that he could bring to his twentieth *Hamlet* or fortieth *Traviata* the same excitement as to his first. Moreover he was able to communicate the quality of his enjoyment to the reader.

He loved the English language, especially Shakespeare and the Bible, and had pages of both by heart. He also retained from childhood a great love – and a prodigious memory – for hymns. Cowper's 'Hark my soul, it is the Lord', was probably his favourite and he would repeat it to himself in times of stress. As he said himself, he needed the feeling of awe in his life. In his *Desert Island Discs* he asked for Verdi's *Requiem* 'to bring me to my knees'.

After the English language, he loved the French language almost as deeply, and Racine, I believe, second only to Shakespeare. The two dramatists could hardly be more different. Was it the sense of strong passions controlled by the discipline of form which moved him so deeply? It could have been. He wrote of a performance of 'that quintessential French classic' *Bérénice*, a tragedy of lovers parted by duty, as 'the eloquence of the heart's politeness strained to breaking point'.

Many of his phrases stay in my mind – how John Gielgud as Angelo 'held the nerve of the audience as tight as a violin string', or Robert Helpmann's King John was 'as clever as a sickly marmoset and as evil as a spider'. His descriptions of the voices of Gigli and Flagstad and many more the reader will find for himself in this book.

He was – without pedantry – deeply interested in words, their origins, their development, their use and misuse. In his last five years he contributed a discursive weekly article to the *Guardian* in which the vagaries of contemporary speech often played a part. A few of these out of a total of several hundred are included in the present collection.

'He grew old gracefully, unwillingly, and somehow incredibly,' wrote William Mann. It still seems incredible to some of us that he is dead. In his life, by the quality of his judgement and personality and the character of his critical writing over so many years, he undoubtedly exercised a deep unobstrusive influence on the taste of a whole generation. Under all the wit and the laughter, he had an absolute integrity and a serious – one could say – a moral purpose in his service to the arts he loved.

Veronica Wedgwood

TIMES AND PLACES

Boyhood in Rouen

Je veux revoir ma Normandie . . . car c'est elle qui m'a donné la vie . . . I never expected to sing that silly song again, having heard it once too often during my days as an Uncle at Radio Fécamp. But here I was, like wheezing Proust tooling along under the apple blossom, on a most Proustian excursion back to Rouen which forty-three years ago seemed to an English schoolboy a miniature Paris, an El Dorado where, the franc being right down at the time, one could live like a prince on English pocket money; go to the Théâtre des Arts for fourpence; see Massenet's heroines twice weekly asking themselves that uniquely French feminine question '*Est-ce ma faute que je suis belle?*'; big busty ladies from the Paris opera cross as two sticks after the train and a quick rehearsal.

Rouen was then – *pot de chambre de la Normandie* – a place of much rain, slithery cobbles, streets so narrow Daumier citizens could shake hands from house to house; the Rouen of Flaubert still, dominated by the three most beautiful Gothic churches, the Cathedral, nearby Saint Maclou; not far the Abbaye of Saint Ouen, where the pink chestnuts point towards the place Saint Hilaire where I was *en pension* in a household of extreme frugality. Next door lived a certain Mme Angamar who, we learned with awe, *se nourrissait uniquement de bananes!* We ate less copiously; Mme the *pasteur*'s wife preparing a soup of hot salt water and crusts openly designed to *couper les appétits* so that the *pensionnaires* should not eat ravenously. Aline, the maid of all work who wept so much and slept in a cupboard in the dining-room, used to get *one* day off a month, waddled to the pastry cook (the best in Europe), devoured *quinze gateaux à la crème* and returned to be sick in the outside privy. What use giving her more leisure, was the view taken.

The house had no bathroom (or perhaps the family slept in it to make room for another paying guest) so I used to go to a bath house on the island. Also on this islet in the curve of the Seine (views by Sisley, attendants by Balzac) there was, we learned with a shiver, a *maison close* but I was too young for that sort of thing. The island is all hideous blocks of flats now, though my feet guided me to the still standing little English church, now closed, where I used to be packed off to attend the *culte anglican*, where naughty finishing school girls under the surveillance of two uncomprehending French mistresses used to sing improper variants to 'Onward Christian Soldiers'. I once attended the funeral there of a British sailor fished from the bassin (drunk drowned). Next day in the *Gazette de Rouen*, not by my hand, appeared a notice in English of these obsequies ending 'all in all there were ten people present which, considering the weather, was not at all bad.'

Not tempted by the patisserie now, more interested in *brasserie menus touristiques*, I still felt drawn to the theatre: the old one, where Emma Bovary admired the tenor Mario, went with the bombs of 1944 (and half Saint Maclou too, how my heart pounded!). There was a ballet gala, with those French ballerinas coming on in a *pas de bourée*, not like angels on castors but like someone digging up concrete with a pneumatic drill. Canned, taped music descended in pitch till the Rouen audience demonstrated their pain, stuffing fingers in their ears and crying *Aie* and *Ouf*.

I love the Normans with their long Bayeux tapestry noses, shrewd eyes, which say, 'It is necessary to make one's self respected' or 'It is not I who eats an omelette like that: no compliments to the chef, take it back!' Into the Cathedral past the Gros-Horloge I went more by instinct than map reading. We weren't, from a Protestant household, encouraged to admire the Cathedral but I used to sneak off there to hear Marcel Dupré making the organ surge and by guile, got to the midnight mass at Christmas to hear the opera tenor belting out *Minuit, Chrétiens, c'est l'heure solennelle.*

'*Des harmonies superbes,*' said the *pasteur* torn between disapproval of Roman flummery and respect for French art: Adam, Saint-Saëns (nearby village), Massenet – how we revered them.

Oh how the skyline has been spoilt; how the camions thunder and scream towards the underpasses. A thing I never thought to see: traffic lights! And even one set which beckoned on the *piétons* when the coast was not clear. What do you think of that? Is it not necessary to make oneself respected, they cried, frowning at the offending robot? If looks could kill in Rouen, there'd be many a corpse.

I walked in a dream: here I used to buy exercise books of fantastic inexpensiveness, ruled sheets of dirty grey paper. But now it's Monoprix and Nouvelles Galleries and *'ville moderne active et créatice qui n'a rien renié de son passé . . .'* Oh come off it, dear Rouen, the wounds were terrible but is not the new building a greater evil? But there, everything changes: that tall, emaciated, round-shouldered schoolboy who had just psychosomaticked himself into and out of a German heart sanatorium and had fled to Rouen has become a portly old gent, too shy to take the newfangled buses. In my day it was the little clanging one-storey tram with its *remorque*. Cheapest ride was on the front platform, also the coldest. 'Absolute *défense* to speak to the *wattman*,' of course. They have floodlighting now: you don't have to await a full moon to see the façade of the Cathedral in its glory. Also those buses and traffic lights. *'Plus de tramvaey, Monsieur.'*

I remembered how Madame Proust had said that she would not like any son of hers to marry a girl who said 'tramvaey' for tramway and I recalled how for the pleasure of my fellow scholars I used to recite the Lord's Prayer in English and when I came to the bit about 'Give us this day . . .' the barbarous sound of the language used by these English *(qui ont brulé Sainte Jeanne, d'ailleurs)* used to have them in stitches. *Calvados, paté de coing . . .* The chief difference to me is I like my food better now. But that hot-water appetite killer had its virtues. Unforgettable, exotic, different city, I can't believe it's forty-three years since I first lost you my heart.

Guardian, May 1971

My Worst Christmas Rush

I have a horror of carrying parcels. So, at this time of year, when nearly everyone seems to be armed with some blunt or thorny instrument, I fear to be taken for a Scrooge. I think of a Christmas Eve in a provincial French town which inflicted on me a Christmas rush from which I have not recovered to this day, though it is long ago now. I was staying, a tall, shy schoolboy, as a paying guest in a family of parsimonious ways and professorial abilities. They were members of a fiercely organized religious minority. Not for them the glorious cathedral which stood protecting the old town: that was a place of trumpery allure for tourists, a place where at Christmas, if you please, the local tenor from the municipal opera was hired to bawl *Minuit, Chrétiens* at the midnight mass. I was in principle allowed to attend the English church, where I sat solitary with eight English schoolgirls from a finishing school, under the tutelage of a mademoiselle who could speak no English and thus did not realize that the words the girls sang to the tunes of *Ancient and Modern* were not those to which the music had originally been set. Occasionally, however, I would accompany my hosts to a tabernacle of wrath in the outer suburbs, reached by a tram which clanged and shrieked on its rails till your teeth ached with the noise. Nor was the musical part of the service at the far end of the journey a restorative.

Attached to this tabernacle was a hall, the scene at this season of a play, or rather a pageant of pious characters, though of course not even faintly idolatrous; far from sumptuous, it was yet somehow extraordinarily exacerbating to the nerves of all who took part in it. The scheme was simplicity itself, yet such is the French genius for mis-organization that the molehill became a mountain of calamity. The little stage was to represent a sort of medieval courtyard, not unlike a touring company's scenery for *Il Trovatore*;

22

a cardboard wall, some ivy and, dead-centre, a clock-face with hands movable from behind by a more or less unseen manipulator. This role was entrusted to my host, Monsieur le Professeur, and he performed it with an indecisiveness pitiable to see, twiddling the clock hands widdershins and back again, and striking on a gong anything inappropriate between two and thirteen strokes.

In a semi-circle, in white crêpe-de-chine frocks, twelve maidens of the congregation chosen for their powers of declamation stepped alternately forward at each given hour, crying *'je suis la troisième heure,'* or whatever it was, and following up this announcement with some edifying sophistry as fast as her breath would take her; after which she would step back towards – sometimes into – the wall and lift her voice with the others in a plaintive chant. In this ordeal of intonation to which a choir of French maidens was not really equal, they were supported by the pianism and off-stage presence of Mme A., a hirsute contralto of astonishing proportions and resentful disposition.

And my role? As a gauche and tongue-tied foreigner I could not of course contribute much. But I was accommodated in a final tableau together with a deaf mute and other handicapped persons who were to enter bearing banners inscribed with legends and form a climactic group above which the bellman, Monsieur le Professeur, would from the back of the clock wall launch over our heads some handfuls of slightly grimy 'snow', carefully hoarded from the year before. It was all so simple. Yet the bearing of that banner on which the words *Mon fils bénis l'Eternel* were inscribed in foot-high letters, was to be one of the most difficult and humbling burdens I ever shouldered.

It was my own fault. I had played truant from the final and desperate sortie of the entire professorial household who were carrying down to the hall by relays of tram rides, the dresses, wigs, snow, and sundry props. I had gone off on the quiet to gaze at the Christmas crèche in the rival establishment and to hear the tenor warming himself up for his evening's yell. But I was at the hall ahead of time and demanding my banner. It was nowhere to be found.

23

Of course, it had been left behind. I knew what was expected of me, and set off post haste to fetch it – twenty minutes there, twenty minutes back; I might just do it, and redeem myself. The journey out there was nothing, but the journey back – alas! I was a tall schoolboy, a head higher than most of the population, dressed as only an English schoolboy can be, and I was at an age when one readily imagines that people are staring at one. And of course they were. It must indeed have been a very strange and desperate figure who hailed the tram at the Avenue of the Victory and thrust his way on to the platform with a six-foot cardboard notice atop a broomstick which alternately occluded his scarlet face, tipped off the bonnet of the stout lady with the parcels, or poked out the eye of the conductor. Public resentment turned to mockery. I began to hear murmurs: 'Ah, how they complicate the life, these English,' or *'Mais qu'est ce qu'il foute là, ce type?'*

I could only hold on grimly and glare, switching my cardboard exhortation this way and that, so that not too many people seemed to be addressed by it at one time. But if I had any biblical thoughts during that ride they were a prayer for the powers of Elisha who called up bears to devour his mockers. A lifetime of chagrin was endured.

I could think how, at the other end of the line, already the maidenly Hours must be mincing and gabbling through their pieces and how soon the final tableau, without my banner, would be forming itself – without my banner which gave cover to the snow-throwing professor, my host. With pounding heart I hurtled up the street and into the hot hall.

It was too late to get on-stage. Cowering back, my banner now upside down an emblem of reproach and unpunctuality, I watched in hypnotized dismay the final stages of what, on any showing, must have been the most catastrophic Christmas pageant ever staged. Bunched together, as though for the massacre, the Hours stood in agonies of self-consciousness, clutching and rumpling their white dresses; some of the fast-withering ivy had become detached from the clock wall and had lassooed Hours Eight and

Nine about their crowns, and at some point it seems Mme A. had plunged her foot into the electric brazier which provided a historical touch to the scene, and had fused all the lights on the prompt side, and the clock-face showed not eleven, not twelve, but a quarter past six! And even as I watched the final tableau form, minus my crucial covering decor, I knew – as one knows in the split second before a bomb goes off – that worse was yet to come; for, unaware of my absence, Monsieur le Professeur here suddenly arose upon a chair behind the clock-tower – a myopic giraffe balancing a plate of artificial snow.

The audience saw him almost before he saw them; a yell of laughter, too long pent in, rent the air, and with it the wall, the clock, Monsieur le Professeur, and every vestige of order fell together in one almighty crash. Ah, futile struggles! Useless goodwill! Though it and I had failed, I now think the rush was worth it. But I am still shy of carrying parcels at Christmas.

BBC World Service, December 1952

Is there Tennis still for Tea?

Ah Wimbledon, ah, wilderness. They've let scrub grow all over the Common – like Ontario. Council houses where once the nightingale sang, and race-track bypasses scream through the silver birch woods once silent save for scampering rabbits. I expect it is all very nice and very much what it was in some ways, but I shall not escape nostalgia by trying to give hard facts about improvements. Wimbledon is more than a place, to me, more than a collection of SW postmarks. It is my childhood. Wimbledon was and is, like Soho, a feeling more than a place.

It was my birthplace; very useful too, especially if your last name is Wallace; it means that every hotel clerk from Totnes to Tokio books you correctly: Me understandee, Edgar Wallace. Wimbledon of the Lawn Tennis.

Where do I begin either in place or time? Do I really remember or only remember hearing about Swinburne kissing my sister in her pram and being beaten over the head for his pains by our Alsatian nanny (no, not a dog-nurse like the one in *Peter Pan* but a worthy body from Alsace)? Do I remember the suffragettes being ducked in the Rushmere? Do I remember being taken to 'hear the guns in Flanders' on the edge of the chalk-seam by the golf course? Or my mother saying to a friend 'Run, Edie, run – it's the sight of your life' and Edie running (in a hobble skirt) to see a flying machine take off by the windmill?

The Common was everything that was not 'common'. Ringed with huge mansions (where starchy servants sulked below stairs), the homes of the U-est rentiers imaginable, givers of mighty children's parties to which you went in Dormer's hired 'growler' with your party shoes in a bag embroidered with the word Slippers and suffered shyness and overeating before being fetched. Dances too: the newly learnt Charleston, and tangerine ices sent all the way from Harrods. From such imposing residences (nothing so common as houses) would issue forth on Sunday mornings family parties wearing holy looks and carrying prayer books, figurants from *The Magnificent Ambersons*. Haymaking for the children after Sunday school no doubt (where are the hayfields of Arthur Road now?) but Sunday morning was silent and sacred save for the bells, silent down the long quiet roads hung deeply over with laburnum trees. Overhung? What would those ultra-respectable residents think of today's film starlets bumping on horseback or the hungover, trousered, gin-swigging, car-washing mommas of a modern Sunday morning?

What an experiment in gracious upper-class living it was: what a memory of hot Sunday afternoons it leaves: like North Oxford, always Sunday afternoon, with the elders sleeping off the beef in deck-chairs under cedars. Of course there was another side to it: the shops for one thing, Miss Frost, the newsagent; Mr Burges, the fishmonger, in his boater; and then soon you came to the horse-trough at the top of the hill where the trace horse (an extra four legs hired at the bottom to help the coal carts make the gradient) used to slake his thirst, poor beast; he worked hard on that hill. All the way down, till the bombs came, the mansion principle obtained; gardens, fences redolent of privacy and creosote, iron railings, still the rentier paradise . . . well, almost right down to the station, after which . . .

Yes, the other side of the tracks as Americans say, the railway cutting where the expresses rocked and thundered their sucking sweep towards exotic places like Weybridge and Portsmouth, there began something called 'Lower Wimbledon' which was . . . well, not quite the same, where it was felt mysteriously that though the Town Hall was there and even the theatre (what a nice cosy provincial sense of occasion that provided during G and S Week), possibly accents might be sharper, life more competitive, livings more obviously worked for. Only just short of it but on the 'good' side was Worple Road where croquet balls could be heard striking one another and, if you were lifted up by an elder cousin and looked over privet hedges, you saw Mrs Lambert Chambers serving tremendous lobs to an opponent in a hairnet, petersham belt, and long flannel skirt. It was 'the tennis' then, until Mlle Lenglen with her legs and her bandeau brought Queen Mary and the marvelling crowds and they moved it all to the concrete monster at the base of Marryat Road. My father thought it overlarge: a passing phase, he said. But the 'tennis weeks' stirred the shops. Luncheon parties were being given in the big houses: salmon and soufflé were being eaten in shaded dining-rooms before the debenture seat holders, like archdukes to the St Petersburg opera, went to occupy their places on the centre court later in the afternoon.

Where are they now? How many of those mansions are homes any more? Converted into flats? Correspondence and missionary colleges? Hotels? I dare say very much more of that world survives than I imagine. No doubt life still centres round the churches, children's parties, and the return of pater-familias from the city around 5.30; walks, even picnics on the Common or the Woods,

27

games of Indians in the sandpits or Caesar's Camp, golf on more than one social level. And the wind coming fresh from the Sussex downs and blue spring vistas out to Coombe and Richmond. I dare say Big Ben is still visible from the allotments at the end of Lancaster Road. I haven't the heart to go and see.

Guardian, September 1962

Hitting the Highest Notes

Ah to be born again . . . out with the Quorn again? Not in my case, I am a coward when mounted. But I'd love to have the treble voice I had when I did nervously ride horseback, as Americans nervously have to add. It would be splendid to experience the thrill of actually hitting the highest note in 'Hark the Herald' on Christmas Day, which made the juices flow, and renewed hunger already dimmed by eating forbiddenly, and so the more sweetly, the glacé plums from your stocking left by Father Christmas (never 'Santa Claus' – would that rejection have been a side effect of the 1914 conflict?)

I did a lot of singing as a boy and when my voice broke I still hung on for a bit in the trebles. I remember nearly having a conniption or whatever it is called while holding the high A in Brahms's *A German Requiem* – we were at peace by then so it was all right, and I was at Charterhouse. Peace! But it wasn't good for my adult voice which sings with unlovely qualities. My father sang baritone, one of my sisters a well-trained soprano, mother played the piano and put in a note or two. We sang much: Mozart, Gilbert and Sullivan, hymns, Scots ballads, border ballads – Mary calling the cattle home across the sands of DEEee and never returning (sucked down). Oh how we cried about that. These things were more a reality to me than the carols about which I wish to speak,

28

some of them having tiresome titles, mock antique sounding (even if genuine). 'What is this goodly odour' or 'This is the night we go singing Noel' (O no we don't, said a rebellious inner voice). Even 'God rest you merry gentlemen', which was spoilt *ab initio* by the pedantry with which it was explained to you that you should take a breath before 'gentlemen' to show that you understood it wasn't the gentlemen who were merry, the latter word being an adverb for prosperously. Same as in German's *Merrie England*, you were told. (That inner voice spake up again – pooh!) But I genuinely loved a handful of carols: the Coventry Carol, whether 'good' music I wouldn't even now care to testify, also any carol where one got a solo to oneself as in 'Last night as I lay on my bed . . .' with some conclusion about 'a song for Christian boys to sing' (myself) and (*tutti*) Christian men to hear!

I doubt if these family carollings were an undiluted musical treat and indeed one could sometimes see as much from the looks of captive audiences: cook, French governess or strangers within our gates. But although there certainly was in the house a wind-up gramophone – which played things like Melba's 'Caro nome' and Harry Lauder's 'Stop your tickling Jock', it didn't seem to run to carols. On the other hand, just as German bands once did, quite proficient gangs of carol singers would themselves gather in the stilly night without and sing until bribed with charity and even refreshment to desist. I trust it still happens though mostly now these ceremonies seem to have dwindled (like Penny for the guy) to a handful of kids (we called them urchins or . . . get this! 'street arabs') raising the letter-box and doing one verse of 'We three Kings', ringing the bell before they'd even finished that, what's more. The Sally Army however comes round, heaven be thanked. It's a part of Christmas I like in St John's Wood when the band plays 'Stille Nacht, heilige Nacht' and all the sentimental Viennese refugees fling wide the windows of their splendid flats and hurl out handfuls of coin.

It occurs to me that they probably brought that particular tune with them. I don't remember hearing it in the 1920s, in this country at least. But I may be wrong. The Prince Consort may have imported it with the yule log. I may be making the subject of carols sound very parochial. Devolution and transposition needed. What about Welsh, Norman or Basque carols?

The truth is that in sixty-five Christmases, and on most other blessed or unblessed days, I have heard so much music, joined and enjoined so many 'Adeste Fideles' that I cannot clear-cut my memories – Gracie Fields made me cry in that one, though, at one point in the war. I had probably had a few in the knowledge that we shouldn't have a blitz that night: illogical in those days, some of us.

But one Christmas I remember well and the contrasts of music that it offered were striking and memorable for a lifetime. It was Rouen, capital of Normandy, in the 1920s.

I was staying and doing lessons with a Protestant pastor's frugal family. We went by tram to the *Temple* (not Mormon nor legal but Norman and Réformé). Brought up on King James's version and *Messiah*, to say nothing of the disembodied sightless lark-song of cherub English choristers, the sheer barbarity of this French *culte* dismayed me. Lines from St Luke which have never failed to make my eyes prick came out in French as quite awful (I don't want to offend anyone but for that matter the Roman Mass in French strikes me as displeasing compared to any Anglican equivalent and I can't understand how the countrymen of Racine can be doing with it). In those days it was only the Prods who used the vernacular and so I blamed them alone. The crisis came with the final hymn. Like fiends and fishwives brawling we joined in '*Mon beau sapin roi des forêts que j'aime ta verdure . . .*' (that last word got a special nasal snarl) and what do you think the tune was? We were near enough in date to the General Strike for me to feel a flush. It was of course the Labour Party anthem, 'The Red Flag' derived of course from 'Tannenbaum' of which this hymn was a translation and destined to serve also I believe as the state anthem of Maryland.

These things I learned later. But I thought how nice it would be to see how the Catholics were getting on in their marvellous cathedral where Marcel Dupré besat the organ console and great singers from the Opera lifted their voices, under cloche hats, in the case of the sopranos – this was before the Vatican forbade such frippery and secularism. Well, in point of fact, on the very eve of the unlovely service in the Temple I had most wickedly seduced the son of the house to steal out with me and hear the Catholic Messe de Minuit and, wonder of wonders, the best French tenor of the day went soaring through *'Minuit, Chrétiens, c'est l'heure solennelle . . .'* (great Caruso number, by the way). They say I haven't much faith but I near as damn grovelled into conversion to the other faith. It was rather reassuring the next year to get back to 'Good King W' and 'Away in a manger'. But I never seem to hear carols at all nowadays except on British Rail. Time to get to church again I see.

Spectator, January 1977

In the Groove

'We know your voice,' they say. A lordly person himself possessor of a lordly voice once said to me with refreshing candour: 'I heard you broadcast once: not an experience I'd care to repeat.' I was humble enough to sympathize with him on that occasion and even later when in an access of candour he incurred a £10 fine for sending a photo of his penis to a Scandinavian sex mag. Those were pre-Calcutta days – *à propos*, are chaps still hauled before the courts for doing on Hampstead Heath what is done twice nightly at Royalty (the theatre that 'replaced' Stoll's Opera House)? But I wander. This is about vox not cocks. I don't think people can do much to alter their native wood-notes wild. Frankly I have never tried. Efforts to modify the arrogant ring and half-crown accent always now strike me as demonstrably phoney. But one thing in extenuation: when I first broadcast there were for practical purposes no tape-recorders. Most people then had no inkling or clue as to what their own voices sounded like: you don't, you know, hear your own voice through your ears but through your front teeth. Till the tape-recorder, the shocking discovery of what others were hearing from you remained a secret perhaps to the grave (except for famous singers who made soup plate gramophone records or the illustrious who gabbled on to Edison Bell cylinders). With tape came red faces. The first time you hear a playback of yourself is like catching sight of your arse in a tailor's mirror. Is it *that* I show to the world?

Actors nearly went mad with self-consciousness. Haughty sopranos who alleged that getting bad notices only proved the critics' spite, wept and fell silent for weeks. To be sure, one may alter one's utterance and pitch (ask any choirboy) but like the eyes which change not at all in an ever ageing face, the timbre remains the same through life.

Now what I am wondering is: if I could have known my own voice as I know it today would I ever have embarked on my first job which was as an announcer in France in a set-up later known as Radio Normandie? *Sancta simplicitas*. I had some French and could read aloud and badly needed a job. What more? So, one winter dawn I found myself taking a bus from Le Havre to a place called Fécamp (where the fig tree that J.C. so bad-temperedly cursed was washed up and where Russian archdukes maintained mistresses in what were described locally as *coquets petits villas* such as only Osbert Lancaster could draw). The radio station did what in Reith's monopoly was illegal: it advertised: Symington's soups, Ballito pure silk stockings, Irish Hospital Sweepstake, plus a Children's Hour of ineffable embarrassment at home and abroad. Three English Uncles lived sulkily in a small part of one of the hotels which had grudgingly been kept open. There was a hut on the chalk cliff serving as an office and bombarded by (no doubt BBC) seagulls scolding and hanging in the air. The 'studio' sounded grander than it was. In a street near the Bénédictine distillery, it was a ramshackle affair put into operation as a toy for the *bonne amie* of the distillery's proprietor. This frank and boldly handsome lady with her fishwife ways crowded us all (one had to sit close round a single mike). She would muscle in on our Children's Hour with cries of '*C'est la tante Fanny qui vous envoie son plus gracieux souris.*' She was the only woman I have known at all well who powdered herself in warm weather with cooking vanilla: Children's Hour was like sharing an armchair with a blancmange.

One of the chores was . . . pirating is the word I suppose, at least copying news bulletins from other stations, since we had no means of gathering our own news except from the *Continental Daily Mail*. It was a period when Japanese warships sank or were sunk. I remember just guessing at the names, issuing Jabberwocky with a shrug. Worse, we had to play twenty-minute sermons by one Judge Rutherford, an American stupefying religious bore, Jehovah from Denver or somewhere. No microgrooves in those days, his records were as big as restaurant table tops, revolving ever slower than the dread divine drawl. We used to put 'em on and descend to the street for a quick one. On return the telephones from London and Denver too were going like the toothache: the Judge's needle had got stuck in one groove and he had been broadcasting the two words 'Christ Almighty' for ten minutes.

The pub wasn't bad though we had a good laugh about its motto: *La maison ne recule devant aucun sacrifice pour assurer le confort de ses clients.* But they did *reculer* before letting us use their loo if we didn't also take in a *consommation*, and there wasn't a loo in the studio. One had to trek to the nearby *vespasienne* or teapot where – the English not being popular tourists in summer – someone had written in letters as bold as those at Belshazzar's feast the lapidary doom *Merde pour les Anglais* and a finer hand had added the footnote *Et la pisse pour les Anglaises.*

I suppose the experience – which ended I need hardly say in summary sacking for being heard grousing crudely before a mike I thought dead but, being so, yet spake my mind to London – was very like what was endured by thousands of Britons far flung by war or Empire. At first when I arrived I was a catalyst to a little company bored to death with each other who found their tongues again with a stranger arrived from home (I had exactly the same thing happen in service messes when I went a-lecturing for the War Office). 'Tell us some yarns, Wally,' they begged. But they seemed to know them all. I had more success with imitations of the inimitable Fernandel, whom I had seen in Variety in Rouen in a sketch about a man from the Midi assailed with toothache on a visit north and finding himself in a *maison de passe* which he believes to be a dentist's waiting-room . . . and why were all these other people, in couples, jumping the queue and looking so happy about it? But you can't tell stories twice. Silences grew longer. I played bits of *Madam Butterfly* on the hotel piano. It was locked next day: *'pour ne pas l'abîmer,'* said the proprietor's wife and I dare say she was right. But the real damage I was doing was rather with my own speaking voice up the road. Where ignorance is bliss . . . but I suppose it wasn't too bad a start.

New Statesman, June 1973

It Was a Gas in Those Days

Chairmen looking me up in *Who's Who* to prepare that 'needs-no-introduction' bit gleefully pounce on my old connection with the Gas Light and Coke Co. Cue for a joke: 'Our lecturer tonight will not run out of gas.' These last weeks too while seeing headlines like 'Gasmen begin to bite' (worse, surely, than Barking Housewives) I have caught myself murmuring in the manner of Sir Andrew Aguecheek: 'I too was a gasman once.' It was in the hungry 1930s when unemployment was for real. I had just lost my job as Uncle Wally at Radio Normandie and was grateful to be taken on in Horseferry Road by the GL & CC. (Take-home pay, £2 18s. Bed-sit was 14s; okay.) Never did a firm pick such a dud. In Accounts, I floundered. No computer yet devised could foul up simple addition as I did. I recall with shame the look of real pity on the face of one 'Jacko' at the enormity of my mistakes. Next, it was Watson House over in Vauxhall, where the trade was learned. To one nurtured on nothing much louder than Wagner the din in this establishment made me literally ill (an ear opener for a cossetted graduate from Balliol). I had to flee. The gas ovens at Beckton were hardly less daunting: a vision of hell by Gustave Doré, an apocalypse to be glimpsed but ducked, even if one learned that, while the mountains travailed, one of the mice they brought forth was . . . the harmless domestic mothball! (I still feel a motherly affection for this *désuète* convenience.)

Much more fun was going out with the fitters, who were kindly disposed to a Little Lord Fauntleroy hopelessly at sea, with a double-barrel name to boot. They were not surly and at first watched their language though there were lots of happy simple jokes: gas fitments include such things as brass nipples and male inserts. Such jokes were rationed to the right company. Mr D. was sternly reprimanded for asking the canteen lady for 'suggestive' biscuits. There was a good deal of repressive discipline; the clerks, even in the dog days, were forbidden to shed their jackets. No smoking, no shirtsleeves. But paternalistic regard was shown even to the extent of a co-partnership mutual; a William Morrissy scheme which would no doubt be sneered at today. I don't remember surliness or disaffection or much shirking either.

As a lesson in sociology, taking out fire-places in bed-sits in Pimlico was an eye opener. The things one found behind them. What are those? I asked (upper middle-class male virgin). '*Those*, sonny . . .' yells of laughter and anecdotes. 'Half cremated some of them,' the story might end. I could only reciprocate with a limerick about the young man of Madrid, who went to an auction to bid, where the first thing they showed, was an ancient commode, and oh my, when they opened the lid. This was appreciated but fitters found it hard to scan. They were wordly wise. Yet I had seen the answers to a written exam they had to pass on entry; no idea of the name of the prime minister *or* the date of Waterloo, in paper after paper.

But I was soon back clerking, clockwatching. Mr F. read a novel in a drawer. Miss S. did her nails. Miss T. wore a cloche hat all day and popped out to excitement meetings with the Gas Council. Little chance for me to pop out, though sometimes one went to an inquest: the relatives of gas suicides would prefer to think it was an accident (watch that). 'A sensible man like him would *never* have put his head in the oven: it must have been a leak.' (But the cooker was serviced last week, madam.)

In those days all London east of Aldgate was gas. But rival electricity was encroaching. Gas was thought to sound unmodern. The word – did you know? – is the Dutch alliteration of the Greek word chaos, the vapours of the void in the underworld. We wanted to make gas sound modern and exciting. The GL & CC began to toy with the idea of advertising. A film was made (by Brunner and Lord Elton). I stood by, morning after morning, in a shabby studio where a rep actress sat day-long in a hip-bath, to show how much more comfy she'd be with an Ascot water heater. Presently a genius called Eric Fraser of the London Press Exchange invented 'Mr Therm burns to serve you'. An advertising, canvassing campaign to the smarties was put into effect.

Soon I was popping out all and every day. It was known as the

Blue Blood campaign, I regret to say, and there was a list of posh addresses where a Balliol voice at the front door might gain an entry for Mr Therm himself. I was not good at this, though not strikingly much worse than other members of the team. In those days front doors were mostly opened by a servant. 'Wait a minute, please.' Message taken within – 'a gentleman from the gas company'. This often produced smothered convulsions inside the house where it was suspected that I had come about the unpaid bill. Presently Major X would emerge, all effusiveness and conciliation

(I even got sherry once). The tone changed when it was found I had something to *sell*. Sometimes it was hostile from the start: 'The gentleman says if anyone else comes from the Gas he'll break every bone in their body.' Sometimes cordial for the wrong reason. 'I thought it was my married daughter. But she never comes to see me now.' Once through the day's list, I avoided the office till the last minute, went to the British Museum, and killed time, put my feet up behind the Pharaoh and read the NS.

I despised the job and when I got the push wasn't a bit surprised. Actually the push was towards Fleet Street. 'What's a man like you doing here anyway?' 'Only job I could get.' 'What do you want to do?' 'Write about the theatre.' 'Nothing like trying.' And this greatest of my benefactors picked up the phone and spoke to a famous newspaper. After a while he put his hand over the mouthpiece and said: 'Do you speak any German?' I nodded. I could. It was true. 'Well, they want a German play covered tonight: it's been sent over by these new Nazi people in Berlin. The editor is keen but their Mr Charles Morgan says, "Over his dead body".' With a heart going like a sledge-hammer I went and collected that pair of first-night tickets, first of many. We didn't say 'It's a gas' in those days. But it was, *nicht wahr?*

New Statesman, March 1973

Bomb Culture

Good reading,* even fascinating reading to some of us oldies: the strange paradoxical history of how a new hunger for culture and a mighty shift in patronage of the arts grew up under the bombs.

Robert Hewison can only have been a toddler when most of the

Under-Siege Literary London Life 1939–45, Robert Hewison (Weidenfeld & Nicholson).

phenomena recorded here were being produced but as in the case (say) of Hugh Thomas's work on the Spanish civil war, it is certain that very true history can be written, if there is the talent, without one's having been an eye witness.

I think it proper to stress that Mr Hewison 'gets it right' and pulling rank, I can add that I vouch for it, having been there, very much so, myself: one of the swelling band of people who felt that if one was going to be killed the importance of hearing Beethoven (that dreadful German) was paramount: that not merely as a way of passing long hours of night firewatching or evenings in the blackout, Tolstoy's great novel *must* be read before one's extinction. Drink was not enough (anyhow one sometimes couldn't get any). One wanted Schubert and Schuman at midday in a denuded, icy National Gallery with Myra Hess presiding, she who, far from running away from the war (no names please), actually came back from safe America to give weary London its ration of really good music cheap.

Also ENSA wasn't enough. CEMA (which turned into what we call now the Arts Council) came into existence. Perhaps those initials don't mean much any more. I don't suppose Mr Hewison remembers as I do that while in tobacconists one saw 'No Cigs', in butchers 'no offal', in bookshops, one saw 'No *War and Peace*'. So we started in on Trollope and queued up for the Griller quartet, all four in RAF blue.

It was only to be expected, I suppose. The outbreak of hostilities, 'the balloon going up' as we said, found us art-starved. No bands even, let alone Shakespeare.

Wolfit (curiously omitted here) tried to remedy that. 'Much ado' at lunch time – no television, but a remarkable series of fine BBC radio drama for the long black evening.

Somehow the harder it was to get a bit of culture written or performed, the more we strove to do it. It was almost as if the argument used by pay-for-museum entries pundits had something in it. The more inaccessible, the more desired.

One need not make a catalogue of all the persons and facets of this revolution on which Mr Hewison touches. It might be said by

some people that he gives unwittingly an impression that the
revolution in patronage and creativity was wider and stronger than
it really was; it was the contrast to the drab picture as a whole that
was so striking. He goes to all the right sources, Connolly,
Waugh's *Put out More Flags*, and Elizabeth Bowen's *The Heat of the
Day*, Willie Whitebait (Stonier) in *Shaving through the Blitz*,
Orwell, Koestler, giving us an uncommonly vivid recall.

Guardian, 1977

Aurora Awakens: Reopening of Royal Opera House after the War

The reopening of Covent Garden was a grand occasion – with
great implications. So let us not bother how the Cabinet Ministers
looked in their exiguous finery, nor count the 'diamond tararas'
nor report what the big-pots bawled at each other in the intervals.
The important things were that the Sadler's Wells Ballet had
brought a new production of Tchaikovsky's most exacting ballet
to the august stage of the Royal Opera House and that the
beautiful old theatre, one of the loveliest in Europe, had awakened
from its long bad dream as a haunt of jitterbugging GIs and,
resplendent with new *carmine* candle-shades, was rededicating itself
to the muses. *The Sleeping Beauty* was a symbolic choice. Immortal
house – it is more than a decade since we heard Beecham at the end
of a Wagner season pronounce its impending demolition and since
then how many bombs have missed it! Who could have been
unmoved, last week, to see the lights fade, to hear the orchestra pit
once again throb with trembling strings and plangent oboe, and
watch the vast wall of faded plush curtain twitch, divide, and
swoop suddenly back, to reveal the enchanted groves of some

40

legendary Versailles? Even if Oliver Messel's sets had less exquisitely caught the spirit of Perrault, it would have been a sequence from a fairy tale.

Time and Tide, March 1946

Paris

Paris, said Gertrude Stein who devoted a book to the subject, is Paris is. Few better definitions exist, though not for lack of trying. But where shall we turn? To Villon and *vieux Paris*, to sigh over bad Baron Haussmann's demolitions with the Goncourts, to drive in Zola's cab or shuffle knee-deep in adjectives with Marcel Proust through the blacked-out boulevards of 1917? Every pen, every pencil and brush has had a go. Paris, her soul, her face, her heart – indeed nearly all regions of her person have been catalogued. And still she is Paris-paradox, a sphinx.

She? Paradox again. Paris is masculine; incontestably it is *Mon Paris* (wherever we were born) and yet at this very instant one of those uniquely Parisian consort of trumpets, known as a *quin-quin* and good for outdoor dancings, strikes up a one-step: *Paris, C'est une blond-e* tempering this in the next line, a semi-tone higher, *Paris, C'est tout le mond-e* . . . And to clinch it a Negro lady, dressed in bananas, brings us all to our feet with a snatch of Vigny rephrased, *J'ai deux amours: mon pays . . . et Paris.*

That is the crux of it. We all hold in our hearts an image of Paris, be it only a paper-weight model of the Trocadéro. Other cities sometimes pat themselves on the back. Dear old London, New York's a wunnaful town or (more doubtfully, and only on Saturday nights) Glasgow belongs to me. But no city, not even lachrymose Vienna, with its wine and women, has so long, so loud, so lovingly, so – above all – successfully, hymned itself and exploited its own reputation. And what more natural? If Paris be a woman, is not the mark of the Parisienne to make the best of oneself, even if no beauty by natural right?

So the swarming 'collection of villages' became, at Haussmann's behest, the capital of capitals; city of this and that, city of love, of light, of gastronomy, pornography, the *haute couture*, the elegance, the leisure, the existentialism, *le jazz hot, le tourisme* (with Eastbourne prep school boys and a frozen begum with a fur coat over her sari atop the Eiffel Tower); *le highlife, le nightlife,* and how much else? Is not Paris also the whore of Babylon, the martyr (bombarded by the boche Big Bertha), the saint saved by her taxicabs, liberated by her citizens, city of barricades, of *s'en foutisme* in the bus queue and of the complacent relaxation in the hour of the apéritif when half Paris sits to watch the other half go by?

Paris at dusk is a theatre, with a backdrop of twinkling lights, a stage where Charpentier's Louise and her lover bawl salutations to the queen of Free Love, female emancipation and *art nouveau: Paris, protège tes enfants!* At dawn Paris is the puddles and cold sky of a film by Carné; in March an Utrillo; a shimmering Renoir in July – that is best.

A million leaves catch the pale sun; everything needs a coat of paint, but roundabouts are turning in unexpected places; the air vibrates with remorseless honking, canary song and the shallow quake of the métro puffing its unique aroma through the grills in the interminable Boulevard Raspail. Over the roofs a *tricolore*, surely the painter's favourite flag, sketches a Manet brush stroke on an opaque sky. Look closer. Between the chimney pots there is a small, sooty garden with rabbits (is it?) or canaries which the proud *locataire* of the twelfth floor, in peignoir and curlers, is nourishing from an old Vichy bottle. Her husband steps out to dry the lettuce in a wire basket. It will be warm today. You can hear them make the statement, banal, sensible, yet said with just expression.

Perhaps the heart of Paris is up there on that roof? The outward show is a capital city, Paris *en fête*, Paris *fleuri*, possibly, indeed often, Paris *en grève*. But hidden away, like beavers toiling, is a race of little connoisseurs. In tiny flats under the mansard roof, innate taste and tireless fingers are making handbags which are a little better, smarter than handbags made elsewhere. Deep in kitchens, it is not considered too much trouble to put the purée once more through an even finer sieve. Yet it is not exactly love which orders life. Kennelled in kiosks, or knitting their widowhood away in cupboards under staircases, lives a breed of harpy quick to short-change you or rail at those who fail to contribute to the saucer for the service. If, on one side, nothing is too much trouble, on the other, *les affaires sont les affaires*.

But we stumble here on Paris-paradox once more. Who shall explain (say) the phenomenon of the late Christian Bérard, or Mistinguett, or *Faust* at the Opéra, other than by saying that the phenomenon is Parisian? And who shall analyse the quickness (combined with, and paid for by, a certain shallowness) of Parisian taste? Who shall pronounce upon the importance of appetite in Paris, the passion for the detail and the carelessness about the whole? And what is the secret of Paris which gives its citizens a gift not found elsewhere – the gift of managing everything, even the heart, the palate and the mind, with *light* sensuousness? The hall mark of Parisian elegance is just that – in all her arts – a light sensuousness.

Elegance? But what about those *Abatjours-Fantaisie*, those unspeakable illuminations in the great boulevard palace cafés? What, if it comes to that, about the *armoire*, nearly as big as Garnier's Opéra, which shuts light and air from the bedroom otherwise so well supplied with *confort* and *bon sens*, with wide bed and *bidet*?

Certainly the light-fittings are a blind spot in *la ville lumière*. But watch the way this *maître d'hôtel* manages the salad dressing; watch how that girl, no beauty to be sure, pins, with an artist's unerring aim, the flower she has bought where it and she together will show to all advantage.

Superficial! Insincere! Such flippancy! Such cynicism! Surely these will call down a judgement? Paris is finished; is old hat; is no more the mother of the arts. Envious and disapproving, outwardly, how we adore you in our secret hearts, Paris, even if your temper is poor before lunch. So this is your birthday? We will not ask your age; even if you are no longer in what Maupassant would call your *première fraîcheur* – with so much wit, such fine eyes, such good corsets and above all so excellent an appetite, you are ageless and much loved. *Bonne fête!*

Vogue, July 1951

Coronation Night

The open-air dancing on the Festival Hall promenade was like a true sampling of the whole day: i.e., it started glum and chilly and ended with deafening cheers, flushed faces, and milling crowds.

The waiting crowds looked youthful, with fewer women than in the route-lining crowds, one thought, where they must have outnumbered men by three to one. Always where there is to be dancing, however, gangs of youths laughing with self-conscious raucousness and combing their hair in the wind are to be seen on their own. The girls in nylon mackintoshes were inclined to sit saving their feet during this wait for what, by the look of the asphalt ballroom floor, was going to be heavy going on the shoes in any case. They too kept in groups.

Presently the lights began to come on, and still unbelievably no rain fell, and then, slowly, cheered to the echo like members of the orchestra at the last Prom concert, the bandsmen and the Lord of the Revels in person. That was better, we all either said or looked. And under difficulties, with every handicap to overcome, the party shyly started, swirled, went into full jive, came to a climax, and then, perhaps cheering itself as much as anything or anyone, broke into those rare, loud, spontaneous, half-mocking, half-congratulating bellows which it can take an English crowd so long to unleash. The effect in the cold was heart-warming. The scene was perhaps less decorous or charming than the equivalent Parisian efforts for the Fourteenth of July, but it was jolly enough, and as one struggled away, looking backwards at the glittering terrace and the strange, diaphanous shape of the Festival Hall (it may look like a hangar but it also looks pleasantly light), thousands of people could be seen patiently squeezing themselves single-file along Hungerford footbridge towards the movement, the clapping, and the queer, overblown, tooting noises which dance bands make from a distance.

And not a soul in that surging mass need have felt that there was any danger of being crushed to death. Surely this is the gentlest mob in history. One word: ''S'no good: you'll have to go back a bit,' from a policeman who looks not a day over sixteen, and three thousand people make genuine efforts to comply.

Guardian, June 1953

Rio de Janiero

Not everyone would agree that the view from Sugar Loaf is even the finest in Rio. Later, on the road winding up to the hill station of Petropolis where the Brazilian Emperors Pedro I and Pedro II held their mid-Victorian courts, I was to see views arguably more spectacular; and in Rio itself, the vantage point of the Corcovado under the giant concrete Christ of 1922 'affords a panorama' (as they say) wider and yet more giddy. But one is as high there as in an aeroplane, higher than some which indeed purr between you and the aerodrome.

On Sugar Loaf you are stuck with The View, as our grandparents understood it. Or rather, perhaps, as the eighteenth century understood it. By one of those quirks of thought I had found the names *Paul et Virginie* running in my head ever since I had set foot in Brazil. Later I was to find that these Rousseauesque lovers – as if I had indeed invoked them – had given their name to a wonderful waterfall and gulf in the forest of Tijuca. Anyone who ever saw an illustrated copy of Bernardin de Saint-Pierre's famous romance will know – although it is about Mauritius – the atmospheric 'presence' of Rio. It is this above all that you enjoy as you gaze from the top of Sugar Loaf, at a distance which exactly lends enchantment without rendering remote and inhuman the prospect of the Works of Man and Nature.

The former include, one must regretfully admit, the skyscraper cliff of hotels at Copacabana, its beach of demerara-sugar sand, its thumping breakers and new look. Gone, all but a few, are the former little Scots baronial or Gothic summer palaces of the ultra-rich. Since the twenties, Copacabana has become the Nice or Blackpool of Brazil. Thousands surf bathe, in costumes of a notable decorum. (Some fearless Nordic maids in bikinis I saw hustled away; and during the PEN congress, a famous literary personage was forcibly restrained from undressing on this famous beach.)

From Sugar Loaf you can see with pitiful clearness too the shanty towns which cling to the hill sides. Here was the home of that Black Orpheus of the film, here those ragamuffin shoeless bootblacks have their homes. Rich beyond calculating, Brazil has her poor, her sore-baring beggars too. Swivelling, one sees the indentations of the bay, the old part of the town, the bootbox skyscrapers marching backwards down the Rio Branco Avenue, the aerodrome which the American Army band's plane missed and plunged with all hands and instruments into the sea, the port, and, beyond, still miles and miles of houses. Then, fantastic in the sharpness of their fairy story, crenellation, and their height, stand the mountains.

At this moment of recent memory, I think this view the most lovely I have seen, though these things are like love affairs. The latest is apt to knock another out. Can it really be more wonderful than the view from the top of the Mark Hopkins Hotel in San Francisco – that bridge, that rainbow, those far-flung lights of Oakland stretching to the horizon? Can it compare with the astounding view from the Peak above Hong Kong? To this it is similar, in its morning haze of mauve and golden island prospects, its evening carpet of twinkling lights. Moreover, the Peak is approached curiously by a Chinese tram which runs uphill at an angle of sixty degrees.

Two thousand feet below Sugar Loaf the waves sucked in and out on the Pria Vermelha (Red Beach) and palms threw thin shadows, as indeed we did ourselves as the car swung out over the sheer rock's edge on the descent. The little shadow chased over the tree-filled chasm and the occupants, feeling a winter chill perhaps unknown to me, slammed up the cabin windows and held shawls and pullovers to their breasts or sealed their popping ears. (The drop is rapid.)

There, I thought, looking at the toy beach below, I'll bathe. And so I did, in cellular pants, none gain-saying me, though a dog barked and a few fellow bathers stared (but they were nutbrown; I was goose-flesh pink). The water was perfect; Devon in August. I got smeared with tar but was filled with bliss, caught an open tram at its figure-of-eight turn-round (the No. 4), and was drawn, fanned by the breeze and scents of Rio, through the congested streets and markets, on a sofa of hard wood, grinding as only a tramcar can through the very heart of the town. I'm told the tramcar's days are numbered. Sad! Second only to a cablecar, this is the way to travel. It took an hour and cost a single filthy five-cruciero note, folded lengthways – 2½d.

Guardian, September 1960

The Lascaux Caves

Lascaux is saved and itself again, the 25,000-year-old pictures glowing with their pristine colour. I know because I have just been there. These old eyes have seen the marvel. I don't know whether to say Nunc dimittis or Eureka (no, not that in truth). Perhaps thank you for a privilege now practically unique since the Lascaux cave is probably barred to the average tourist for ever. I am feeling like the pleiad sonnet about Ulysses who had made a long voyage, though this was a short one, more perhaps like Aladdin or Prince Florimond in *The Sleeping Beauty*. Getting to see that tantalizing wonder of the world, now again in purdah, something which millions luckier than I had seen but which I feared I had left too late, was about the best present I have ever been given.

The story is one you know as well as Aladdin: in 1940 three boys saw their dog suddenly disappear. Scrambling through the bush they disturbed the serene sanctity of a grotto which had lain inviolate since before the beginning of history: how the cave lay open for eight years, was then enthusiastically exploited and by 1951 was the Mecca of every tourist with an archaeological bent from every land on earth: how their warmth and breath in hundreds made the colours begin to fade and the walls to grow fungus. Then came the Draconian decision: better lose the tourists than lose the pictures, this marvellous legacy, which if lost would lose the tourists anyway. With what agony, for the practical French, the decision was made to shut the cave and turn the tourists away.

Fermé; no more bods. So why little me?

At most, one heard, a handful, once in a while. Imagine then the shout of excitement when a tiny group of us in a minibus learned that by special dispensation etc. the cave would be opened. '*Un rêve se réalise,*' I said, showing off. A highly educated lady from an even posher paper said that she too had always dreamed, but despaired, of getting in, and she wasn't as young as she had been.

There's many a slip etc. At Montignac we heard the worst: that at most two thirds of our party had a chance of getting, so to say, seats in the lifeboat. 'Bash on,' we said, thinking they might relent. But faces grew glummer. Heads on the site were strongly shaken. Six at most. 'Do not insist, Monsieur.' Insistence was tried and failed. Unselfishness vied with longing – and lost. It was a Henry James story under the thundery marble sky. Finally we drew lots. A long straw meant: in. A short one: stay out. I got a long. Educated lady got a short. I knew she wouldn't blubber, as she was of the suffragette generation. 'Perfectly fair,' she shouted, gulping down a lifelong disappointment, and we males began to feel a bit worse than Judas Iscariot. I shuffled my feet and thought of that other unsung Edith Evans, children's nurse, who stepped out of a Titanic lifeboat to cede her place. Suddenly in this Henry James situation, the heavy afternoon silence was rent by a searing telephone call. A race back to the hut: Paris, appealed to at the last moment, had relented: all might enter.

The air of Périgord seemed lighter. We stepped to the bronze door, then stood in Stygian black for five minutes so that our eyes accustomed to the dark needed only the minimum of electricity to see. Next, feet into the formaldehyde bath. Prince Charles could have been invited, it seems, with his tutor. But, I was told, 'question de protocole'. They didn't like to ask a future monarch to thus demean himself. As for myself, I'd have stood up to the waist in that refreshing fluid, had I been asked.

We went forward and I did not know what size to expect. Like the Sistine Chapel perhaps, big vault, far away, famous designs? It was much more like arriving at a Sussex coaching inn, blundering down passages of uneven levels ('Mind the step, sir'). Soon, quite close above you, at arms' reach, those amazing bulls and rhinos: marvels I am not equipped to speak of. Only I will say no guide more lovingly described them. The rather intransigent young man, about thirty-five, who had barred our way, became the infatuated proprietor to whom no question was worthless. 'Conservateur', he seemed to own the place.

I mentioned this later that night at dinner with the professor of pre-history, Dr Sarradet, as a neighbour. I heard a lot more. 'It was I who had to decide to shut the cave,' he said, implying that touristically he might be the most unpopular man in France. And who was that young chap, the conservateur, I asked. But he was one of the three little boys that made the initial discovery and you didn't know it? I laid aside a truffle and like Winnie in *Happy Days* murmured 'Great mercies, great mercies.' How comes luck like that?

Guardian, June 1969

Skegness Unvisited

Unknown, mysterious Skegness calls to me. The Call is clearly connected with a growing disenchantment with the exotic. I used to crave lagoons, royal palms, alps, nights in the gardens of Spain. I holidayed in a hotel which boasted 'the most suggestive terrace in Italy'. I don't want to go back there. But all too long, I see, I have travelled and holidayed for self-aggrandisement, just in order to send home boastful postcards from Rio de Janeiro or even Lesbos, where I made landfall almost entirely for the post-mark value. It is in this anti-romantic mood that I feel the pull of Skegness.

Or is it something more deeply imbedded in my mind? There can have been no part of my conscious life when I did not hold a mental picture of that Old Salt bounding along the sands. 'Skegness ... is so bracing': first and best line in the whole litany of travel literature. Braced is what I now want above all to be. The old idea of a holiday as a 'change of air' appeals every year more strongly. Alpine air can fortify, it is true, but heights make my pulses race. Lethargy succeeds sunbathing. But to be braced in Lincolnshire seems most desirable.

I should want to go by train if possible, with golf clubs, for surely in this of all counties there must be links, and some quite heavy luggage in the van. I should eschew a hotel and prefer a boarding-house, or 'rooms' in a villa with some highly improbable name such as 'Haslemere', where the landlady spent her honeymoon. It would be traditionally a 'stone's throw from' or 'in easy reach of' the sea, but not quite on it, so that at night, though you could hear the tide sucking the pebbles, in Dylan's phrase 'singing in its chains', you would be spared that irritating, rather than bracing, nocturnal symphony of the acorns at the ends of blind-cords tapping the panes in the breeze.

The beds are hard but healthy, with many blankets (such a relief after French *duvet* or German bolster). The food is copious but plain: just as well, because enormous appetites are born of the bracingness. At lunch there will be hot apple pie with cloves and gamboge custard. For our morning bathe from the dunes we are given a packet of bloater-paste sandwiches which go excellently with the sand, which is there, and stave off premature pangs of hunger. The water, like the air, is bracing in the extreme. Bathing is a venture, a triumph, a violent operation to keep warm. The pleasure of resuming dry clothes can be breathless. I see myself under a cloud-covered but light, high heaven, plying a shrimping net at dawn, or heaving on a slow swell, with a line out, 200 yards from shore. The shrimps we will be allowed for tea, the 'fish', if caught, only grudgingly. Mrs Blank the landlady has strict ideas. 'No washing to be done in this bathroom, by order' proclaims a notice, and the outward and visible drying of bathing costumes, which despite the keen, uplifting breezes dry slowly, is much frowned on.

Before tea we putt, on verdant turf. After tea we walk into the gloaming and count the winks from a lighthouse. There is good walking either on shore or on the low cliffs, once you have skirted the tamarisks (bent westward by the prevailing winds) and some outcroppings of nettle and bramble. It is, as they say, unspoilt, so very close to where we lodge. Yet in the other direction – so I fancy – one will come on a kiosk where no doubt sometimes a band strikes up selections from *The Arcadians*, and on the pier, frivolity ensures some seaside delights, views of the parade in 1911, postcards depicting bottles of Guinness and peppermints which the famous air seems to render twice as powerful as elsewhere.

It is not romantic, not picturesque, in no wise quaint or even cosy. But it is clean, free, clear dry, mildly sunny, and I cannot wait to make my first meeting with it – Skegness my goal.

1977

Ageing in the Wood

Where does the heart of St John's Wood beat? Is it in the High Street where village shops still defy the supermarket age with windows full of corsets and boiled sweets? Or is it in Hamilton Terrace to the west where the rich publishers and richer pop pianists look down – but only literally of course – on the Vale named after the Battle of Maida (we are very historically minded in 'The Wood', as you must call it). But Hamilton Terrace is too much like residential London, a cousin of Wimpole's or Gloucester's, very much *coté* St Marylebone. Politically we are all that in The Wood, and at election times one sees posters saying 'End Tory Misrule in St Marylebone'; but we don't.

I find the true heart much further east, by Ordnance Hill (say) or down the lovely curve of Acacia Road where the new lamps are sprouting, alas, but which on a spring day, with almonds in blossom against a blue eggshell sky, is a sight for sore urban eyes. Specifically, I would locate the heart of The Wood in Woronzow Road, especially under lying snow when you might almost fancy yourself in Pushkin's St Petersburg, especially if you can hear a distant bugle call and the stamping and snorting from the RHA barracks where the most expensively stabled horses in the world still haven't yielded their huge parade ground to a million pound block of 'luxeree' flats. Oh, the flats are going up everywhere, ruining all prospects. But here in the Woronzow world you can still see the original dream, the airy suburb of stucco and tree, the little villas and their discreet gardens, with perhaps a concealed or covered passage to the gate in the high wall; architecture with just the faint Italianate touch which makes you think of Rastrelli palaces by the Neva. These charming villas are very much like the ones where people are 'leading lives of quiet desperation' but they have an air which slightly differentiates them from the kind of villa where 'Mrs James of Sutton' visited the Pooters. Something *what?* A little bit racy, a little *coquet*.

Since the time when a large part of St John's Forest was sold to the Eyre Family – from the time, say, when Marylebone Park was converted into Regent's Park and Sir Edwin Landseer pioneered northward – a certain piquant reputation for 'fastness' (which means, like so many English words the very reverse, here, 'naughtiness') has attached itself to the district. Here George Eliot lived in such respectable sin that even the strictest felt themselves permitted to accept her invitations. But there were less serious minded unmarried women, too. Hear Bulwer Lytton in a positive orgy of meiosis: 'And thus I fled to the sanctuary of the Grove of the Evangelist where Poetry and Music environed Philosophy and even served to glorify (and excuse) Phryne at her ivied lattice-window.' One recalls, too, the father of one of Evelyn Waugh's heroes who, living here, hated the then new buildings and gleefully heard the butler's report of 'tarts in the flats'.

Of course that is all long ago. But there was once a reason for those discreet garden gates. Fair, and thought to be frail, were such ladies as Mary Moders, Lydia Rose, and the Miss Howard whom Louis Napoleon admired. But if it is name dropping we need, The Wood has always been much more than a home for hetaeras; the arts were honoured, too! Poetry with poor Thomas Hood who died so quickly; science with T. H. Huxley, Bradlaugh, and Mme Blavatsky at one end of the spectrum of respectability and Mrs Henry Wood at the other. Romney, Haydon, Tissot, Alma-Tadema, yes and even Phil May: the list of painters and illustrators is long. Theatrical folk then, as now, abound ('so handy for the theatre, darling'), and amid the silence of the early morning, the birdsong and faint rattle of milk floats, you may sometimes hear a current Valkyrie getting up steam. The great Tietjens lifted up her noble voice in that self same studio in the garden of a house since owned by Bernard Miles where Flagstad helped get the Mermaid Theatre venture off to a good start with a 'Dido' which I could hear clearly by opening my bathroom window at the back of the house. The Wood has certainly had its history; its eccentrics, too. Not for nothing, one feels, was Joanna Southcott of the Box buried here; or did the scoundrel Maundy Gregory live, characteristically, in someone else's house and on her money.

Are today's denizens less colourful? Who shall say. Certainly they are friendly. There is quite a strong community or clique feeling among long-established residents. But it is changing. I feel that Swiss Cottage, with its floating, often foreign-speaking population, is pressing down on us from the heights. The late Richard Capel wrote once of 'St John's Wood polyglottery'. One has always heard a lot of furrin' talk. There are many practising Jews (who like to be near the synagogue) and this has the excellent result that delicatessen remain open on Sundays and shopping is more cosmopolitan than it would otherwise be. I have heard some very odd tongues being spoken. But the great wave of refugees from the Hitlerite abominations cultivated the politeness of speaking English even to each other from the first; in the lean days of the war I heard a woman inimitably say, 'Ven I am direkt hungrig, so I become a slice of bread and drippings.' And only the other morning in the dairy I heard this exchange: 'How are you, dearie?' 'I'm *much* better thanks. I've taken up this new religion, Zen – have you heard of it?'

The great heart of The Wood is beating still. Most residents seem to like it, wrong side of the park or no. And when the Eton and Harrow is on at Lord's, some of the best people imaginable can be seen taking a patronizing stroll in our casbah. On such an occasion a bus conductor, the wag who calls Swiss Cottage the 'Schweizerhof', sang out as we came down Finchley Road, 'Next stop, Sinjohn Boyse!' Evidently we have a remnant of past glory still.

Guardian, April 1962

OPERA

'Potty about Singers'

'Potty about singers' was how I heard myself described the other day, and serenely accepted the impeachment. I like singing, rate it the most human of the arts and in moments of elation have been known to talk slightly sacreligiously of Music Made Flesh. I think the nearer music approaches to the condition of singing the better it is likely to be. Not everyone would subscribe to this view. I know of a child of a great singer (who died untimely) who grew up to be a superb flautist but flatly rejected the 'sound of the human voice'.

I like the therapeutic side of singing, its expressiveness and, more controversially, its sex appeal. (Don't start in on castrati and countertenors just yet, please). But the voice is after all a secondary sexual characteristic. *'Mon coeur s'ouvre à ta voix,'* Samson was told, and believed, with what dire results we know. Seeing a billboard as I often do inscribed 'Famous singer dies' I rush to buy the edition. Who can it be? Aren't they all gathered to Abraham's bosom long since (though not Carrie Tubb, now 98: she who continued with the 'Jewel Song' in *Faust* after the bomb fell outside the theatre in the *First* World War)? But usually it is only some pop idol, who, yowling into a microphone for twelve thousand a year, has overdone the heroin. Tiresomely I have now invoked the microphone for of course great singers use that wretched thing for recording and it has been found better than the acoustic horn before which Melba advanced and then retreated for a high fortissimo.

Well, Melba did just make it into the era of electrical recording (the *Traviata* duet with Brownlee and the final and farewell *Bohème*). But I rather wonder if we can 'deduce' Melba from her legacy of records, as we can I think Caruso from his or Galli Curci from hers (alas when she, wildly popular from her 1918 records, actually appeared here in the flesh, people were equally dashed by the smallness of the instrument).

The gramophone has proved a valuable archive for vanished executive musical art – indeed of acting too: some Shakespeare speeches, even Sarah Bernhardt (if you adjust the speeds). But the cinema camera, from the same epoch of great opera and Lieder singing, has very little to offer: Olga Knipper, Chekhov's widow, snippets of Pavlova which make the younger ballerinas of today gasp and giggle.

Me these same snippets make weep. Why? Because I am using the filmed fragments merely as a key to my own memories of seeing her for myself. This is my point: a gramophone record of a singer whom you have *heard* may be a stimulant to memory, like a photograph of a loved and long lost face (but see Proust on this dubious belief). But how safe is it to base judgement on a record only, especially in the circumstances in which many records were made in the distant past? It seems to me hazardous. For one thing you cannot judge volume; or not accurately: nor the combination of sound and personal aura which comes into it very much. Callas on the stage threw at us such powerful personality that any blemishes in her vocalization were somehow scrubbed from awareness. However, please do not think I am not grateful for the legacy of vocal gramophone records. They are the only things that nearly made me a collector (a role I dislike). They have made me richer than any Emperor who could command a nightingale to sing for him alone.

I have just been reading a fascinating book called *The Grand Tradition: seventy years of singing on record* by J. B. Steane (Duckworth: £10). Reading with delight and envy too, because although I could not have done it so well I would have been in the position if less lazy to do something similar.

It is part a catalogue *raisonné*: take a famous song or aria and compare some of the best accounts of it. In this sense it has an element of *The Record Guide*. There are 122 illustrations, all apt, many off the beaten track. The book otherwise is in three periods, the second beginning with electrical recording 1925–50 with the first chapters headed menacingly 'New talents and declining standards: Pertile and Pons.' The third part is headed Renaissance: the long-playing record and the words Wagner: every note every word, followed by the name of Flagstad.

So it is a history of great singing as deduced mostly from records and here Mr Steane has been perceptive. To take one example, he pinpoints the recitative from Melba's Ophelia (*Hamlet* by Thomas) beginning '*Des perles de la nuit*' as explaining the Australian diva's supremacy; and it is exactly the moment to choose from all she put on disc. On the other hand where I think, being older and of longer experience in the opera house than Mr Steane, he is making false deductions about singers I actually heard perform, I begin to wonder whether you really can write a true history of singing in this fashion: the proportions go slightly agley.

Still, as historians often point out: it is not what really happened that matters: it is what people thought was happening. I should be less than human to feel dashed on finding some pet of mine slightly denigrated or to gloat, in however mild a degree, when it seems to me that the author could not have described such and such a diva in that way if he had heard her in the flesh and at her best. Old man's privilege I trust. Mostly like a love-sick swain wandering through a field of daisies, I savoured name after name (name dropping is memory's only comfort as you get on). And what names: Alma Gluck, Lubin, Pampanini, Cigna (a trumpet, hers) and Muzio, ah Muzio . . . but he only judges her from the decline and I want to say that after she made those records I heard her in Rome and was bewitched.

Yes, and the reason Destinn only had a short career was that she died in a dentist's chair. The paths of glory etc. I could go on for ever and haven't even reached Ponselle. I believe Mr Steane and I could talk for a week.

Guardian, 1974

Norma after 20 Years

Bellini's opera *Norma*, that *désuète* masterpiece of the *bel canto* era which set the salons of the eighteen-thirties sighing and languishing with its innocent harmonics, its mild, suave accompaniments, and its marvellously extended, plangent melody, came back to the Royal Opera House last night after an absence of more than twenty years. It is a singers' opera, and it was sung in Italian as it should be – if one reflects that the German for *Casta Diva* becomes *Keusche Göttin* and that the English would hardly be more acceptable – and for the greater part by Italians, at least the four main parts.

The conductor was Vittorio Gui, who made the very best of the score. The accompanying was flawless; it is long since one heard this kind of music (at which superior persons permit themselves to smile) played with such tenderness and respect. The introduction to the third scene was a poem. One recalled how Toscanini changed opinions overnight by his handling of the third-act prelude to *La Traviata*. Mild, and even at times naïve, this music may be, but the limpid classical beauty of the whole takes us rather into the world of Gluck than of the energetic young Verdi. It would be a dull ear which failed to respond to the delicately moulded 'line' of *Casta Diva*; and if the duet in thirds for the two priestesses arouses a smile today – in spite of the similar duet in *Semiramide* the device seems more proper for comedy than for tragedy – at least the final pages, from *Quel Cor Tradisce*, impose themselves as some of the most deeply-felt and noble music of the lyric stage.

Norma, in her self-immolation, is an Italian Brünnhilde of another age and no less magnificent a creation. Under Signor Gui's inspired control, this was a noble performance in many ways, not least that the production and the scenery and general stage management acknowledged that nothing should be allowed to interfere with the singing; even at the end there was, in the literal sense, no fire. Norma's funeral pyre in flames was merely implied, not exhibited. But there was much fire of another kind. One performance in particular, that of Adalgisa, the heroine's rival in love, was sung with great classical beauty by Mme Stignani; a lovely voice, perfectly placed. The tenor hero (who is as despicable a fellow as Lieutenant Pinkerton and leaves Norma in the lurch in much the same fashion as that later hero left Butterfly) was efficiently sung by Mirto Picchi, whom we have heard in Edinburgh to better advantage. The heavy father of the erring druid priestess was sung by Giacomo Vaghi, also a little off form.

Yet these three, even without further consideration, were so much superior to the general run of the mill at Covent Garden that the audience was already well satisfied. But of course Norma, which is to the opera what *Phèdre* is to the drama or *Giselle* to dance, stands or falls by the prima donna herself. The role has been the test of all operatic tests since Pasta first sang it; and part of the pleasure it gives is the pleasure of comparing the present performance with those of old. There will be much discussion of Maria Meneghini Callas, last night's Norma and the most admired singer of the role today. Mme Callas, of Greek extraction and American birth, now married to an Italian, comes to us with a great reputation. Clearly, as far as most of her audience were concerned, rumour had not lied.

She looks most impressive. Tall and splendid, like one of Millais's pictures of mid-Victorian Divas, she dominated the stage with her deportment and with acting as vigorous and vivid as that of a Tosca. She enunciates with dramatic power. Her phrasing was often memorable, arresting and even perhaps exaggerated; though she is a most musicianly singer. Yet the flawless vocal emission which is the cardinal quality called for in this exposed and perilous role was not vouchsafed. The voice is uneven. Some things, such as the gliding runs in the first scene and the attacked high notes in the second, were dazzling and amazed the audience. There were some beautiful soft phrases. But the voice did not ride the big final ensemble as it should. Much of the proper resonance was 'boxed in' and uncomfortable and though the performance she gave was impressive I myself cannot feel that she is more than a plausible Norma. The classical dimension was wanting.

Guardian, November 1952

Faust after 38 Years

You know Gounod? But the chances are unless you're an oldie Francophile like me you don't know him very well. *Faust* used to be *the* opera, the absolute top of the pops where it remained for years until gradually dislodged by Puccini's *Madam Butterfly*. Box office number one and the opera in which every operatic star wished to shine and did. Mario and Patti (still doing it when already forty years before the public), later the de Reszke brothers with Melba was the sort of casting GBS greeted again and again.

Every opera house in the world depended on it for true attraction. But now? Well, in France yes. But last seen by me in London with the Carl Rosa, strongly sung in English. I begged Norman Tucker to restore it at Sadler's Wells but he simply said 'You can't do it nowadays.' Can't you just. Today we shall know if you can. Odder restorations have occurred. I never thought to hear either *Norma* or *Lucia* in my postwar lifetime.

Faust when it arrived from Paris rhymed with ghost. Hence the parody Faust On Toast which supplies the bandstand to this day with a jolly quadrille. But how the amazing fount of memorable, singable tunes gushed and spurted. Now people know the ballet music which is splendidly danceable and comrades in arms have all roared through *Déposons les Armes* to the unsuitable words 'Drunk last night, drunk the night before, so drunk we couldn't get off the floor.' I suppose the 'Jewel Song' would be recalled because so much parodied, it being the lyric equivalent in the hackney stakes of the adage in *Swan Lake*.

Berlioz greatly admired much in *Faust* as only a fool would not. The lightly sensuous music of the garden scene is lovely operatic poetry. The last few minutes where Marguerite tells her love to the night sky *'Quel émoi dans mon coeur'* struck Berlioz particularly (in Paris the final C is not sung, merely a swooning silent sigh; I shall be interested to know if it is tonight – Italian heroines sing it).

Faust which started as an *opéra comique* with short spoken scenes had by the time it reached Garnier's great Grand Opera acquired not only ballet but a church scene to show off the organ: a scene moreover far too good to skip. Then there was Sir Charles Santley, our first knighted singer: so Gounod wrote him 'Even Bravest Hearts May Swell (*Avant de Quitter ces Lieux*)' and you can't drop that, or Valentin's death which is I think the most impressive page in the opera. You must leave Siebel her little contributions; the exchanges at the end of the Kermesse are not only crucial, in some opinions, i.e. those of James Harding, they gave sung French a new and highly original 'turn'.

One other thing I trust will be recovered: difficult to define but there is a Gounod style and I wonder if it has survived the long neglect. Just as Dinu Lipatti playing Chopin or Brendel phrasing Schubert are felt to catch those styles with complete inevitability, so unquestioned in *Faust* were those two supreme Gounodists: Percy Pitt and Thomas Beecham.

And how will the French be? Good: is my bet. In a way I shall miss the comedy of the familiar English translation where everything is inverted: Loving Smile of Sister Kind; Years How Many have I Behind Me; and best of all the rendering of that gorgeous swinging finale to Scene one, *A Moi le Bonheur, les Jeunes Maitresses*, which comes out Be Mine The Delight . . . and no mention of young mistresses! I think it will still work.

Guardian, November 1974

About Verdi

The trouble with doing a job – if you can call critical journalism a job – for a long time is that people get tired of ploughing through you and say, phrasing it with tact and charm, 'Don't you get *tired* of writing about . . . so and so.' Well, the answer is: No, I don't. Just as I don't get tired of going to *Rigoletto*, as I have done regularly for fifty years, I do not tire of reading about Verdi or of writing about him. But one gets – how shall I say, to avoid the dread charge of elitism? – 'choosey'.

I think I have read all the books on Verdi and written about a few. Some are a lot better than others. Still they come, thick and fast. Many in the pipeline and Messrs Budden and, I believe, Andrew Porter have undisclosed treasures in store. Today Gollancz publishes one which took me by surprise: first of two studies of *The Dramatic Genius of Verdi*, a title which stakes a claim later vindicated. It is by a name I only know obliquely from *The Gramophone*, Vincent Godefroy, and he has been wasting his life as a headmaster when clearly he ought to have been an opera critic. For on this showing (if he could have worked fast enough i.e. a good notice in eight minutes from curtain fall) he would have been a very good one.

The book which lacks an index as yet, because it is only a half-way house (first of two volumes) takes us up to, and includes, *La Traviata*. I don't know of a better description of the last minutes of that work than his; Budden or Toye or Dyneley Hussey do not miss points at such a crucial time but Mr Godefroy seems to me to have an ability to describe dramatic action and its springs (*ressorts*, in the French) which is superior.

This of course comes from insight and deep knowledge but those advantages do not always produce what I am extolling here.

It is the gift which I horribly envied Kenneth Tynan when he was a drama critic in competition with myself (and very generous in my direction let me remember). I often thought his judgements faulty but he could describe acting so well. Not acting only. Do you remember how he wrote of that rather absurd (now) Lady Chatterley case and of the distinguished, wonderful, literary figure who gave her evidence 'in a manner at once firm but rambling', and how we saw Dame Rebecca West spring to life off the printed column?

That's a gift, not a skill. I can sometimes bring it off myself but not at will. Mr Godefroy does it again and again. 'Immediately the full orchestra crashes in with a punch of uninhibited vulgarity and the distraught victim turns at bay amid her heartless captors and lashes at them in a mini-cabaletta of superb venom. Soon the Count and Ferrando, backed by the chorus are striking back vigorously, with a trumpet ripping along to rivet their abuse and their fiery threats of destruction. It is a little *tour de force* for the mezzo soprano who, ringed round by male warriors, can fling up her manacled arms and behave like a newly-caged tigress, throwing about in their midst her lone woman's body and female voice with two As to back up her hysterics.'

You won't need to be told: it's Azucena the gypsy in *Trovatore* Act III. I like every bit of that quote (matched easily *passim*). Possibly the tigress simile is dangerous: I once, not in this paper, described a Tosca who had slipped as being like a 'tigress robbed of her whelps' but the editor, a feminist, changed it to 'tiger' and the printers altered whelps to whelks. So I am shy of that word. But I think the passage tells you what a Verdian scene is like.

Reading Mr Godefroy on the last act of *Rigoletto* explained to me, more fully than I guessed, why in fact anyone with any instinct for the theatre knows it to be the unsinkable masterpiece of its kind that it is: no mean feat, but only to be illustrated by quotations too lengthy.

Thinking about it, I wonder if one of the reasons that most drama criticism is so un-illuminating (if you don't know, or have not seen, the play in performance) is that possibly some people who write drama or opera criticism don't know in what dramatic music or musical drama consists. Bored and disappointed by plays which were hailed as epoch-making and masterly by my colleagues of yore, I used to sulk and say: 'But it isn't theatre.'

Yet when challenged I could seldom say what theatre *was*. And would come up later (too late) with words like 'It is surprise, it is agonized anticipation; theatre is Sonia Dresdel, alone in the house at last, hesitating whether to go and open the private drawer of her stage-husband where lies . . .' O let her not do *that*: we hug ourselves in ghoulish rapture. Too late. Her hand is on the secret spring-lock when, suddenly, the front-door bell rings, and could that be the Inspector again? That's theatre for me, I am afraid. Verdi can do that kind of thing by making music do the action, 'rev up' the emotional key, and that's opera.

The Dramatic Genius of Verdi: Studies of Selected Operas (Vol. 1: Nabucco to La Traviata) by Vincent Godefroy (Gollancz £6).

Guardian, June 1975

Otello

Many of us feel that the world of opera (nay of drama, quite simply) has few experiences to offer so powerful in their effect as a good performance of Verdi's *Otello*, noblest of operatic agonies. Covent Garden's revival on Saturday had the house in tumult – quite rightly. This was just that: a good performance. Mr Solti drives hard and too fast and he does not in my view always trust Verdi to make the lingering dying fall, the muted, almost unvoiced pain. But he hatches out the showmanship, the febrile excitement, quite splendidly and he won full co-operation right from the storm chorus (roof raising) to the last broken heart beat.

Tito Gobbi's Iago makes such an impact that he quite blinds me to any other interpretation. Volume in every sense is here, yet a sickeningly jaunty, spring-heeled malignity too. Again, as we had learned before, Raina Kabaiwanska proved to have something more than the essential qualities for Desdemona (how much bigger a character than Shakespeare's boy heroine). She looks right; with dignity, beauty yet pliant fragility, and without necessarily having a very beautiful voice, she has it placed in such a way (right in the mask of the face as singing teachers love to say) so that it 'speaks', rings, 'bells', or whatever word you like, quite tirelessly and with instant audibility at all strengths. Her dynamic control was most beautifully managed, in the *prime lagrime* duet no less than in the monumental ensemble at the end of the act. She could have been allowed a little more space round her 'Salce' and 'Ave Maria' but she too deserved her ovation at the end.

The unpredictable triumph, however, was that of James McCracken who comes from the state of Indiana and has been a word of mouth legend for some time (he sang here in the Verdi *Requiem* last year).

He has been singing the role of Otello in New York with Mr Solti and went on, here, without rehearsal. The house knew at once that this was the voice for the part: large, inclined perhaps to splay a little, but sonorous, the emanation of the true Otello from Tamagno onwards (he looks like the first Otello's photographs) – with the pain and the ferocity implicit. I would have him keep stiller during the monologue, but his *Niun mi tema* was overwhelming, like Melchior's. He seemed genuinely shaken by the yell of approbation which greeted his solo curtain. (Where did we English collect our reputation for coldness?)

Guardian, April 1964

Boccanegra: La Scala

The visit of the opera from La Scala Milan went on to a perfectly glorious presentation last night of Verdi's *Simon Boccanegra* which I would never expect to see bettered. The orchestra under Abbado played wonderfully; in the last scene – enough to draw tears from a stone. Giorgio Strehler who since the death of Felsenstein must be accorded the status of the finest of all producers in this field, makes a marvellously tense and even swift presentation of an opera which we have so often known as slow and sombre.

The prologue, with its dark, perpendicular, brooding scenery (Frigerio), the great Council Chamber, with its assembly of solemn heads and the last scene with its sad, lowering sails, make up a magnificent picture.

The singing was La Scala in Verdi at its noblest; Cappuccilli, in the name part and the bass Raimondi as Fiesco especially gorgeous. The tenor Lucchetti, whom we know from *Bohême* here made a fine strong Gabriele and Mirella Freni turned out greatly advanced and rich in voice. Two of the trios and the quartet were as grand as you will ever get them. A great occasion, much acclaimed.

Guardian, March 1976

Zeffirelli's *Tosca*

TOSCA. Two seats any performance. Cash or FOUR seats for Nureyev offered in exchange.

So reads an agony column. Could tribute be greater? As a rabble rouser Callas might put Garbo or the Beatles themselves in the shade. Yet the triumph is understandable. She is a spellbinder. The vocalism may be erratic; those who hear the broadcast tomorrow may well wonder what the fuss is about. You should have heard what singing teachers were saying in the intervals at the first night. Perilous corners were taken on one wheel. But how Callas wore her clothes was what most of us noted. Perfectly she enters into the character, into the period, and into the age. Slim as a pencil, she is a Tosca in her twenties. It is altogether a histrionic marvel – macaw squawks and all.

The tumult of applause was also for old friend Tito Gobbi, a mellowed Scarpia, acting splendidly and singing rather than shouting this time, with magnificent presence and effect.

Productions as elaborate as this tend to slip. The detail is just now quite perfect: it catches the very minute of the day, just as Visconti does in *The Leopard*. Zeffirelli, moreover, does not intrude; there is none of that distraction which in my view mars his *Falstaff* and *Don Giovanni*, nor are any liberties indulged against the musical planning. The sets are sumptuous.

The church of Sant' Andrea may be slightly oversized; but what a wonderful feeling is conveyed of huge marble pillars rising into the vaulted roof above the clutter of bondieuserie. (Yet the stoup is nearly as wobbly as the old one!) Tosca stalks in from the body of the church but her first question *Perche chiuso?* is meaningless. Nothing was locked. This is a detail which hardly seems to matter when set beside the way Zeffirelli directs the Scarpia-Tosca encounter. Instead of standing cheek by jowl as is usual, Tosca turns her back on him and falls on her knees at the long *priedieu* bench. He sidles up, half kneeling, beside her. It is exactly how secular conversations in church do occur. The truth of it is remarkable.

No stick or bonnet for this Tosca; instead Emma Hamilton white muslin and a perfectly carried orange stole. Scarpia's costume is much toned down: no silk breeches or red-lined cape; more a squire's working dress; similarly Cavaradossi-browns and greys. Tosca, who has been singing before Queen Caroline, comes in to Scarpia in Act 2 in gorgeous claret, with train. His room is firelit (not moonlit). It is the Farnese to the life; but an office. It would need a fire for dinnertime.

The sinister little procession, the torture party, files past Tosca and we can see each one in turn scanned by her. Instead of endless sitting on that sofa, this Tosca ranges the claustrophobic chamber; her lover's groans come up a trap door over which she crouches, her face lighted from beneath. At the moment of reluctant consent, Tosca is down on the prompt side. Scarpia and Spoletta beyond, in diagonal: we *see* everything. And anyone who doesn't twig what *Simulato . . . come Palmieri* means, this time has only himself to blame.

Callas sang 'Vissi d'arte' mostly on her feet, but after the tiresome applause (which breaks the action) gets to her knees for the most beautiful passage in her whole second act, beginning *Vedi* . . . There is no physical 'chasing' of Tosca – the *thought* of her submission is enough. The agonizing wait *before* the murder (with rather limp orchestra under Signor Carlo Felice Cillario) has never in my memory seemed less ritualistic. The stabbing happened almost on the spur of the moment and took Scarpia completely by surprise! Think what that means to anyone who has seen fifty or more *Toscas*.

In the third act I missed the old set of the platform of Sant' Angelo with the cupola of St Peter's in the dawn distance. The new scene is set in the narrow defile between battlements and the tower, whose ellipse runs in a curve out of sight. The night is cloudy: so that that wonderful dawn, with bells and goatherd, seems unmatched by the visual scene (which does not lighten until O *dolci mani*). Tosca has picked up a travelling cloak *en route* (feasible and even probable for this energetic young girl, convent bred but before that a goat girl). I could multiply instances of imaginative thinking. Mr Zeffirelli has done nothing better. It should hold up even without Callas and Gobbi to focus our attention. But for how long?

Guardian, January 1964

La Fanciulla del West

Puccini's pistol toting *Girl of the Golden West (La Fanciulla del West)* is a sure-fire, bang-on hit at the Royal Opera, one of the best of revivals in this splendid Jubilee season. A stranger on this stage, since Destinn in 1911, it simply grips the public as verismo opera melodrama, done with total credence in the style.

The final setting may not be quite right and there is one moment where the tension, after the poker gambling scene, snaps. But the snow, the blood dripping from the hidden fugitive, and all that, is superbly managed in a full-blooded and rich production by Faggioni, with Ken Adam's gunfire 'visuals'.

The conductor Zubin Mehta got maximum effect from this score, one of Puccini's most detailed, imaginative and modern (it looks towards *Turandot*, without missing a trick or two learned from backward glances at *Tosca*). Aaron Copland did not begin to rival the Californian atmospherics until years later. Perhaps the first act is over-extended, and strangely enough it is not until the second and third acts that the bandit-hero's characterization is clinched with the typical Puccinian drive and pith in one of those 'tell you all' arias.

But the saloon scene has great style all the same: not a weakling among all those small 'bit' parts for the home-sick miners who sing of the old folks at home and their poor dog Tray and whom the Girl (Minnie of the golden hair and heart) mothers and bosses.

This part is taken by Carol Neblett and seemed to me splendidly cast, though it was said she was still struggling with a cold. The real right *lirico spinto* style was there, the phrasing sensitive and appreciative, the melodrama given believable expression. Her last scene was most touching.

In the Caruso part, Placido Domingo was unselfish, exciting at the big moments, just about the best you could find. The Venetian baritone Silvano Carroli had also just the right voice for the sheriff-villain, with a Scarpia snarl and potent projection. The reception was enthusiastic. I wish they could start earlier. The evening is too long. Puccini was a quick one and should be honoured as such. But he is otherwise honoured by this grand revival.

Guardian, May 1977

Tristan und Isolde

Culmination of a great reign at Covent Garden, Solti's new, long desired, long awaited *Tristan und Isolde* at the Royal Opera House was vouchsafed last Monday, a stunning five and a half hours of music, leaving souls penetrated lastingly – you are never the same after a good *Tristan* – and the senses racked with Wagner's chromatic ache.

Orchestral playing of unbelievable beauty was heard. True, Solti does not let the first prelude flow like Furtwaengler. But when, since Beecham, have the Tryst and the Watch so glowed and throbbed? About these things I find it difficult to exercise critical sobriety: it would seem like 'having reservations' about the very stuff of the universe. 'Ich sehne um Sterben': Jess Thomas singing as superbly as I have not heard him since his Bayreuth *Lohengrin* sent a shaft through the heart at that point. If any tenor has sung 'Wohin Tristan nun scheidet' better on this stage I was not there, alas, to hear it. Later he was made to spill out his sheep's spleen, like a wounded nag in the bull ring, a painful sight, the only one.

Too often one has to avert the eyes from Wagner's lovers because they look like upended Chesterfields in a Knightsbridge shop window. But Jess Thomas and Ludmila Dvorakova looked beautiful, both lying on their backs in guilty duplicity, arms lifted to the stars beyond the branches of the tree which had lifted at Tristan's high A entry (one of Peter Hall's most marvellous strokes) and dropped to brood over them as, in shame, they sang 'O sink, hernieder' among the roots of the dominant tree. Earlier, waiting for the potion to work, they had bafflingly stood, back to back, fumbling hands. Not quite 'Er sah mir in die Augen' but never mind: it, *and* the potion, worked.

Ludmila sang beautifully, effortfully, successfully, with opaque tone and not enough 'follow-through', to give you the heavenly lift of Flagstad or Nilsson at 'Frau Minne's Macht' ('Mrs Love's power', in English, I regret to add) – but once you've heard Flagstad, of course, comparisons are absurd: like matching Southend to Chamonix.

Veasey perfect as Brangäne; McIntyre, a Kurvenal whose dying fall was like the death of chivalry itself, a Last Post in the rags of a red sunset. Best of all, David Ward's immensely dignified discovery of the guilty pair in the garden: one of producer Peter Hall's finest touches. King Marke 'took root' by the tree; 'Dies mir?' (I was off again, gulping.)

How did Wagner, given the great story and the themes of the Wesendonck songs, actually create a magnum opus so potent in its erotic discharge that it makes every other work of the stage, everything in this silly permissive age, sound like piffle before the wind? Bury's dark sets are beautiful, with heavy Constable clouds of late afternoon and a water-satin swell of tide, also a genuine castle keep, bless him. But the benediction is on us: *ausserordentlich rührend*.

Guardian, *June 1971*

Die Walküre

In the case of the, after all still pretty rare, big Wagnerian red letter nights the critic finds his position more insecure with every passing year. The light of other years gathers around him. Impossible, if you have a memory at all, not to think 'I heard Melchior and Lehmann do this present passage "better", Hotter and Flagstad that passage.' Like some lachrymose member of the wedding, one is softened up by nostalgia. The danger of course is that your memory may be playing you false, that the impression was anyhow subjective and may have seemed better only because you were younger, fresher, had more appetite.

But this said, I must simply speak as I find to best honesty and say that I thought this revival of last year's *Die Walküre* was a very fine and much improved achievement, for me, perhaps for me alone, lacking the last blaze of sheer glory but splendid, stirring, and supremely lucid. Visually: the movements of rocks no less than creatures human or godlike were extremely effective from a dramatic point of view (viz: the fight and Brünnhilde – the splendid Lindholm – for once standing up to her father, with scarcely any kneeling).

I found myself quite undismayed by what seemed the too self-conscious modernity of the stage pictures when I first blinked at it last year. I didn't feel that opportunity was even wasted in act one, settling for such suggestion of tree and spring night as are vouchsafed. Further I believe the sight lines have been newly

74

OPERA

respected and hope that others had as good an eyeful as I did. Then I like the Valkyries' flamingo wing Greek costumes, approve the Greek hovering divinities, find the *Todesverkundigung* more intimate than usual (and of course increasingly moving as one gets older oneself).

The Covent Garden orchestra played most beautifully for Colin Davis once more. One of his great merits is gauging the volume and texture so that the singers really penetrate, with their words and their meanings (Beecham just drove on till Melchior would be yelling sometimes). More flow is easily demanded. All I can say is the music did not stick as it did last year in that long, long second act, made glorious this time by Donald McIntyre's tremendous quarter of an hour of laying down the law (mid stage, high up, between huge boulders). He is a very fine Wotan indeed now. How fail to admire Veasey's Fricka too, so much opened up as a character? Cassilly (Siegmund) has the impressive stature. Eszter Kovacs (Sieglinde) has not yet quite what it takes, and was nervously below pitch sometimes, but crucial things did not fall to the ground. Aage Haugland was a splendid dark, metallic Hunding: the Valkyrie team champions to a girl.

Guardian, September 1975

Götterdämmerung

There must have been many people (if you include the home listeners as well as the rapt auditorium of Covent Garden) for whom Georg Solti's *Ring*, concluding in the formidable rites of Saturday's Twilight or Decline of the Gods, has offered a contact with the sublime seldom afforded anywhere in the theatre. Moreover, there are always many people for whom it is a first time. Indeed, as the Gibichungs' Hall began its cosmic crumble in flame and flood, a woman near me let out such a heartfelt gasp,

75

such a whoops and golly that she clearly thought the whole theatre was coming down (as, in a sense, it was) – a tribute to what is at best, I am sorry to say, a poor spectacular match for the overwhelming grandeur of the music.

But it reminds me how I used to resent, when the *Ring* was new to me, the kind of regretful intellectual sighing criticism which used a gambit ending in the words, 'but you should have heard So and So.' Of course, for regulars there are always other competitive memories. But I don't know that I can recall orchestral playing more eloquent, sheerly beautiful with the balance so perfectly held between excitement and quality, of a fulltide, yet not impossibly boisterous volume, as that we heard in some of the two hours of act one – the scene where Waltraute (Veasey) comes to tell Brünnhilde of Wotan's lonely reclusion. Two other wonderful episodes: the giant bass Martti Talvela summoning the vassals and the electrical tingle of the oath of vengeance trio between him, the betrayed heroine, and Günther (Shaw). It has been a *Ring* with many grand moments – the sum of the parts greater than the whole.

I found the Siegfried (Hering) reliable but not quite inspiring, though better than the previous week. He flunked one climax in the penultimate scene and the hero's death has certainly been made to yield more drama and draw on deeper emotional responses – though the savage pain of the ensuing funeral march was acute. Miss Dvorakova has nobly stood the course – a warm personality, strong, indeed solid sound (but no very clear diction). She remained valiant to the end (where we often have to settle for a frantic half-fainting fight) but did not put on those extra inches of stature which the greatest of all culminating scenes can sometimes bring forth. But in grey chiffon, she might be a Magdalene as well as a Valkyrie; her torch is ludicrous, the ravens and the steed are merely apostrophized unseen and the heroine merely patters off. Better leave the stage in darkness than display such a miserable paucity of illustration. You should have seen Leider leap to the stirrup . . . but there I go again.

Guardian, September 1970

Lohengrin

Lohengrin, since the First World War at any rate, has not always been one of Covent Garden's more frequent successes. On paper, names such as Lotte Lehmann and Melchior may suggest thrilling nights but I assure you they were often what is called 'dicey'. Fine in places, dubious in others. Not enough rehearsal perhaps? The new production is marvellously brought up to its full potential, musical, vivid and intense, full of reward and at crucial difficult places fresh and exhilarating. Visually some old hands may find it a bit odd but should, I think, come round to the idea that it is highly successful on this side too.

The producer is Elijah Moshinsky who has original ideas about movement, mostly effective though, to make a tiny cavil, is it not better if Elsa sings 'Euch Lüften' on a tower or eminence of some kind, with Ortrud crouched at ground level? Here they were seen like two stately *vendeuses* in a fabric department, mourning one side of the gauze, bridal gold on the other: good for ballet, less good for mid-nineteenth-century medieval fairy story drama.

But the insistence on white in John Napier's sets – a mighty shoe-box some might call it at first sight, imposes itself steadily as an idea: the absolute minimum of props, not even a thalamus; the newly marrieds simply kneeling on a vast silk spread, gauzes again and acres of white Terylene in service make a memorable effect and a dramatic appeal. There are a few totem poles here and there which look faintly Byzantine and not at all like the traditional oak girt shore of the River Scheldt and King Heinrich might almost be a priest out of Verdi's biblical opera *Nabucco* or Rossini's *Moise*.

But if the styles are, let's say 'mixed', I found them beautiful and the whole thing persuasive in a way difficult to analyse but very much the product of original artistic thought. A lady in the interval said: 'I don't care if there is no scenery when the music is done like this' – and like so many unprofessional critics she put her finger on it.

For Sir Bernard Haitink got really wonderful results, over-whipping the Third Act prelude perhaps but winning poetry from passages often seeming stodgy. Wagner's score of course has at first much of the notorious and proudly extolled 'German Andante' which the irreverent late Prof. E. Dent said was nothing less than the breathing rate of the average corpulent German bourgeois audience. On Thursday we were thinking how exquisite this music, even when slow moving, can be made to sound.

The orchestra played for the new (hon.) conductor Knight with the greatest delicacy and splendour: Haitink balanced, caressed the music, nursed the singing to admiration. No wonder the house roared for him. The cast had a most distinguished Elsa who made the role grow in every way, from a shy start to ecstatic and tragic grandeur: she is Anna Tomowa-Sintow from Bulgaria.

The Lohengrin himself was René Kollo, known to us well already. His presence, bearing, expression of the 'holy' role, the son of Parsifal, are most taking and have the rare 'numinous quality' Wagner clearly wanted: the tone is never hectoring. A slight defect is taking some notes slightly under par and tuning them afterwards.

Eva Randova, vivid actress and beauty as Ortrud, was less powerful in volume than I thought she well might be (also a newcomer – from Czechoslovakia). Perhaps she had a little cold but her second scene duet was beautifully subtle and true. McIntyre as Telramund gave one of his strong performances and Robert Lloyd sang out magnificently as King Henry, with Jonathan Summers too, as the Herald. A memorable evening.

Guardian, November 1977

Massenet's *Manon*

Who said, 'I would give the whole of the *Brandenburg Concertos* for *Manon* and would think I had vastly profited by the exchange'? Beecham, of course, who reminds us of the Duchess in Alice: 'Speak harshly to your little boy and beat him if he sneezes; he only does it to annoy, because he knows it teases.' Still Beecham did love and appreciate *Manon* as only a fool would not and I like to add that I love it too, defensive-like, because *Manon*, Massenet's masterpiece, is an intensely French work and French art or much of it – opera, classical drama, even neoclassical art – has many sneering detractors *chez nous*. It is the Frenchness of course which allows it to catch so perfectly the spirit of the Abbé Prévost's love story. Just as Massenet would hardly be able to mirror, say, Defoe's *Moll Flanders*: which we might entrust to Vaughan Williams were he still with us.

Puccini knew this and in spite of his effrontery (as it seemed to some) in writing his own *Manon Lescaut*, which tells us a lot about Puccini's love of the passionate, did not capture the French essence and admitted as much. The third *Manon*, by Auber, we can ignore though the 'Eclat de Rire' (laughing song) is still sung; nor need we drag in Massenet's attempt at a sequel many years later: *Le Portrait de Manon*. What is interesting is that Puccini himself, feeling his way into French atmosphere when confronted with the Paris of Murger's *La vie de Bohéme*, went to Massenet's *Manon* for a model for his own frail Mimi. Manon's 'Je suis encore tout étourdie' clearly inspires in its wilting way the 'Si mi chiamano Mimi', that wan appealing revelation of character at which both composers so instantly excelled, what Puccini liked to call his 'povera facciu' or fallen faded mode.

Incidentally Puccini, with two exceptions, brings on his

heroines as voices off-stage initially. Massenet lets his heroine tackle us direct in duet and solo. She has got to be an actress and a charmer but for long periods the insinuating, coaxing charm of the vocal lines makes few strenuous demands. Spirit – certainly: the decision to elope with the new admirer in the final duet of Act 1 ('Nous vivrons à Paris') has an irresistible optimism. But right down to the barely more than intoned 'Farewell to the little table' (where she and the lover she is betraying have had such happy suppers) there is little very exacting singing; it is character work, not vocal brilliance that one remarks.

With the heroine's worldly triumph in the *Cours La Reine* scene the role grows far more showy – too much indeed for some otherwise highly gifted singing-actresses. Lina Cavalieri, arguably about the most beautiful woman to have graced the operatic stage, did not please in this role at the huge Scala, Milan. The posters reading *Cavalieri: Manon* were added to – *'Ma non si senti'* (But she is inaudible).

Even the great duet in Saint Sulpice where Manon wheedles the Chevalier des Grieux out of the seminary and back into her arms is within the province of quite a low-powered lyric soprano: the quintessentially Massenet quality of the leading line 'N'est ce pas ma main que cette main presse?' can be sung quite quietly, though I must admit to liking the way such people as the late Mme Boussac (of the Derby winners) as Fanny Heldy used to turn up the volume here: to say nothing of Schwarzkopf, De Los Angeles, Adèle Leigh and McWatters among postwar Manons at the Royal Opera.

It is a crucial phrase in the whole opera and how it caresses the French words, taking the little sprung resilience of the mute (but not unsounded) 'e's.

Ah, there's the rub! The Sadler's Wells version will be in English. Manon in the story is sentenced, as a thief and a harlot, to be transported to South America and dies there (or alternately, on the road to the ship of transportees in Massenet's version, likening the evening star to a diamond, her last 'Je suis encore coquette'). One sometimes wonders if *Manon*, the opera, can really survive translation into any other language but her own. I have heard the opera many times and in more than one language – Italians, Puccini notwithstanding, love Massenet's *Manon* and Italian tenors such as Schipa and Gigli revelled in the dream and 'Ah, fuyez douce image'. But somehow I find it difficult to dissociate the music from the French words in a manner wholly exceptional.

But we learned at the Coliseum (though some of us knew it before) that Wagner can go perfectly naturally into English if you have the translator with the right gifts. I shall go 'unprejudiced' tomorrow. Don't laugh; this is a fiction all critics like to keep up, except Bernard Shaw who declared that a critic who wasn't prejudiced was no critic at all. Fair promise anyway.

Guardian, January 1974

Meditation

'Prison holds no terrors,' said the wag, 'for those who have survived Eton.' Similarly I do not think that anyone whose first delighted and sustained contacts with the art of the opera house were made at the Grand Théâtre des Arts in the town of M——
will ever be surprised, dismayed or angered by any of those declensions from artistic grace to which Mr Newman, with his flair for the psychologically true in the world of the music drama, has been calling attention for what seems (indeed is) the whole span of my life. It is with this thought that I raise from my own past a few of the happy experiences I underwent while a *pensionaire* in the exceptionally frugal household of a Protestant *pasteur* in that town.

I was not, of course, in those days unacquainted with opera entirely. I had seen a Carl Rosa *Carmen* from the front row of the stalls and had been astonished by what happened to the hoop of Carmen's semi-crinoline dress when she was stabbed and fell over

backwards with her feet pointed in silent reproach towards the
conductor's desk. (I have seen many undignified demises upon the
stage, but this one remained for my mind the *locus classicus*.)

What is more, I came of an opera-loving family; my father
would often make buzzing sounds which he would presently label
as some bass aria from Meyerbeer; my mother could be persuaded
to show upon the nursery table something of the abandon with
which Mme Calvé, of whom we possessed a grating gramophone
record thick as a soup plate, executed the 'Danse bohèmienne' in
Bizet's opera. Opera then, as a genus, fascinated me as it still does,
D.G.

But opera every night of the week and twice on Sundays was
something new, intoxicating, wonderful. I had the barren soul at
that time of a boy but newly out of public school. The void was
rapidly filled . . . by *Manon*. '*Ah Manon, Manon, perfide Manon.*' I
was soon unable to do the simplest thing without fitting some tag
from Massenet's opera to it.

The repertory of the Grand Théâtre was immense: it had to be;
the town was of exactly that convenient size which means that
unless you play a new, or shall we say, different opera every night,
the public will be too quickly exhausted. Unlike London, where
all we get is *La Traviata* at both houses at once, Le Grand Théâtre
de M—— rang the changes. Everything was attempted. *L'Or du
Rhin* was followed up with Messager's ballet *Les Deux Pigeons*; a
night's money's worth being more important than congruity in
that part of France. Next night, it would be *Les Noces de Jeanette*, on
Thursday *La Dame Blanche* and then *La Valkyrie*, known jocularly
at the box office as *La Vache qui rit*. But mostly of course it was
Manon, of which the public never seemed to tire, though it was
always *avec le concours de* Mme this or that, *de l'Opéra, de l'Opéra
Comique, du Trianon Lyrique* – even once amazingly (and that did
bring it home to me) *de Covin Gardens de Londres*, an unending
torrent of talented Manons of all ages and with many widely
disparate hair styles.

In those days I was still innocent about Massenet and liked him
just as much as everyone else did. I did not know that the mere

mention of his name in my own country was enough to set the table in a roar; to make lady members of the Bach choir turn pink with disapproval; to induce apoplexy in the most bloodless cathedral organists. And it was still to be years before I discovered, over the august initials of E.N., the revolutionary notion that *Manon* was, after all, an out and out masterpiece of its kind.

Whether Mr Newman would have written that blinding sentence (for which I shall never cease to be grateful) if he had seen all the Manons *I* saw at the Grand Théâtre I do not know. I know I quickly learned to size them up on that first entry to the wilting little tune of 'Je suis encore toute étourdie . . .' Sometimes it was we in the audience who were the *étourdi* ones. But one could see at a glance: this one cannot sing; she will merely be *gracieuse*, speak the role until the gavotte and then stake her all on one spine-chilling scream on the climactic high B. Another would be heavy of jowl, old in years and wonderfully loud of voice and she would sing it all, every note of it, without so much as deigning to look at the conductor let alone the local Des Grieux who was nearly always constant in the programme, a somewhat abashed Belgian dwarf on four-inch heels who waved ineffectual babyish hands and sang quite charmingly through his nose in The Dream, a page of which three to four repetitions were always demanded and generally conceded. This usually brought out a jealous burst of application from our guest Manon who had bided her time during these *entrefaits* and would then step forward and 'show 'em'.

The household where I lodged was supposed to be, besides a forcing house for public school French, a good influence. To explain to them why I was spending everything I possessed and each night at the opera was not easy. I did not reproach myself; seats were to be had at the equivalent of fourpence, and I sensed that it was an education of which my parents would have approved. I had gone so far indeed to smooth my path by taking the whole of this highly Protestant family to *Samson et Dalila*, which was selected on moral grounds. As an outing it had its less successful aspects. The *pasteur*, failing to *couvrir les bronches* on the tram ride, took a chill. Madame greatly enjoyed *le grand duo* of the seduction scene and joined now and again in the *fameuse mélodie*, breaking off when the vocal line went out of her reach to cry some critical comment such as *Enfin – des harmonies superbes, mais superbes* . . . But she was much less sure about the ballet and bacchanalia *du temple de Dagon* – though it was on another occasion at this theatre that I saw the Samson who had been covertly practising his hand on the pulley with which to set in motion the destruction of this same temple of Dagon, inadvertently pull down the pillars thirty-two bars ahead of time; which made the actual *débâcle* when at last it arrived *in the score* something of an anti-climax.

But the ballet dwelled in Madame's mind; and the fancy that I was being corrupted by the voluptuous appeal of French opera raised its ugly head. I had to take to subterfuge, pretending I had been to *Les Huguenots* (permitted, since it showed the Roman Catholics in a poor light) when in fact I had been to *Thaïs*.

This *Thaïs* in fact made life very difficult for me. The local paper carried a criticism of the performance which, in its careless critical way, pointed out that the lady's personal charms exhibited at the end of the great scene of her attempted seduction of the Monk more than made up for certain vocal deficiencies in her portrayal of the Alexandrian courtesan. If I recall, after all these years, the words were something like, '*C'était une petite voix bien exténuée par la grande reprise en bémol, mais à la fin on a vu son nombril qui, ma foi, valait bien le reste.*' Or some such. This mention of the diva's navel made it for ever difficult for me to own up to visiting *Thaïs*.

I did, however, do so, by what fibbing I will not now recount. It was a very special performance, given on 11 November for *les fêtes de la victoire* in the evening. The matinee of *Rigoletto* which I had also attended had been the stormiest known for many years. This was the period when France's relations with Italy were for some reason strained to the utmost. The tenor, a Sardinian, had most rashly insisted on singing both his first aria and 'La donna é mobile' in Italian, whereas, of course, the audience, especially on a Sunday afternoon, wished to hear it in French as 'Comme la plume au vent' and resented any other version. Anger which had been banked down broke out into violence. Earlier the Gilda, who was rumoured to be the *bonne amie* of the *chef d'orchestre* and who really couldn't sing at all, had pretentiously tried to *faire l'oiseau* in Caro nome, had broken down, and had got what in this country would in fact be called the Bird. When the audience jeered at the tenor, however, he strode forward and said something rude to the conductor, whereupon this Gilda, sensing the feeling of the house and seeing a chance to get on the right side again while defending *la musique française* in the person of the greybeard at the podium, ran on stage and smacked the Italian tenor's face. Order was not restored for a long time, and then only by an impassioned speech from the *chef de clacque*, an acknowledged authority.

So it was with nerves a-tingle that we took our places for the gala *Thaïs*. In the event there were no riots, but I remember that the theatre, during the hushed scene of the invocation of Venus, 'Vénus, mystérieuse présence, dis moi que je suis belle, etc.', the stertorous breathing of the extra police and *sapeurs-pompiers* who had been brought in to keep order, rather detracted from the magic of a scene which still to this day strikes me as beautiful and apt.

The firemen breathed even more loudly some minutes later. Perhaps they did not know about *Thaïs* and were expecting it to be all *Méditation*, without any of the very ninetyish Parisian grand effect in the middle of Act II. Admittedly, nothing much had prepared us for a scene of such daring. I should explain perhaps that the Grand Théâtre, being a sensible and ancient opera which put first things first, did not bother much about its chorus. There were four loud, superannuated singers who were known as the *chefs d'attaque* and who really knew the music; the rest was made up of *figurantes*, that is to say, ladies recruited one knows not how, who did not attempt to sing let alone act, and who wore their own shoes irrespective of the work in question. This was the period of short skirts and bobbed heads, and the effect was much less incongruous than you might suppose, for a toga well worn over such a fashion goes a long way towards suggesting the abandoned voluptuousness of the Alexandrian court.

All the same, we (that is I and the firemen too) had not looked for quite such an *exposé* as we were treated to. I suspect that the manager, in view of the matinee disturbance and also perhaps a little from patriotism (was it not 11 November?), had told the guest soprano not to pull her punches in the matter. And she did not. I do not know either how far it is customary to go in this matter. Mme Edwina, I have been told, at Covent Garden, used to compromise – flinging off Thaïs's cloak to reveal herself dressed impeccably in one of her own ball dresses underneath. Not so at the Grand Théâtre.

I quote the description of the great conversion scene from *Opera Nights*.

'She makes a last desperate stand against the doctrine of the monk, swearing that she is and will remain Thaïs, believing in nothing . . . (and) breaks down in a hysterical mixture of laughter and sobs . . .'

Not a word, you see, about taking all her clothes off. But Mme X on this occasion went one better. As the curtain came down amid thunderous applause she also ripped the bed hangings from their attachments and flung herself, ill shrouded in these hessian remnants, in a series of the most incautiously executed rolling movements I have ever beheld towards the footlights. It was a great curtain and the applause for a *bis* was still on when the *Méditation* began.

The theatre was bombed out of existence in the war. I have lost track of the diva. But both of them live on in my heart.

Guardian, 1955

Pelléas

'Il faut parler a voix basse maintenant' sings the sorrowful king hushing the agony of Mélisande's dying and Golaud's remorse. The ebb of tension in Debussy's opera is one of its many marvels, realized with such immense distinction and penetrating poetic beauty in the revival of the opera at Covent Garden last night. But never did an opera so little make one wish to fling oneself at a typewriter and size the achievement up in a jiffy. The spell lingers with you for hours. If applause seems vulgar how much more do petty quibbles about the kaleidoscopic stage pictures of Svoboda being a mite too restless or the French enunciation of the non-French cast just occasionally (but very rarely) lapsing below the plausible and intelligible.

The fame of Pierre Boulez's realization, much fanned by the gramophone records and the word of mouth from the previous revival of 1969, had brought out a packed audience (including the PM) who listened in a pindrop hush to the fantastic, clear, vibrant, even vigorous exposure of this once mocked incarnation of Maeterlinck's twilit idyll. Listening to the infinitely touching way in which Elisabeth Söderström, her tiny pale face and luminous eyes full of dismay, half whispered 'heureuse et triste' it was difficult not to remember that the line got a belly laugh at the Paris first night – how little a time ago, all things considered! The Swedish soprano makes a wonderful heroine. George Shirley lacks something seraphic in the tone for the hero but his is a superbly devoted performance. David Ward's king and McIntyre's Golaud – the latter making a very powerful thing of the spying scene with the child (Richard Cooper) – were also deeply imagined.

The production by Vacláv Kaslík strikes me as more assured than before: the lighting by Robert Ornbo is a matching visual poetry and the score which one has heard almost lull itself to sleep in some very exquisite performances here comes out and fills the big house with a miraculous clarity of texture and dramatic thrust. If one had to pin all praise on one single moment it might well be the cumulative effect of Pelléas emerging into the daylight at the words 'Je respire enfin' with an extraordinary effect of liberation and soaring. A lovely performance.

Guardian, January 1973

Cunning Little Vixen

Glyndebourne opened with a stunning performance of Janacek's enchanted woodland drama *The Cunning Little Vixen*. It is a score with short, sharp bouts of nature poetry from which you emerge possibly humming Dvor.ák, yet the music is like nothing else but that of Janacek's other operas – notably the garden scene in *Katya*. The night-time breathing of vegetation, the snapping of twigs, and the burrowing of lonely animals combine to produce an atmosphere which can be deep and consoling in its continuity: this in spite of a jerky way of conjuring the impressive moods.

These are homespun or sometimes pleasant as in the episode of the foxes' wooing, or heart-searching as in the scene of remorse after the gamekeeper has reluctantly shot the Vixen, and her cubs have come wandering out of the earth to stare at the new spectacle of death. I found the final scenes deeply moving and, as one who saw the now legendary Felsenstein production in Germany, I should at once say that Jonathan Miller has brought off an artistic success of comparable beauty: miles away, of course, from Disney archness and more human in its portrayal of animals than one would have believed possible.

The human beings are earthy, the animals more witty. None, it should be noted, is ever on all fours, more like princes or peasants from a fairy-tale book of the last century, nearer in fact to Alice in Wonderland in Vercoe's stage pictures. These are largely projections of damp woods or rank vegetation with a twisting scaffold of stairs in front to make a space for acting. Mark Furneaux's choreography is of great ability; you never saw better hens doing pecking embroidery or a more strutting Cock (Hugues Cuenod).

Norma Burrowes is perfectly cast as the Vixen; Robert Hoyen, an American who is the star of this role in Germany, is also most impressive as the Fox; and Benjamin Luxon was very fine and moving as the Forester who finally had to shoot and live to regret.

Raymond Leppard conducted with great affection, getting fine sound perfectly scaled to an ideal theatre from the London Philharmonic, though the problem of getting the words over (Tucker's English translation) is not yet solved. Cellos and bassoons can kill even the strongest baritone at times. Yet the drama came over with some force. The weather, which is important at Glyndebourne, was poor: it was oysters in the cloisters for the famous dinner interval, but the story is one of success.

Guardian, May 1975

Monteverdi

The first half of last night's Prom came from Westminster Cathedral, a basilica which you do not have to be a Roman Catholic to feel, in its very stones, ennobling. The vast, calm interior, with its wide nave and deep vista, has often inspired in me those thoughts which William James called 'numinous' and the genius loci is strongly present. Music here is heard to great advantage with a reverberation which is seldom confusing. Monteverdi's *Vespers of the Blessed Virgin* conducted as at one former Prom by John Eliot Gardiner, was given a most vivid eloquence; so much must have been evident to those listening on the radio, but the huge congregation heard something made strikingly dramatic by reason of the distribution of the sound.

The orchestra and antiphonal choruses were under the great hanging cross, the choristers in the clerestory and many of the solo contributions reached us from afar off, from the west door, the south wall pulpit or simply disembodied, like those voices from

Heaven beloved of romantic opera composers. These devices, which Monteverdi himself would surely have approved, made one realize that it was not Berlioz and Verdi who invented such showmanship; the tenor *audi coelum*, with a mysterious hidden party echoing his cadences from behind the High Altar, was in the most reverend manner of speaking pure opera – and in the year 1610.

But then, the appeal of this music is exactly its dramatic realism. The sudden rushing up of voices at the words, 'He has raised up the poor' in the psalm *Laudate Pueri* is only one of many such effects. The Monteverdi Choir, the Wandsworth Boys and various consorts and ensembles, together with a fine roster of soloists, achieved perfect unanimity of feeling: an extention of the Prom idea for which one can only feel gratitude.

Guardian, August 1972

Wozzeck

At last tonight at the Royal Opera House we had the first stage performance in England of Alban Berg's *Wozzeck*. This street-car has been twenty-seven years a-coming, and along the tracks meanwhile has passed the oddest procession of theorists, enthusiasts, and those of us who saw the work abroad: dragging much cart-before-the-horse stuff, meaning those concert performances and broadcasts. For *Wozzeck*, a Strindbergian spook sonata, is of, and for, the theatre. Taken with its stage action the wonderful great score need offer no 'difficulties' whatever, even with *Sprechstimme* in English in German accents. Time has mellowed the once aggressive-seeming modernity of the idiom, now so clearly Viennese and of its day; behind the experiments we hear the traditional German musical speech of late Strauss or Mahler easily enough. In the theatre it seizes the imagination by the short hairs of the scalp. One does not in any case stop to question how such shudders are produced.

In the last quarter-century we have had 'under-dog' heroes in plenty: recently Billy Budd and the victims of *The Consul*. But no one, not even Wedekind or Strindberg, could have provided an under-dog in uniform more palatable to the despairing German mood of the twenties than Büchner with his Private Wozzeck, driven to madness, murder, and suicide; here was the 'little man' in the old German play waiting to be exploited. Time has not rehabilitated Wozzeck (to use the jargon) as it has some other operatic figures once deemed sordid: Carmen, for one. The subject still remains pathological, repelling pity: nightmarish and sick. Most important of all, the despair of the twenties is found to be quite unlike the despair of the nineteen-fifties; *stimmt nicht*. It no longer quite rings real. Seeing *Wozzeck* tonight was like re-seeing one of those silent masterpieces of the Ufa film studios with Jannings or Werner Krauss: still exciting but very much of another time and mood.

To be fair, the present interpretation, quite apart from the wonderful handling of the score by Erich Kleiber (who conducted the original Berlin performance), does not try to exploit the mood of the twenties. Sumner Austin's producing is homely, at least once to the point of muffing an important entry: the Drum-Major's in the barrack scene (though the role itself is poorly realized by the singer in any case). Caspar Neher's settings, too, though eerie enough, coming brilliantly so in the scene by the pond, are quite free of heavy expressionisms, indeed as bland sometimes as a watercolour by Morland. This is Büchner's Germany and no nightmare land, to look at, at least. But to hear? How quickly one is put under the spell. The one real trouble is the 'speech melody' (speech given musical notes and phrasing but not vocalized with held 'tones' as in singing). Berg uses a lot of this: and it translates with great difficulty into a mixture of Old Surrey melodrama-hamming and Burgtheater declamation, making a ludicrous effect, which is disturbing, though of course Berg's score has much grim humour of its own.

The principals are, in fact, foreigners. Marko Rothmüller's English is good but in a curious way he seems unable to communicate, or at least 'project' into this large house Wozzeck's essential feebleness. We get too much of the 'dumb ox', too little of the pitiable victim. As Marie, Christel Goltz underlines, as she did in her Salome, the purely animal side of the unhappy slut to a point where she becomes far the most energetic figure on the stage. She sang with poor English but very fine and powerful musical and dramatic sense – especially the Bible reading 'fugue' – but was apt elsewhere to rampage so much that she quite missed the pathos of the poor creature. The odious Drum-Major (Thor Hannesson) is unfortunately weak; so diffident that one felt that it had been Marie who had seduced him, rather than he her. Best at getting the words across was Parry Jones (Captain). Frederick Dalberg as the Doctor and in a minor part Michael Langdon also did well.

But the honours go to Dr Kleiber, a great artist. At first one thought he kept the pressure too low; but he had his reasons, reserving the power for the last orchestral interlude when Berg steps forward, as it were, to speak to us directly about the sordid melodrama we have seen. It is the opera's most moving passage and it underlines the peculiarity of *Wozzeck*, which is that it is not of its nature a musical tragedy so much as a grand guignol reflected upon by a man of great compassion. Like some fine spirit who lays down a newspaper in which he has just read a bare and nasty little crime paragraph, Berg weeps for all poor wretches.

I hope another and wiser pen will later comment on some of the riches of the score. It is important to point out on this occasion, however, both the enthusiasm of the reception and the theatrical pungency of the work. Until one has 'seen' and identified that persistent and finally agonizing B natural (in the murder scene) with the rising of the blood-red moon, one has no idea how strongly it will light up the dark corners of the imagination.

Guardian, January 1952

Wexford Opera Festival

The Emerald Isle is full of noises, none sweeter I trow than those proceeding from the 'driest and warmest corner' . . . just don't heed that equinoctial gale, now, will you? It's a long, long way to County Wexford and a long and vexing wet way it can be, but the heart of the matter and some surprises await the pilgrim. The sheer incongruity for one thing: the near Glyndebourne price of seats, and the smarties, the tiny opera house, where wonders are worked on a shoestring, the air of cautious prosperity which has in twenty years of this festival pervaded some of the shabbier streets: the charm, architectural and social, for the Irish make wonderful hosts and enthusiastic audiences. 'A night at the Up-a-roar' brings out what ermine and rhinestone tiaras may still lurk in the mothball-dark cupboards of the local establishment. It brings also sober suited critics from overseas generally agreeably pleased at what they find, even if it is not quite Salzburg or Aix-en-Provence.

Wexford has its vintage years: two years ago I wrote with disfavour. This year (proceeding now) it strikes me as a *very* creditable shot: two bull's-eyes and an inner: three contrasted operas done with a lot of style and sympathy. You could go further and fare much worse. But what problems have to be overcome and what is the outlook? For, the fact is, the charm of the thing *is* its incongruity, its smallness, its shoestrings and, with broadcasts, world coverage, and the Irish Tourist Board, not to say that delicious refreshing fluid which sponsors the festival in some degree, the thing shows every sign of attracting too much rather than too little attention.

Also they have a good conductor, Kenneth Montgomery, getting fine results from the Telefis Eirean Orchestra and a charming cast in what is the chief collector's item: the nineteen-year-old Mozart's *Il Re Pastore* whose loveliest aria, 'L'amero saro costante', is sung by the Shepherd King himself, always has been in the repertory (e.g., Melba with Kubelik doing the obbligato) and was this time ravishingly delivered on one knee (an elegant object too) by Anne Pashley. The shepherdess was Norma Burrowes, who sang with agile bravura through an even, full range: just what your real opera fan will cross seas to hear. The whole pastorella was staged by John Cox, as it were in a salon in Schönbrunn, and managed to be pretty and 'amusing' without being arty or precious.

The Pearl Fishers in French looked well too in a frugal imaginative way which can't always be said about this opera, which finds Bizet emerging at times gloriously and always superbly singably, from the formulae of Gounod and Meyerbeer. Singhalese deep sea divers, hero called Nadir, no less, don't always look right when they are blacked up Belgian tenors. But here all was plausible, neither chum (the other is baritone Zurga) looking too obviously a meal for the sharks.

Their duet of old boys' solidarity where they bawl out their remembrance of the *blanche déesse* at the end of the Temple was a show stopper as done by John Stewart and Marco Bakker, stalwarts both, and the dusky all too-human goddess a temple maiden prepared to turn her back on Brahma for a very French love duet 'Ton coeur n'a pas compris' was most fervently and idiomatically phrased by last year's Lakmé, Christiane Eda-Pierre whose big scene 'Comme autre-fois' with the haunting horn which enchanted Berlioz, had the real right spell. I much admired Guy Barbier's conducting. The whole evening, which, O joy, included Benjamin Godard's trio, made me feel as I did forty years ago in the gods at the Opéra-Comique.

La Rondine, Puccini's one ignored mature opera or operette (see Greenfield and Carner's books on the fascinating story of the 1914 war and Ricordi's ill judgement, not to say the Master's own diffidence and uncertain handling of the genre) makes a collector's piece also, but it's a difficult proposition. Musically it looks back sometimes to the larkish bohemians, even to the soulful Butterfly but lies more often in the genre of the *Trittico* – pre-echoes of Sister Angelica and the *parlandos* of *Il Tabarro*: very interesting but a difficult wave band to tune.

I think Meyer Fredman will get it more idiomatic and dovetailed at the second and third performances but the Anthony Besch production seemed restless and though John Stoddart's sets are pretty the intended picture of Parisian gaiety somehow didn't quite come off: the Bal Bullier was more like a Waterford *Merry Widow* – a work incidentally much admired by Puccini which by and large sustains a much more suitable style for such a tale.

Guardian, October 1971

The Trojans

The ghost of Hector Berlioz in this centenary year was well and truly laid by the Royal Opera's splendid assumption of his huge double opera *Les Troyens* which was loudly acclaimed at a five and a half hour first night on Wednesday. I would like nothing better than to heap superlatives on this immense enterprise. Certainly the word Splendour can be used. As one expected, Colin Davis got a splendid response from a mighty cast and fine orchestra (though I think co-ordination and balance will improve greatly after a few more performances). Splendid too is the word for the heavy, jewelled, and richly coloured costumes of Mr Georgiadis even if not all his stage pictures can be called successful; and his fellow Greek Mr Volanakis's producing brings off some scenes with great effect – the departure from Carthage for instance.

But he is no more, perhaps less, successful than Gielgud twelve years ago with the apparition of Hector's ghost or the arrival of the wooden horse. The stage often looked cluttered rather than peopled. Better not illustrate the Royal Hunt and Storm at all than do it with so forcible-feeble an affair of gauzes and bogymen and pantomime lighting. I find nearly all the choreography has to go on the debit side. But perhaps you always have to have *misères* as well as *splendeurs*.

For that matter the score in its virtual entirety finds Berlioz nodding at times. Against the swooning ecstasy of the love scene, the throbbing passion and the sheer effrontery of the pomp and circumstance, one has to set some hit or miss devices, a failure to come to terms with the right operatic length. True, Berliozians will not tolerate criticism of this score, but certainly it has some strangely defective passages: not least the self-indulgent riding of a good idea to the point where it fails to tell any more.

Last time Covent Garden used Dent's English translation, not satisfactory in many ways, but I think it communicated more than Wednesday's largely incomprehensible French as sung by a non-French cast. There were honourable exceptions. As Dido, Josephine Veasey, pouring out tone of the most beautiful quality, managed to make much of her grief-stricken farewell intelligible. Mr Vickers as Aeneas makes a forthright and even idiomatic impression. They are very fine interpreters.

But the chorus and Cassandra (Anja Silja) do not succeed in making themselves effectively understood. The latter, however, exhibits a stage presence which dominates the episode of the mass suicide of Trojan women and, French singing apart, many of the secondary roles were assumed with great dignity and striking visual effect, not least Heather Begg as Dido's sister – their duet together was lovely; and Ian Partridge as Iopas whose courtly song was one of the evening's unquestionable successes. Ryland Davies seemed scared of his chance as the sailor Hylas whose 'Vallon sonore' is often accounted a highlight in the fifth act.

Some minor deficiencies must be put down to first-night nerves – as no doubt to that alarming débâcle of the scenery which almost decapitated Dido – a magnificent refusal to be upset on Miss Veasey's part. In short the musical performance will be better yet. What we have to accustom ourselves to are the often rather clumsy and fussy production and the sets. The garden scene is lovely, but

Dido's room, with those hissing lamps, as in this designer's uncomfortable Amneris scene in his *Aida*, are with us to stay. Imagination boggles at what it must have cost. But it is a glorious eyeful to match a gorgeous operatic feast. The balance is all admiration.

Guardian, September 1969

Billy Budd First Performance

Benjamin Britten's new and best opera, *Billy Budd*, commissioned by the Arts Council for the Festival, was given its first performance at the Royal Opera House, Covent Garden, last night. Few operas can have been cradled in so much determined goodwill; few composers of Mr Britten's age have won such acclaim. But then, few composers, since the eighteenth century, have done what he has done.

This stern and beautiful opera enhances his repute. Turning again to full-scale opera of the size of *Peter Grimes*, he shows a new mastery of that essential craft of managing operatic 'attention', and with it an originality, effectiveness, and fineness of musical creation altogether magnificent. If only one could laud the distinguished librettists, E. M. Forster and Eric Crozier, in similar terms, one might be saluting a masterpiece instead of a qualified success of esteem.

Herman Melville's fragmentary tale tells of a pathetic incident shortly after the Mutiny at the Nore: a young conscript, Budd, who suffers fits of stammering rage, the only flaw in an otherwise almost divinely innocent character, is falsely accused of sedition by the Master-at-Arms, who has taken against the lad's natural goodness. Budd strikes his accuser; the blow kills him; and the unlucky seaman is duly hanged at the yard-arm: all of which

Melville invests with his own kind of potent, moral, and cosmic significance.

It is the collaborators' hard task to convert a pathetic incident into a four-act tragedy, and one has to say that their solution, however conscientious and emotionally responsive, seems to give rise to a cardinal defect in the opera, considered as a work for the stage: 'seems' because critical first reactions to opera (where so many elements are involved) are notoriously insecure. Until the music has fully flowered in the mind the bare tree stumps impede our view of the whole wood. But where a defect sticks out so clearly it should be spoken of, even if the sheer musical virtues of the score finally 'carry' the opera.

Briefly, it is that the effort to turn a pathetic incident to tragedy has been entrusted to a third character – the moralizing tenor part, sung by Peter Pears, Captain 'Starry' Vere, the much hero-worshipped and nice-minded arbiter of Budd's fate, whose stern duty it is to string up the trusting seaman. Captain Vere is identified with the narrator in a prologue and an epilogue and is given a heavy burden of philosophical disquisition, together with prayers for that light which distinguishes right from wrong.

This gives the opera a core of almost German earnestness and is a brave effort to find an equivalent for Melville's voice in the proceedings, but it has the effect of weakening the 'natural' hero, Budd, and the villain, Claggart, in spite of their monologues and self-revelations, into little more than abstractions of good and bad, far less sharply and humanly characterized even than Scarpia and Cavaradossi, let alone Peter Pan and Hook; while Captain Vere, in a false position dramatically, fails to catch our sympathy for his dilemma of conscience to a notable degree, appearing rather as a sanctimonious, not to say priggish, character nearer to the perplexed prefect of some story by Dean Farrar than to Melville.

Perhaps the music redeems the flaw, so immediate and telling is the poetic atmosphere (not, unfortunately, matched by the dark, claustrophobic settings by John Piper or the dull production). But Mr Britten makes us sniff the salt air with a single cunningly spaced arpeggio; he holds a scene on a single rocking chord. The first scene of the second act is a masterpiece and as nearly as anything – would things had been left at that – springs the Captain's dilemma in our minds. A chord and the whole ominous calm of the ship is imaginatively projected. The officers drink (trio); from the orchestra the dreaded word 'mutiny' creeps into the conversation; then, with one of those effects of which only opera is capable, the answer is given – far off – by the happy singing below decks.

The ensuing scene, below decks, is no less brilliant. The songs and games, the brawl, the irruption of the villain, his Iago-like monologue (otiose, strictly speaking); the rousing of Budd from his sleep and his temptation by a suborned shipmate, the whole scene overlaid with the drowsy reminiscence of Budd's dream (which recurs in his farewell ballad in the fourth act) and ending with the fast, free, catchy duo with the elderly sailor – here, indeed, is mastery. But the climactic third act shows up the flaw. The opening, with the mist lifting and the ship going into action ('This is our moment') is superb; so, too, the change of atmosphere as the mist descends and, in rancour of disappointment, the false accusation is made. But from there to the end of the act events move jerkily. The 'accident'; the drumhead court-martial (quartet); Budd's plea for mercy, especially the captain's solo self-accusations, a quasi-Verdian outburst, are curiously implausible.

It is only when the captain leaves the stage empty to break the news of his fate to the poor seaman that the composer, freed from the fumbling libretto, can bring off a really effective operatic stroke: the reiteration, on the darkening stage, of a ponderous succession of related chords, like bell strokes (or 'ear tests'). On paper, dubious; on the stage, how triumphantly successful! They are like the ripples widening out from a marine disaster, and nothing could touch the imagination at that crucial point more effectively. What follows is anti-climax in the sense that it holds no chance of a surprise. But Britten reserves for it his most poignant music, the ballad of farewell and resignation for the prisoner and the mute, shambling procession towards execution, pierced by his cry of blessing on his captain. Then the decks are cleared of murmuring men, the mists come down, and we are back with the old narrator again. It may not have been the tragedy of conscience aimed at, but it has certainly left its emotional mark.

We shall hear later better performances. Theodor Uppman in voice (light baritone) and in person is ideally cast as Budd; Peter Pears and Frederick Dalberg as the Captain and the Master-at-Arms rather less so. Some of the small parts are well done. The composer conducted.

Guardian, December 1951

Billy Budd in 1979

Since 1951 something has happened to my reception of musical eloquence; nothing strange, or even interesting generally, about that. Such changes occur, but I must say it to qualify the intense response I had on Monday to Britten's opera *Billy Budd* which seemed to me enormously powerful; whereas in 1951 I felt like the late Neville Cardus, that the score though immensely clever, did not somehow pack a vigorous operatic punch (in the way, for example, Verdi's *Otello* had done during a lifetime).

Monday's revival seemed to me overwhelming, strong, affecting and searching. Or could it be this interpretation? I cannot say: only that Thomas Allen's performance in the name part was obviously and incomparably fine and touching. The scene of the acceptance of death was enough to draw tears from a stone. Captain Vere was taken over at short notice from Richard Cassilly who was not well enough to sing a role that should suit him. Richard Lewis, with his fine expressive line and perfect diction, totally convinced us that this was *his* part too.

Geraint Evans made the evil Claggart 'tell' with the strength of a Scarpia. A dozen other roles from Richard Van Allan, Norman Welsby, Handel Owen, Rouleau, Dobson, Leggate et al, and many more came up in perfect proportion under the baton of Edward Downes and the fine chorus too, of course. The decor strikes me as too uniformly dark now; there is *sea-light* in the music but not in the scene. Yet it is great stuff to take in.

Guardian, March 1979

Britten's *Midsummer Night's Dream*

Nice for lovers of Shakespeare that this play does not arrive as a Tin Pan Alley musical called 'Bottom!' whatever some people may say about Britten's beautiful opera (his ninth) – for instance that there is a certain lack of 'getting there' about the music, a certain negative, Ravelian diffidence, a certain want of sustained lyrical singing for an opera of this length – the work cannot be faulted for lack of a true feeling for Shakespeare. I, who dare to criticize in both fields of opera and straight drama, declare that this opera has more true feeling for the play than dozens of straight performances I have seen. To put it broadly: all that is concerned with the supernatural elements, all the music of sleep and dreams and woods bewitched, is quite marvellously successful, from the first heaving, snoring sighs which creep out of the orchestra and seem to hang in the air (such is Georg Solti's conducting) above the magic glade which John Piper has devised. The music is never more ethereal than in this: that it seems detached from the players in the pit.

Let us go straight to the heart of the play in the middle act (the best in all ways, musical, dramatic, and visual). Here the magic works strongly, but defies analysis. The components are the silvery top of Joan Carlyle's voice as Tytania; the unearthly counter-tenor (the most appealing I ever heard) of Russell Oberlin as Oberon, King of Fairies; the hoarse speaking voice of the boy actor and dancer Nicholas Chagrin, who plays Puck ideally and even, by remaining slightly outside opera, bridges the piece perfectly towards the Shakespeareans, especially in the Epilogue. There are seven urchin choirboy voices too, and working the simplest strokes of celesta for eye-drops, a swooping arpeggio or a flicker of woodwind, Britten conjures the magic irresistibly. If the scene of the translation of Bottom (with, be it noted, the help of a detail for lack of which I've seen more than one 'Dream' go wrong, i.e., a very good ass's head) – if this scene and Tytania's cozening of her monster is not perfect Shakespeare, may I too grow a mighty pair of ears? What does it consist of? The genius to make Bottom's voice break into a hee-haw at the right moment in 'The ousel cock . . .'; Tytania remembering, as it were, the sylphs of Berlioz as she adores the Ass and then when he has proclaimed his 'reasonable good ear for music' and requested a song with accompaniment on 'the bones', the sudden snatch of 'Boys and girls come out to play . . .'

An operatic composer can have his way with Shakespeare and defy false interpretation: I do not see how this scene could be better done. With the quartet of lovers, however, doubts come in. Are they well enough characterized? Is Helena's dilemma placed? Does the quarrelling quartet in Act 2 really make its dramatic point? I think it is the characterization which is at fault, and possibly the vocal performances, because Britten has done wonders in keeping the lovers' intrigue on the right plane, neither tragic nor stupid, but a level between both (again something possible in opera as in no, or few other, media).

Britten conveys the perplexity of love but not surely its ecstasy which is what I meant by saying that one does not always feel the music is getting anywhere: hints, allusions evanescent ideas compose the dream feeling but leave us rather lost with the mortals when fully awake. The Mechanicals' rehearsal is very funny: funnier I thought than 'Pyramus and Thisbe' as enacted with its parodies of Italian opera and Thisbe as Lucia. This is not quite to match the subtlety of Oberon's 'I know a bank where the wild thyme growes . . .'

The reception was rapturous. Georg Solti and the orchestra

deserved every cheer and so in the main did the cast. Sir John Gielgud's direction is tactful but lacks the touch of genius which a Felsenstein might have provided. Mr Piper's middle act set is a beauty. Geraint Evans (Bottom), John Lanigan (Flute), Michael Langdon (Quince), André Turp, and Marjorie Thomas, Louis Quilico and Irene Salemka as the quartet of lovers were all commendable. But it is the fairy part of it which makes the evening: the artless-seeming valedictory, a fairy chorus, was one of the most delightful moments of all.

Guardian, February 1961

Death in Venice

The revival of Britten's opera *Death in Venice* last night was conducted magnificently by Steuart Bedford, the final scenes charged with a distant yet poignant emotional force stronger than I have experienced hitherto in this work. It is in any case a most beautiful production, a model of what lighting (John B. Read), suggestive yet economical settings by John Piper together with the gifts of producers and choreographers such as Colin Graham and Frederick Ashton can achieve when the piece has been perfectly rehearsed, as it must have been in this presentation by Richard Gregson.

Britten comes to a searing eloquence in the latter half and always and everywhere the sound picture was arrestingly beautiful and interesting, even if a hostile critic might say that at times it is flimsy, or even 'filmy'. I thought it most movingly managed last night and of course not the least cause of that was Peter Pears himself, aged sixty-five and living Thomas Mann's ageing hero with a total identification which we get in operatic artists far more often than is generally assumed. Think of some of the *Boris* or *Traviata* impersonations of recent years.

Mr Pears acts it without shirking anything, even moments of dubious jauntiness, and brings it out to the full and moving close. Thomas Hemsley is the multiple 'traveller', seven roles in various guises. Greatly to be admired in this protean exercise. Very much admired too was the alto Voice of Apollo, John York Skinner, a fine sound well placed, Robert Huguenin was the alluring and beautiful beach boy who torments the hero and Deanne Bergsma was his Czarina-like mother: both splendid mimes. The audience listened in rapt admiration.

Guardian, June 1975

Don Pasquale

Donizetti's *Don Pasquale* has always seemed to me a touchstone of operatic taste in this country. It comes back tonight after nearly four decades to Covent Garden (never its natural home) and will no doubt fare very well, for a present generation has 'caught it' – this most catchy of scores – from the gramophone, from many revivals, not least those by Sadler's Wells and the Welsh National Opera.

But for those whose memories don't reach back much before the war in this field, it must be hard to imagine the contempt in which Donizetti as a composer was held in the late 1920s and early 1930s: grudging exceptions were made for *L'Elisir d'amore* ('The Love Potion') and for *Don Pasquale* where it was allowed that Donizetti's 'weak sentimental and conventional' formulae were not inappropriate to the light-hearted intrigues: whereas, it was implied, these methods were totally inadequate to sustain or express such dramatic situations as those brought forward by *Lucia di Lammermoor* or *La Favorita*.

Well, that notion is all changed now. It was a view held as a
reaction (by those who wanted more Richard Strauss, say) that the
nineteenth-century adulation of the prolific maestro from
Bergamo now needed a good snub (that is the English way of
dealing in musical stocks and shares). He was to be devalued. When
Toti dal Monte sang Lucia at Covent Garden in 1925 there was but
a single performance and the nobs rated it ludicrous. A rather
different story was to be told after the war when Callas and then
Sutherland created sustained furores of acclaim and Zeffirelli
mounted the piece with genius and a lavishness hardly matched
until then. Of course, it is a beautiful opera taken in its own right:
Bernard Shaw pointed out that though the mad scene is in waltz
time it is not either incongruous or anything but devastatingly
exciting theatre. The sextet speaks for itself: and the tenor melody
in the last act 'Tu che a Dio spiegasti l'ali' is one of the most
beautiful in all romantic opera.

But it can certainly be argued that Donizetti's music is never
more perfectly fitting than in the opening scenes of *Don Pasquale*
where in a family-comedy of sentiment, deriving in a straight line
from the *commedia dell' arte*, the rich old bachelor announces a
desire to get married ('un fuoco insolito') and the disinheritable
nephew tenor descants above it his farewell to dreams of his own
betrothal ('sogno soave e casto'). It was at that point, in the gallery
of the Teatro Reale in Rome, that I first heard the heavenly,
floated, dulcet half-voice of Tito Schipa, a voice small but so
perfectly projected that it 'spoke' in even the biggest opera houses.
Donizetti goes from good to better all through the work: wily
Malatesta, Pasquale's friend arranges a 'bride' for old Pasquale and
describes her 'Bella siccome un angelo' which is as good as any of
the baritone music in *La Traviata* and the rehearsal duet where
Malatesta and Norina (the tenor's fiancée who is to pose as a bride
at a mock wedding and then give the old man hell till he gives up
the idea of finding bliss in marriage) marks a real high spot in all
comic opera.

With the great Stabile and Alda Noni in the Jay Pomeroy
Cambridge Theatre seasons it brought down the house in a way

that meant, to my ear, that Pasquale was back for ever: I remember sighing in print at the time that I supposed a return of Lucia was unthinkable . . . but I had only to wait in patience: (shares go up again, please note.) I won't continue with the story of the comedy of *Don Pasquale*: even those to whom it will be a total novelty certainly won't find it obscure or boring: but the quartet is a masterpiece, not any less than the great sextet in *Lucia* nearly a decade earlier: people are apt to jump over it and cite the quartet from *Rigoletto* as the next landmark. As for the servants' whispering chorus, the garden scene (*Notturno*) with the lilting serenade 'Come è gentile la notte mezz-april' and the billing and cooing in thirds and sixths, a love duet deliberately sung to be overheard by the old dupe himself, they are instant charmers, and you would have to despise *Figaro* – either Mozart's or Rossini's which Stendhal preferred – not to surrender. The succession is such. Only the patter duet for baritone and bass seems to me on a slightly lower level than Rossini at his best.

But it must be remembered that *Don Pasquale* fell out of fashion among the austere British between the wars – and when it was done at Covent Garden in 1937 I well recall the rictus of dismay on the face of Sir (then Mr) William Glock on hearing the cornet solo-like introduction for the tenor's lament 'Cerchero lontana terra'.

Next year Glyndebourne made a real success of it with Audrey Mildmay, John Christie's wife, and Stabile too. So even before the war the opera had got back some of the fantastic popularity it had known in Paris in the middle of last century, where at the outset of Offenbach's *La Vie Parisienne* we find characters enumerating the chief glory of the French capital – Adelina Patti in *Don Pasquale*.

The favourite cast however was the handsome Mario (pin-up tenor, a Piedmontese guardsman whose legs were noted by Madame Bovary in Rouen), Grisi his wife, and, of course, the fabulous Lablache; 'never was nobler organ, never a grander head set on mightier shoulders' than his. He must indeed have been ideal.

Illness (syphilis) was closing in on the fantastically fertile

Donizetti (sixty operas or more). In a year or two general paralysis of the insane would confine him to a living tomb. It was a radiant sunset.

Guardian, February 1973

Mathis der Maler
World Premiere at Zurich 1938

How far is an artist justified in standing apart from the common struggle of mankind? What is his place in an afflicted world? That, in effect, is the question asked and answered in Hindemith's *Mathis der Maler*, which was brought to the stage for the first time at the Zürich Opera House last night. To Mathis Grünewald, working peacefully in the protection of the Cardinal Archbishop of Mainz, comes the harsh thought that art is vanity, an escape from duty. The times are grievous. Man's misery cries aloud. The dawn of the Renaisscence comes too slowly, and the skies are red with the fires of peasant insurrection, the burning out of heresy and the strife of creeds. Leaving his work, renouncing love and patronage, Mathis joins the peasants and seeks a hero's death. But here is no fulfilment, only perplexity and sense of waste. Artists, he finds, make poor soldiers, and the noble-seeming cause turns to futility.

Hunted and homeless, he wanders in the forest, and in a vision sees himself as St Antony tempted by the world and tormented by despair. He sees the Cardinal in the likeness of St Paul, who brings him comfort and an answer to his perplexity. Artists are not as other men: their special mission is divine. 'Return,' says St Paul, 'return and paint.' Taking these visions as his subject, Mathis creates his masterpiece, the Isenheim Altar. It is his final offering. At last, all passion spent, his mission justified, he can seek death in his time, alone and content.

It need not be emphasized that artists of our day too must face a like dilemma. To draw modern parallels, however apt, would be superfluous. What is significant here from the point of view of music is that Hindemith has been able to make of such a theme not a remote and intellectual oratorio, but strong, compelling work for the theatre. Nothing at first sight could seem less apt for operatic treatment than this conflict in an artist's mind. Yet by allowing the claims of the opera of action and emotional conflict, by weaving his main theme into three subsidiary plots, Hindemith contrives to give it forcible expression of a kind effective in the theatre.

Mathis's conflict is linked with the fate of Ursula, his renounced love, Albrecht, his rejected patron, and Regina, the peasant child whom he befriends. We see him not only alone in the dark night of his soul, but also as others see him, as painter, lover, friend. That is what brings the character into relief. Unlike Gerontius, Mathis is felt to be a real person. The only weakness of this – a weakness in Hindemith the librettist – is that the by-play is too fully treated so that it lengthens the work unduly, and somewhat weakens the impact of the main idea.

But the music of these minor characters is some of the most arresting and could not easily be cut. Nor is there any lack of theatrical effectiveness in the scenes of action. Mathis helping Schwalb to freedom is no less exciting than the almost identical scene in the church in *Tosca*. The horror of the times, peasant war and persecution, is evoked with a power which the composer of *The Huguenots* might envy.

That Hindemith should thus show himself a man of the theatre is surprising, in spite of the evidence of *Cardillac*. But much more surprising is it to note the wealth of feeling and sentiment which springs from this many-sided score. Those who found nascent romanticism in his early works will regard *Mathis* as a return to the composer's true self. But those who have come to think of him as a dry, intellectual composer addicted to tiresome doctrines will have to revise their opinions. The term 'romantic' cannot be resisted, though compared with the overblown romanticism of Strauss this taut, spare writing seems austere and even formal. These long, expressive vocal phrases, this economical orchestration recalls rather the late Verdi. Nor need the modern idiom dismay. However strange the use of musical language, what it expresses is readily perceived.

To praise the enterprise of the Zürich Stadttheater in opening the June Festival with this work would be superfluous. Enough to say that the composer has been fortunate, and to make mention of the excellent musical direction of Herr Denzler, the imaginative production of Herr Schmid-Bloss and the fine settings of Herr Roman Clemens. The teamwork was admirable. No singer of importance failed, and the four principals, Mmes Hellwig and Funk and Herren Stig and Baxevanos, acquitted themselves splendidly in an arduous but rewarding undertaking.

The Times, May 1938

Mathis – 35 years on

Thirty-five years ago Hindemith was under ban and in exile. He got his stern, fine, vigorous opera about Matthis Grünewald, the painter of the great altar at Isenheim, put on in Zürich. Furtwängler, to his eternal credit, risked much to leave Germany and conduct it. I had the privilege of flying, in a plane unpressurized – as they were in those days – and came down to earth with altitude sickness only to find this imposing score much above my critical head. I have had special regard for it ever since.

Camden gave us a concert performance, last of three (earlier in Oxford and Cambridge), a confident, dedicated performance by the Chelsea Group under Roderick Brydon. All credit to them too for putting their hand so firmly on a tough job. Perhaps it is not a work for concert performance but at least in such circumstances you don't notice that as a staged opera it seems uncertainly timed, with some tender moments which take the attention immediately, but others which might be the musical equivalent of a long conversational scene in Bernard Shaw getting rather piled up, from a musical and dramatic point of view.

Still, it is always interesting, never factitious or flimsy. With the staging in mind I could feel the dramatic argument: the despair of an artist (always a difficult subject – see Ibsen or, in opera, *Benvenuto Cellini*), the pains of insurrection – this is the peasants' revolt and Lutheran faction of the sixteenth century – to say nothing of the pains of love: the women are a Cardinal's daughter and a sort of Mignon waif as a second soprano. There are choruses of book-burning: think what *that* meant in 1938.

Guardian, February 1974

Fidelio

The beautiful *Fidelio* which opened the Glyndebourne Festival last night, reminded us again, as it had twenty years ago, that this is a good stage for the wonderful but difficult opera. In Peter Hall's staging, perfect but quite unobtrusive and unexaggerated, in the plain and effective settings by John Bury and in the characterization throughout which had integrity and no over forcing of dramatic points, this was the performance which one had hoped for.

Furthermore the conducting of Bernard Haitink, vital, forward-going but capable of heart-stopping delicacy in the great moments of reflection as at the start of the quartet or the emergence of the prisoners, helped to achieve what is so difficult in this opera: to make a whole of music which is often sublime, with a down-to-earth melodrama and humdrum domestic excitement which are often ill-matched and break up the continuity of the piece.

It is as about as finely managed a *Fidelio* in this respect as I have ever encountered.

Elisabeth Söderström is strong if not specially substantial as the rescuing wife. But she manages always to make the point musically with great effect without resorting to what Germans call a heavy dose of the 'high dramatic'. Ian Caley and Elizabeth Gale were an excellent secondary pair. Kurt Appelgren was a wholly convincing Rocco and there was a finely cut and vivid portrait of the governor Pizarro in the person of the Australian Robert Allmann, full voice, slight blurring of the lines sometimes, but most effective also.

Michael Langdon making a sort of farewell to the operatic stage, put much into the small part of the Minister at the end. And the Dutch tenor, Anton de Ridder, imposed himself most powerfully in the dungeon scene which was thrilling from first to last. The LPO and chorus were in fine form and the reception was ecstatic.

Guardian, May 1979

The Threepenny Opera

Die Dreigroschenoper is the Brecht that everyone loves. Some of us were humming 'Mack the Knife', the hit number from this Kurt Weill masterscore, in the late 1920s. It seemed like the echo of a lifetime last night: an elegy for all those long ago, far off unhappy things. *The Threepenny Opera* stands to modern theatre somewhat as the films of Pabst and Pudovkin do *vis à vis* the modern cinema. You just have to know it. It is a gutter gem, a slum classic, and those who miss its desolate pathos must be groping in the dark in pursuit of truth in the labyrinth of our culture.

The Ensemble's production dates from 1960 and as far as I can trust my memory it is in nearly all points an improvement on the famous original which swept Europe on stage and screen. Certainly I find it hard to imagine a better Mackie than Wolf Kaiser who is simply magnificent; contained, sardonic, the spring-heeled masher of imagination – with his low forehead and gentlemanly leer, he puts into his performance such a wealth of detail that not a point falls to the ground. Voice, face, presence, height, volume of personality – there is no substitute for such qualities in an actor. If I could see and re-see a hundred times this Captain's shifty slow foxtrot with treacherous Jenny while the coppers tiptoe into the hall of the Wapping brothel to arrest him, I feel sure I should not tire of it: one of those little moments of perfection that are born only in wonderful theatrical companies, whether the occasion is trivial or tragic.

Polly in this event was a treat, too. Christine Gloger has the classical look for the part: Dresden doll, with a temper like a macaw. Her enunciation is so perfect that she can sing Polly's 'Und sagte nur immer "Nein"' without any force on a thread of sound and yet make every component tell. The wedding breakfast scene was perfection: its high point the duet between Mackie and Tiger Brown of the London Police (Siegfried Kilian), an old-boys-together ballad of quite appalling cynicism. (In the original production these now world famous ballads were wickedly ascribed to Rudyard Kipling!)

Peter Kalisch as Peachum deserves a mention and so does Felicitas Ritsch who put over that wan, haunting Salamo song with great effect. Erich Engel's production is unobtrusively right: witness the playing down of the whore house atmosphere so grotesquely badly done in some revivals. The musical direction under Hans Dieter Hosella also spoke of complete professional accomplishment. The performance was greeted with rapture.

Guardian, August 1965

The Gondoliers

With *The Gondoliers*, all this week, the D'Oyly Carte company completes the chronological display of their repertory and must now in a matter of days stand up for the first time to metropolitan, professional competition from Sadler's Wells and Her Majesty's where Guthrie's *Pinafore* and *Pirates* are due in the first weeks of February. Some say the traditionalists will take an awful beating: others, including myself, that they will still take a lot of beating.

Not that last night's was a superlative revival of the least dated (indeed completely undated) of the operas, a fantasy as topical as Mozart's *Cosi* and rather more so than Mr Eliot's *The Confidential Clerk* (which are two works which come a little to mind). The chorus and the orchestra were professional and perky as ever; the chocolate box view of the lagoon – there's a wasted chance – was hard and bright and the words at whatever cost were audible. There was one understudy on: Peggy Anne Jones, who had a sporting shot at Tessa. And Jean Hindmarsh sang prettily as the other soprano sister. But almost everyone else sounded as if he or she had just recovered from or was about to succumb to a cold in the head: it might have been Covent Garden opera and not Savoy. Still, much pleasure was given.

On the first night of the present season I unkindly enquired: 'What has happened to the principals of the company?' I retract the innuendo that they seem much diminished. I have found a great deal to admire in their style. Their size and volume seem to me still too small. But isn't that something perhaps to do with age? At the time I was first seeing these works with singers like Darrell Fancourt and Edna Thornton, the very policemen in the streets outside were all eighteen-stone giants with handlebar moustaches. Perhaps it is only that I have got bigger myself. So don't let any head shaking or repining on my part put you off.

A stern borough councillor took me to task the other night: 'They,' he said, meaning G and S, 'are a waste of time.' Being a peaceable chap, I said, 'Like cricket,' but said it under my breath. 'What?' said he. 'More rewarding than train-spotting,' I said, and we left it at that. It is true there is more in Schubert and Mozart. What one did resent about the fanatics of old was that while wallowing in Savoy operas they wouldn't cross the road to hear Offenbach or Mozart or any other silly foreigners. But that situation is surely less stiff now. The beloved works are in fact passing into perspective: a corpus of elegant, witty, tuneful light operas which should be a useful stock in our national lyric theatre.

Guardian, January 1962

Samson and Delilah

Like a trusted old firm of haberdashers *Samson and Delilah* (one can almost see the name on the shopfront) produces yards of fine quality stuff. Never was music less rubbishy, yet so little touched with spiritual magnificence. People who slightly disapprove of Saint-Saëns anyway are apt to complain that this is 'empty' music; and so it is if compared to late Beethoven or indeed early Verdi – beautifully composed and yet ineloquent. On the other hand there is a secret audience that digs all that jam in the second act. I have long noticed this and I have every sympathy with them; the grand seduction scene, of which 'Mon coeur s'ouvre à ta voix' is the particular plum in the compot, is quite irresistibly voluptuous and exciting. The conservatoire 'exercise' choruses and the ballets may be taken or left as you please, but all French opera and indeed perhaps opera altogether will likely remain a closed book to those whose hearts are not melted in some degree by this famous central scene.

Guardian, November 1963

DIVAS AND
OTHER SINGERS

Solo Voices

I love a soprano, a loud soprano, even a lame one. Those who cannot share this enthusiasm had better cease reading at once. One swallow doesn't make a summer, nor one nightingale either (leave the macaw for later). But it does seem to me that this has been a splendid season for sopranos in London: all colours, shapes and sizes, giving the lie to the moaners and praisers of bygone golden ages. 'Singers' in the lunch-time evening papers' sense usually means pop stars, *I* mean concert artists, if that didn't somehow suggest the winter-gardens world.

In summer we have three even four opera houses going (if you count Glyndebourne and foreign visitors to Sadler's Wells). For the one you slip into a boiled shirt just after lunch: for the Royal Opera on the other hand, bare feet and an any-more-for-the-skylark neckline suits the stalls. On top of all this, indefatigable single concert versions of obscure operas get put on on Sunday nights and savoured in the five-guinea stall bracket.

One such of these remains gloriously in memory for the super singing of the Spanish soprano Montserrat Caballé. Postponed and substituted once – she had broken a leg in old New York – but at last we were to hear her.

'La donna é mobile?' we asked anxiously. 'Well, only just mobile: she's on crutches you know.' This did not sound too incongruous for an opera called *Il Pirata* by Bellini. Visions of Long John Silver came to mind. But when the handsome diva appeared, the stateliness of her progress from wings to stage centre (where else after all?) awoke a royal cheer. Nothing brings out the gallantry of a British audience like the sight of a handicap on stage. Erect before a score upon a music stand, she proceeded to sing with the utmost brilliance – making old buffs think if not of Galli Curci at least of Mercedes Capsir – disdaining the succour even of a voltapagine or turner-over if you insist on Anglo-Saxon. This, however, involved transferring the right crutch to the left to free an arm – dextrous and deft work even in the andante, and it became borne in on us that an allegro prestissimo was at hand. When it came, hey presto, I don't believe any such piece of juggling since Cinquevalli kept six billiard balls in the air has ever been seen – and *he* didn't have to sing scales, roulades and hair-split divisions while he was doing it. Dear Mme Caballé, when you are mended we shall love you all the better for this memory of you in adversity.

All this pleasure came by way of the London Opera Society who had earlier introduced us to some others in this mighty handful, my nest of singing birds. For it was at a similar freak-out Meyerbeer revival – *The Huguenots* – that I first heard Martina Arroyo and decided she would figure as my ideal Aida (after Leontyne Price at least). And so she has proved. She is black (the word I suppose) and comfortable looking, not to say matronly. 'Tremble thou dusky one,' cries the equally dusky Princess Amneris, her rival (a case of pot calling the kettle, surely?). But black Aidas have the edge on their white sisters. Verdi wrote the most taxing of all roles here and one of the longest. 'We must not,' he said to Ghislanzoni, 'ask too much of our heroine but we may not ask too little.' The third act makes fantastic demands. Miss Arroyo sailed over the hedges like some great thoroughbred, climbing in the solo to a high C which came out like the evening star, bright as a diamond, clear and steady. You don't get it much better, I heard my inner self decide. As for the descant during the splendid (but rather untidy) Triumph Scene (so like those stills of Griffith's *Intolerance*) with all the supers and chaps from Kneller Hall, at the big crunch Miss Arroyo was going such great guns that one was simply overwhelmed by sheer admiration of her physical courage – bravura, no less – like a partisan stopping a tank bare-handed.

You will be saying that I admire sheer power in a soprano and though I can worship a Schwarzkopf or an Elisabeth Schumann I do rate power pretty high. In these days of electronic amplifying, I dare say this taste is on the way out and old hat. But there is something to me wonderful in a really gigantic voice in full cry. As many people are simply horrified by the phenomenon I make it plain that I award myself no special marks in the matter. But I do like power *evenly* distributed and capable of real control. In this matter the Greek soprano Elena Suliotis has me worried: her chest notes come out like a paper seller announcing the outbreak of war: her top is not of the same piece and wiry. Verdi specified that his Lady Macbeth (which she has been singing at Covent Garden) should not have a conventionally 'beautiful' voice: but I bet he expected, as of right, an even scale. Still with her bulging eyeballs and imperious strut she throws a lot of Callas-style personality at you and that I fear often suffices for the general public.

Last but best in a wonderful season: Birgit Nilsson as Strauss's *Elektra*, with Solti drawing marvels of sound from the Royal Opera Orchestra. This was a performance which ultimately earned thirty-six curtain calls (do I care for nothing but size?) and sent some of us into a rigor of applause. Dramatically, musically, it was a masterly assumption but when all is said the quality which made this *Elektra* so electrifying was the sheer voltage and ease of the vocalization regarded as something in itself: there were times when I could find no simile except that of one's astonishment on looking up at a crane, watching it hoist a mighty steel girder, swing it round and lower it into position without a single bump or tremor. Kolossal! as the krauts used to say.

Punch, July 1969

Montserrat Caballé: *Il Pirata*

Il Pirata looked as if it might be a non-starter. Substituted for a Meyerbeer work and then postponed because Mme Montserrat Caballé broke a leg, it finally got off the ground at Drury Lane last night. So too did the prima donna, who managed crutches with enormous skill and dignity, looked not in the least like Long John Silver, and in the closing pages of Bellini's uneven (third) opera, sang with a perfection of delivery which brought the audience also to its feet.

She gets better. I have burned my boats about her Rossini. I declare that last night's was some of the best *bel canto* singing we have heard since the war. It is secure. The strong voice is so perfectly placed in the 'mask' that loud notes and soft ones ring out like the strokes of a bell, with no sort of puffing or blowing, and the accuracy and precision of the ornaments is a delight, because one feels a total sense of security. In fact, a singer of real schooling; moreover, a fine musician and a moving actress – as far as that goes in a concert performance, with your hero and villain in evening dress, like two impressive maîtres d'hôtel. I don't think *Il Pirata*, founded on an Irish play slated by Coleridge, is ever likely to go down big in the modern repertory, but when it is the occasion for such a display as this on the part of a splendid prima donna it seems highly rewarding.

The conductor was Mr Cillario who did wonders, giving a feeling of having had ample rehearsal (which he probably had not). The tenor, Rubini's role originally, was sung in forceful but by no means inadequate style by the tenor Bernabé Marti. Vicenzo Sardinero was the baritone and Glynne Howell the basso, a hermit, who when the hero is shipwrecked – wouldn't you know it? – turns out to be living in a cave nearby and to be his ex-tutor as well! The London Opera Society puts us in its debt.

Guardian, June 1969

Montserrat Caballé: *Norma*

What an irony that with our two big opera houses, it should be a concert hall which framed the début of the magnificent Caballé, in that supreme test of the *bel canto* diva, Bellini's masterpiece *Norma*, which towers above his other works. Still the Festival Hall could hardly have heard more beautifully fashioned singing nor more riotous applause. There are those who find Bellini wan and wiltingly elegiac. But the kind of performance which Carlo Felice Cillario elicited from his soloists and the New Philharmonia, with the Royal Choral Society, had that grandeur and passionate nobility which our ancestors heard in it (it nearly killed Queen Victoria).

This was a performance which sustained the rigours of the great female duets, the bravura solos, but also knew how to provide the big 'crunch' for the most elevated moments of what is, after all, a tragedy as much as any by Racine. The lightweight finicking conductorship we have sometimes heard at the Garden was blessedly absent.

If the score does not everywhere stand scrutiny on its own, critics should bethink them that the score of *Giselle* is lovely in as much (and no more than) it provides peerless opportunity for great dancing. Likewise Bellini, for his singers; and no one who heard Mme Caballé in the opening scene of Act II – where Norma, gazing at the children which Medea-like she means to slay ('Dormono entrambi'), takes up the magnificent maestoso lament of the celli in the introduction – will ever be likely to call this prima donna too placid a perfectionist, or Bellini a watercolour artist.

Here perfection of vocal delivery was infused with a tragic distress – perfect of its kind. Mme Caballé looks like a portrait by Ingres and draws a vocal line like that of this painter; not overcharged with colour but riding on the invisible breath like the bow of the violinist on his string. When it comes to the thirds and sixths of the ladies' duets of rival sisterhood, it is of a violinist's double stopping that we think. Mme Cossotto, also in splendid voice, has a vocal grain different from the soprano; more vibrant and, one would say, 'Verdian'. But while not stinting herself in her own numbers she fined down her tone for a good, if not ideal blend in both the big duets.

The memory of Mme Caballé's 'Ah rimembranza' spiralling out in a perfect arabesque will stay with me, I hope, for years. Both singers had beautiful steady held notes. The soprano as she showed first in 'Bello a me ritorno' has a flexibility and both a glide and a staccato which admit no peer. Only the trill is weak and there is a slight tendency to linger beyond the call of the rhythm. But a more classical *Norma* it would be hard to imagine.

Husbands of these two great ladies, the tenor, Bernabé Marti and Ivo Vinco the bass druid respectively, sang generously. Indeed, the Druid's 'Ite sulle colle' presaged accurately the kind of performance we had hoped for and heard.

A well-meant effort to suggest some stage atmosphere – lowered house lights, a sort of village-hall 'stone' screen, and sundry comings and goings of dinner-jacketed Romans and electric-blue druidesses may have quickened imagination in some people. But of course the drama hangs on Norma's legato line, as a *Giselle* hangs on the ballerina's balance. For this kind of vocal miracle a thousand pairs of ears did not listen in vain.

Guardian, April 1971

Montserrat Caballé: *Adriana Lecouvreur*

A superb concert performance of Cilea's *Adriana Lecouvreur*, one of Denny Dayviss's presentations which have made quite a lot of operatic history these past years, brought us Caballé in the very rose and perfection of her art. In haste now I can only describe Adriana's death scene, 'Poveri fiori' and the duet 'No sulla fronte' as sublime singing, the line pure, expressive, poised and able to swell or retreat as if under the bow of a master violinist. But her whole performance was exquisite: her entrance aria running gently to the climax of 'un sofio di mia voce . . . morir' was as one dreams of hearing it.

In the celebrated recitation, too (which in the play, Bernard Shaw would always expatiate upon, for the benefit of his favourite actresses), Mme Caballé put on the grand manner to a sumptuous degree. Now *there* is something to act: the lack of which a famous stage actress of our time was bewailing to me the other day. However this was a concert performance with only token acting. One missed some dramatic effect: e.g. the scene of double assignation in the darkened drawing-room and the 'I saw him first' duet for the rival ladies: incidentally Bianca Berini as the mezzo also made her mark; a fine voice and presence.

But the faithful Michonet, the Comédie Française stage manager who adores Adriana from afar was a little diminished by concert conditions: all the same the baritone, D'Orazi, was excellent. As for the tenor Carreras, who recently made so good an effect in *Traviata* at Covent Garden, he played up magnificently to the diva; both had great dignity; both sang gorgeously where the pressure is needed. Hers was the refinement however.

Cilea's music derives a bit from Verdi's *Falstaff* in its chattering ensembles and from Puccini's *Manon Lescaut* in its erotic swooning. But it has a flavour of its own. Maestro Gina Franco Masini conducted the NPO with honour.

Guardian, May 1974

Kirsten Flagstad's Isolde

Tristan und Isolde is the ideal of Wagnerian music drama and the most monumental and potent realization in terms of voice and orchestra of the pain and ecstasy of love. But like the love which is its subject it binds a spell not to be explained by rational analysis of the aching, chromatic progressions, the delayed climaxes, the incomparable power of translating mood be it bliss or desolation into sound. *Tristan* is a milestone in the education of the senses, and to pass it for the first time or to come upon it after an absence of ten years is a deeply moving occasion; it is like suddenly sighting the huge, forgotten-about Atlantic: overwhelming, mesmeric. No one who is not fatally genteel or frigid or completely tone deaf can ever remain indifferent.

The Covent Garden Trust, mounting the masterpiece in German in a steady production by Schramm the Swiss producer and with orchestra under Dr Rankl, gives its best yet; the performance, a noble one all considered, is made possible by and revolves around the greatest heroic soprano of our day, Kirsten Flagstad. A truly magnificent singer! We have heard more dramatic Isoldes, with a quicker rage and a keener anguish; curiously this great singer's personality goes into an eclipse when she is silent. But for sheer flawless splendour of singing, this Isolde has no equal. Besides the sensation she gives of having limitless reserves, two other peculiarities must strike every listener; her enunciation remains classically pure whatever is demanded of the voice; the words, so interesting a clue to the whole of the German tragedy, words which continually build up a meaningless self-deluding romantic mystery, are quite beautifully sung, just as every note value is sung as Wagner wrote it. And just where nearly all heroic sopranos fail, in the upper middle reaches of the voice, Mme Flagstad positively seems to be at her easiest: the effect of her F or her G effortlessly riding the full flood of orchestral tone astonishes, as nothing else. Where we have learnt to accept from others a desperate wailing yodel, Mme Flagstad rolls us a note like the Atlantic sending in a breaker. There is not, and there could not be, any question of failure; at one moment this peerless diva calmly put the erring wood-wind back on the right note!

Her Isolde is deeper and tenderer than a decade ago, and the things one has remembered across the years are still there – the greeting to Tristan in the second act when above the bubbling horns and fever of the strings, she turns on us a jet of sound like a fireman's hose; and with what serenity she later follows the twinning chromatics of the love duet.

Time and Tide, February 1948

Sena Jurinac: in *Rosenkavalier*

Rose-bearing, breeches-wearing mezzo sopranos who can carry off the title role of Richard Strauss's sumptuous score are not perhaps the rare birds I once thought them. All my life my Oktavians seem to have been stunners. But this does not lessen the enjoyment to be derived from the latest to take the stage at Covent Garden where Visconti's jugendstil (or slightly art nouveau) production is now to be seen, gorgeously run-in and smooth working.

The Rose Cavalier is Brigitte Fassbaender, daughter of about the best Figaro we recall from Glyndebourne, Willi Domgraf Fassbaender, with his hint of menace and temperament, the latter quality having been passed to his remarkably personable daughter, a most sympathetic boy-actress, with a beautiful dark lustrous voice. Yet such is the measure of this revival, conducted with a fleet and authoritative mastery in which nothing seemed forced or feeble and every detail shone, that the new Oktavian merely took her place in a superlative team. Michael Langdon's Ochs is now a marvel of fine operatic characterization, beautifully turned, immensely funny, imposing and important especially in the great scenes which conclude the middle act: a great assumption. Sena Jurinac's Marschallin, every word audible, every nuance echoing a deeply-felt understanding of Hofmannsthal's grand dame seemed to me to reach a new and even higher level in a career which, time tells us – and time is the Marschallin's admitted enemy – dates back to budding Glyndebourne Dorabellas and (for me) her first Vienna Eva in which for once – exception to prove the rule – she did not launch Wagner's quintet successfully. The best since Lehmann? I think so.

Dr Krips elects to take the Strauss trio rather more slowly than can afford maximum comfort to the three sopranos, but on Friday night, if it sagged at one moment, it still sounded like an elegy, a threnody for the world which came to an end in 1914 – as is the case with few other pieces of music save Elgar's Cello Concerto. Mme Jurinac was under strain at one moment to be sure yet the whole house hung upon the soaring sound in a hush of lingering ecstacy. The Sophie was charming Lucia Popp, who makes a person of Miss Faninal and sang with the ease of a lark and the gleam of the 'unearthly' silver rose in question, but must beware of too much, too fussy stage business. Gillian Knight's Annina, Derek Hammond-Stroud's Faninal, Gwynneth Price as the duenna were but three others in a magnificent cast to whom I would dearly love to give detailed praise.

But we must be brief: we are dealing with a work of immense length, of volume of feeling, richness of texture (how thin the operas of 1970 will seem in forty years!). The performance takes nearly four and a half hours and so defeated even the most determined of on-the-night critics. To those who only know the Waltz Suite and the Trio (from records) it must, I fancy, be something of an ordeal. Yet a lifetime of love is stored there. All in all one of the best *Rosenkavaliers* at the Garden in the past half-century. Glorious.

Guardian, November 1971

Janet Baker

Another evening of fine singing on the South Bank. After Gedda's 'Dichterliebe', Schumann was honoured again (and with the same piano partner Geoffrey Parsons) by Janet Baker singing the 'Liederkreis'. Same thronged and hushed audience, same enthusiasm. I think this is a recent phenomenon. I don't remember Lieder getting quite such avid attention in the old days. Miss Baker has a great following and rightly. Her spun tone itself is a thing to go miles to hear, delivered without falter, pure legato, mordents coming in as natural as you could dream: *Intermezzo, Mondnacht, Die Stille* – the nature poetry of Eichendorf was again and again rendered with the utmost delicacy. *Waldesgespräch* (the meeting with the Lorelei), the first song which really, literally made my hair stand on end as a child (when I had some to stand) now finds me incapable of balanced criticism.

Miss Baker thrillingly goes for the high option of course at the words 'Wohl irrt, das Waldhorn . . .' and 'Es ist schon spät'. All one might ask for is a little more *swing* at the start. The one (Auf einer Burg) about the stone statue and the mysterious, indeed mystical 'Zwielicht' were pure mood-painting. 'Frühlingsnacht' produced the same sort of effect and triumph of inner joy that Mr Gedda scored in a not at all dissimilar song, Rachmaninoff's 'Water of

Spring', the night before. In a minute Miss Baker had come back with an encore in elegant, smiling French 'Mandoline'.

But she put her greatest heart into the dramatic scene by Haydn 'Arianna a Naxos' (in Italian, two recitatives and two arias). We recently heard Teresa Berganza do this: clearly it is a grand but taxing effort and Miss Baker encompassed it with dignity and fervour, but I believe that with piano it seems not quite big enough for this hall, a *cantata di camera* rather. The recital began with a Schubert group of which the best was Litanei, but the much admired mezzo was at that time not yet in fully warmed up voice, nothing like the even, full, ubiquitously beautiful tone and scale of the later part of the evening.

Guardian, March 1973

Janet Baker in *Mary Stuart*

It may be idle speculation but I wonder if Malibran herself ever sang Donizetti's *Maria Stuarda* as well as Janet Baker did on Saturday at the Coliseum in the revival by the English National Opera Company. Miss Baker sang with such beauty of phrasing, such delicate and persuasive inflection of tone, and projected the character so radiantly that scenes of confrontation, of shriving, and of progress towards the scaffold belonged in the exalted realm of great tragedy, even on the same plane as Schiller's drama from which this not wholly plausible libretto derives.

Such a performance of the title role transfigures a score (long out of the repertory) which is always effective and often exciting but can sometimes sound like the routine pot-boiling of the great and prolific Master of Bergamo.

Guardian, August 1975

Josephine Barstow in *Salome*

The English National Opera's new *Salome* is a really stunning theatrical success. Richard Strauss's opera, which once shocked all decent people, has of late – in the cussed way that happens – come to seem a bit tame, lurid and restaurant-dance-floor-show-off. This production by Joachim Herz gives it back all its proper or improper pungency. It is suggestive, horribly real seeming, dubious in a few places, such as the ending, but mostly a complete triumph of imaginative realization.

The scene by the late Rudolph Heinrich who died here in London when fitting up his set is the epitome of all one could wish for a near east interior: exactly the thing, not arty or 'kitsch' but extremely realistic, a 'cistern' house palace, brooding and oppressive, without cheap romance. Mark Elder conducted splendidly and drew out of that magnificent singing actress Josephine Barstow a mighty impressive performance of the lustful princess, commanding the stage and all the business of the dance and the grovelling with the sheer bravura of a Sarah Bernhardt which is exactly as it should be for what derives from Oscar Wilde dripping jewelled French fancy.

If you are used to a very big Swedish or Bavarian voice in the part you may think she lacks all the weight, and certainly her words in the excellent new translation deserve to be clearer but the performance carried great conviction and power – to me at least. Not since Welitsch, in fact, has a Salome so gripped me. Ramon Remedios as Naraboth, Emile Belcourt and Elizabeth Connell as the Herod pair, Neil Howlett, a really impressive visionary Baptist and splendidly cast groups of Nazarenes and Jews were rightly acclaimed. A night to remember.

Guardian, December 1975

Josephine Barstow in *La Traviata*

Josephine Barstow is once again singing the famous role of Verdi's *La Traviata* with the English National Opera at the Coliseum, an experience to be treasured. I would be glad to go on record as asserting that she is the best singing actress in our language in this part ever to be heard in the last half-century. Her Violetta is deeply affecting, realized with intensity but no exaggeration, acted with total conviction and beautifully turned, in every sense.

She moves on stage with stroke after stroke of credibility and phrases the music, through the English translation, in a most dignified and successful manner. She stands up well to the memories of some of the most eminent international stars who have impressed us in this role and very properly wins the plaudits of admirers from all parts of the big theatre. It is a performance which everywhere bespeaks the keenest artistry. Tastes may be divided on judgement of the tone quality here and there. There is too much personality in the voice for it to seem, at every point, ideal.

The sheer melodic and lyric instrumental quality of a Melba is not to be found, nor for that matter the often reckless projection of personality heard in the late Maria Callas in this role, but the intensity, the hold on the drama, the musical assurance of the crucial phrases will not be lost on any true connoisseur of the famous lyrical creation.

The staging is intelligent and effective, without silly, producer's freakishness. Mark Elder conducted with responsive results right through the cast list, which included the tenor Brecknock in fine, clear, ringing form as the young hero, Norman Bailey as the father (with a most persuasive way with the over-celebrated second act passages).

Guardian, March 1978

Maria Callas in *Norma*

Mme Callas delighted everyone except those who find their admiration for her magnificent and flamboyant assumption of the role constantly disconcerted by faults of vocal emission. In this part, as in *Aida* and the Leonora of *Trovatore* (both seen in London) and likewise in such parts as Lucia and Fedora, Mme Callas never fails to hypnotize her audience. She takes the stage as Rachel must have taken it. Visually she is magnificent. Musically she exerts so much will-power and bends art to her fashioning in such an imperious manner that one guesses that even if she were to whistle the music or play it on a violin instead of vocalizing it, she would still make us hang upon her every phrase.

She is, in short, the very antithesis of your canary soprano, your empty unmusical prima donna. And yet those with critical ears can scarcely fool themselves that she was not often singing sharp on Saturday: that her *tutta forza* was invariably sour and that her climactic high notes often developed a zagging beat like the sound of a plank being sawn. Moreover, the actual timbre of the voice often sounded nasal and 'blocked'. Free emission, the sound of a voice of natural beauty vibrating in perfect harmony – the noise, say, made by Mme Flagstad or the late Kathleen Ferrier – was simply not in evidence. But such is Mme Callas's witchcraft that one was utterly resigned to including her second scene of Act 2 among the supreme experiences of opera. Here – but not in the hooty 'Casta Diva' – Mme Callas abandoned herself with perfect simplicity to the lament, which echoes the big cello tune of the orchestra, sitting and singing with her forehead propped on her hand. In the duet 'Mira, o Norma' (with the stalwart – but no longer young – Mme Stignani) she gave proof that whatever one may think of her as a singer or as a 'voice' she is a mighty performer.

Guardian, February 1957

Birgit Nilsson: A Mighty Brünnhilde

Well before midnight on Saturday the Wagnerian rites were accomplished; the second cycle of *The Ring* came to its majestic close and the Royal Opera began slowly to fill with the stunned applause of the audience which had been immersed for five and a half hours. There was a heart-felt ovation for the orchestra and its conductor, Rudolf Kempe; never have they done so well. Four soloists took curtains. Mr Windgassen who had made a heroic recovery for Siegfried's death scene, looked relieved to hear such cheering. Mr Frick (Hagen) looked frankly tired, though he had not sounded so in his splendid last act. Only Miss Birgit Nilsson, however, looked really undaunted – as if she could and would be quite ready to start off again.

Few Brünnhildes in recent memory have had so evidently the stamina for the role. The voice is aquiline: it soars, swoops, wheels, pounces. It peals like an unsilenceable bell. It pierces the darkest Wagnerian tutti. It vies with the massed brass in the scene where the heroine's grief breaks into rage. It has perhaps less of the specific gravity (in terms of gold) than Flagstad's noble, more deep-sounding organ. But it is the voice for the role in a way which does not occur more than once or twice in a normal life span. The audience tried to show its owner what they thought of such an exhibition: doubly dear, of course, to a British audience which responds to the element of athletic contest in such affairs.

It is indeed like watching a show jumper; 'She cleared that fence with a lot to spare: how will she do at the water jump? Over! Gad, sir! The woman's a stunner.' And so she is. Subtlety? Well, some Brünnhildes get more wisdom and pathos into it. But few in the audience cannot but have thought themselves lucky, even blessed, to have been present at this mighty display.

Guardian, October 1960

Birgit Nilsson as Elektra

Birgit Nilsson's Elektra last night was even more stunning than before. The sheer vocal stamina leaves me without words to describe it: it is a force of nature. After an hour and a half, full tilt over the Straussian whirlpool, the gleaming soprano tone was still cutting like a great sword. The shades of expression are now fined to a hairsbreadth. The whole assumption of the punishing role in its acting, its plastic, its realistic tenderness in the recognition of Orestes and its maenad dance of vengeful triumph at the end, is a feat of histrionic mastery to find the like of which sends you searching the archives of operatic memory. To make the occasion even more thrilling and set off salvoes of applause and cheering which surpassed anything heard this year, Solti (Sir Georg) came back to conduct the Covent Garden orchestra which rose above itself to give the most tumultuously exciting account of the score you could imagine. This was the first opera I heard Solti conduct (in Frankfurt) and he is a miracle-worker. There are other ways of doing it: i.e. Kempe for the lyrical Lammers. But if it is sheer electrical charge that you want – like me – then this is the *ne plus ultra* and that doesn't mean the desolation and sentiment are neglected.

What a heavyweight of decadence and vocal murder it must have seemed in 1910. André Gide reports Frau Strauss, the world's most tactless wife, as saying in Paris, 'So you French don't like my husband's *Elektra*? It's time we Germans came back . . . with bayonets, this time.' Even today the piece is properly awesome: if *Salome* has faded, *Elektra* still touches the ultimate in decadent, barbaric force – for all that a superb realization of Greek tragedy. Helga Dernesch, recovered in voice, was the sister, McIntyre the brother, Craig the adulterous lover and the still wonderfully vivid Klytemnestra of Regina Resnik added much to a thrilling occasion.

Guardian, June 1972

Elisabeth Söderström in *Capriccio*

Glyndebourne is ideal for *Capriccio*, that conversation piece, as Richard Strauss called his opera, which illustrates the age-old battle for supremacy between the words and the music in the art of song and opera. It is illustrated by an incident of rivalry between a young poet and a young composer, both suitors for the hand of the lady of the house. It is a *conversazione* about the aesthetics of music and it demands intimate attention. I knew it would be good having seen it here before but did not expect anything quite so assured, calm, full of feeling or poised.

John Pritchard conducted a performance so well prepared and performed that the balance of word and music never seemed at fault. The complex numbers, the intimate give and take of social encounters and the big set piece solos were completely secure, achieving the final epitome of operatic poetry. John Cox's production is extremely graceful. The period, which should be 1775 – during the lifetime of Voltaire – is updated, neatly, prettily and without vulgarity to the 1920s; I imagine to avoid a suggestion of Dresden shepherdess artificiality. It works. But, and this is a major cavil, it makes slight nonsense of one of the figures in the party, namely, Mlle Clairon who was a real historical character, queen of the French theatre in her day and age. Perhaps nobody minds such an anachronism or knows who Clairon was. I soon swallowed my own objection, as a matter of fact. The taste and discussion all round became so pleasing.

The opera belongs to the lady of the house, the Countess to whom Elisabeth Söderström brings a lovely glowing warmth of voice and person. Her last fifteen minutes were the rose and perfection of the Straussian love affair with the soprano voice. But all the casting is from strength. Marius Ritzler was magnificently mellow as the deeply concerned professional man of the theatre, Richard Stilwell a most striking figure as the poet, Leo Goeke, another American, likewise as the tenor-composer, Kerstin Meyer as Clairon and Haken Hagegard a young country squire as the brother of the heroine. All these performances were rounded and telling, the very reverse of stereotyped operatic acting. Signora Ratti, Senor Cassinelli, Thomas Lawlor as the butler, and of course the incomparable Cuenod as the forgotten Mons Taupe, the prompter whom no one remembers. This is self-evidently good. A bit of German will help however.

Guardian, July 1973

Valerie Masterson in *Manon*

Manon, that little masterpiece of *opéra comique* which so perfectly catches the mood and delicate sentiment of Prévost's novel, gets a lovely new production at the Coliseum by John Copley. Henry Bardon's sets are completely right in period, simple and effective in style. The bustle is unexaggerated, the dramatic skill and craftsmanship given every chance, but unobtrusively. In the grateful role of the beloved heroine Valerie Masterson gives a truly exquisite performance, so effortless seeming, so apparently easy for the voice, yet fully expressive and touching to look at as well as to hear.

Massenet would surely have found her ideal, the only inevitable disqualification being that the music and the words are so affectionately wed that they do not make their full effect in any language but the original. There is no way of translating that cardinal phrase 'N'est ce plus ma main que cette main presse?' But Miss Masterson in the matter of vocal deportment is as good as you could wish.

As her chevalier, John Brecknock finds a role which lies very happily for him, Niall Murray is excellent as the cousin Lescaut, Van Allan also, as the heavy father and if Sir Charles Groves's handling of the score is not as light as Beecham's and drags a shade in the Saint Sulpice duet, it is tender and elegant.

Guardian, April 1979

Elisabeth Schwarzkopf

Something very moving about the way Elisabeth Schwarzkopf came on for a second encore to the tumult of applause at the end of her recital of lieder at Euston Town Hall last night, a *clou* in the Camden Festival and a sell out. This proved to be Richard Strauss's *Zueignung* with the climax. 'Heilig, heilig an's Herz dir sank' sung full out with an ardour which had been long held back in the preceding Wolf group from the Italian Song Book – among them two which have wonderful ironic overtones, one which is downright bitchy, one which leaves you in doubt of the piqued lover's real feelings. I don't remember ever hearing the latter 'Wohl kenn ich Euren Stand' better sung, certainly not since Ria Ginster who was a great hand at it. Here is miniature opera, a perfect little vignette.

For the first part of the programme, which was superlatively well partnered by the pianist Geoffrey Parsons, the singer remained cautiously 'within limits'. But with Liszt the familiar, pristine sheen began burnishing the pressed notes; soon with Loewe, we were thinking of the diva as Gretel in Humperdinck's fairy opera: this was 'Kleiner Haushalt' and it grew majestical in its sly humour and mood setting. There were two of Strauss's 'mother' songs, finely done. Nothing failed. This Marschallin knows about the passage of Time. All one was feeling, night long, was how, if you are artist enough, it matters not the least. From where I sat the artist, in a flowing pre-Raphaelite gown of turquoise, looked young and beautiful and sounded so.

Guardian, May 1972

Shirley Verrett in *Orfeo*

Shirley Verrett, the most remarkable of the new generation of black operatic artists, assumed the role of Gluck's Orfeo last night on a stage which has seen the triumphs of Giulia Ravogli, Clara Butt and Kathleen Ferrier but has not, I think, seen a more dedicated artist than this, in dignity, immediate dramatic impact and a quality of voice which is exceptional and so individual that the hearer finds it difficult to place (unlike its possessor, who has it firmly and perfectly pitched and riding on a long easy breath).

The top of the compass strikes as loud as a clarinet, the middle is firm and spare, rather than luscious, the bottom register 'speaks' with power quite unforced or 'melodramatic'. We know this singer's strong definition of Verdi roles, but as Gluck's hero she showed us a new facet of her art. The conductor was Charles Mackerras, which meant that everything went for the best in a version which he himself has based on the Berlioz rescension with, for instance, the ornamentation in one aria derived from Saint Saëns! The total effect is idiomatic yet fresh sounding. Never once did the opera sound marmoreal, and the support from chorus and from Elizabeth Vaughan (Euridice) and Anne Pashley as the god Amor was keen and dramatic. 'Che faro' was taken fast but rode perfectly on its sprung rhythm.

Guardian, May 1972

Maggie Teyte

Dame Maggie Teyte is eighty today. Born Tate, one of eleven, near Wolverhampton, she became world famous, Debussy's favourite Mélisande: '*Encore une écossaise?*' he said in bewilderment. (Mary Garden had 'created' the role.) The 'baby prima donna, rose bud prima donna', etc. duly schooled was presently taking the platform with her great teacher, the legendary Jean de Reszke (remembered now as a cigarette perhaps) and with the indomitable old Lilli Lehmann who bequeathed a name to *her* great pupil, Lotte, who is still with us.

Not wishing to be called Mlle Tatt (she has a sharp, even dangerous sense of humour) the aspirant changed her name to Teyte.

Jean de Reszke kept her singing '*Depuis le jour*' daily (perfect for head tone and pianissimo). Debussy couldn't quite believe the sight of her (perhaps he was expecting someone heavier). He kept staring at her suspiciously. '*Vous êtes bien Mlle Maggie Teyte de l'Opéra Comique?*' He pronounced Maggie with soft g's like the Italian soup cubes. Always her sense of humour was tart and dominant. During the blitz at one of those National Gallery concerts, with Gerald Moore accompanying, she shattered the spell of a Fauré song with the announcement: 'Damn. Start again. I swallowed my eye lashes.'

She said somewhere that singing is nine-tenths nervous energy, one-tenth technique. But this hardly explains either the penetrating skill in poetic identification with a song – Mozart, Berlioz, Offenbach, it is always perfect – or the individual timbre of the voice, literally inimitable in a way which, say, Callas's is not. Instantly recognizable, this timbre: whether the case is 'Oft in the stilly night', or Butterfly, which she sang at the Old Vic in the old days. She was proud to have her Mimi likened to Melba whom she says she did not scruple to imitate, thinking, like all people sensitive to singing who heard it, that *that* voice was really heaven-sent in its even, silver purity.

But it was with Debussy, Ravel and Fauré that Maggie Teyte established her supreme position. Luckily the gramophone attests and preserves much of her art. The initial success, with people saying 'Not since Adelina Patti . . .' did not, Hollywood fashion, mean a career which was an uninterrupted triumph. Far from it. Dame Maggie has had a great many downs as well as ups, rediscoveries and 'returns'. She is very funny in her book *Star on the Door* (Putnam) about her American adventures. Great value as a person, fine artist, lovely singer.

Guardian, April 1968

The Swedish Nightingale

Jenny Lind's birth 150 years ago is being celebrated by a concert given by her fellow countrywoman Birgit Nilsson in the Festival Hall tonight. Appropriately in London where the Swedish Nightingale knew some of her greatest triumphs and where she settled in the days of her charitable age and affluence as the wife of

Otto Goldschmit, the German-born conductor. Mme Nilsson at one time lived in the same Stockholm house as Jenny Lind but is thought of as a bird of a different feather, more Wagner's Valkyrie than the Nightingale who enchanted the generation of Mendelssohn, who extolled her in oratorio, when she left the sinful stage, but had meant to write an opera for her though he never got round to it. Meyerbeer did, however: the work we know as *L'Etoile du Nord*; and Verdi, for the only one of his operas given its première in London, *I Masnadieri* (from Schiller's *The Robbers*) stipulated that Jenny Lind should be the prima donna.

This was in 1847, her first year in London where she made a début in *Robert the Devil*. Already the talk of Berlin and other capitals she was hired by Lumley at the Italian Opera in the Haymarket as a rival attraction to Grisi and Mario at Covent Garden. Her hold on British audiences was powerful. Since the days when the world fought for hours at the pit door to see the seventh farewell of Mrs Siddons nothing, it was said, approached the scenes at the entrance to the theatre for Mlle Lind's appearance.

It was probably a voice very different from that of the powerful Nilsson that was heard then, though it is important to note that a soprano in the days of Lind – a pupil incidentally of Garcia, the father of Malibran and of Viardot, Turgenev's friend – a soprano was expected to tackle *all* the roles – not just a limited and specialized corner: so Donna Anna, La Vestale, Lucia, and Norma (admittedly in a very soft feminine reading of the part) were among Lind's triumphs. Not least perhaps was the charm of her appearances as the relatively short-skirted *vivandière* in *The Daughter of the Regiment*.

But an urge towards the godly and the do-gooding transformed this diva. With the profits (astronomical by those standards) of her American tour, she endowed scholarships (introducing the Mendelssohn Scholarship here), founded the Bach Choir (and some hospitals), and became a professor of singing at the Royal Academy of Music. Her mastery of such things in oratorio as the 'Bird Song' from Haydn's *Creation* and the 'Sanctus' from Mendelssohn's *Elijah* were remembered with awe.

Of course, a single gramophone record would speak louder than any collection of pictures and notices can do (Patti managed to leave us a souvenir of her voice: Lind just missed recording of even the most primitive kind). The exhibition on the upper level of the Festival Hall is full of relics, lurid music cover pictures, raves from the newsprints, with engraved fancy pictures of her portrayals.

Guardian, September 1970

Yvonne Printemps

Reportedly full of resentment, as can be the case with a darling of the public when they get on a bit, elderly certainly, in her eighties – and that sounds old when your name means 'Spring' – *Printemps, tu peux venir*, Agate was always quoting – the legendary Yvonne died last week. Should one feel sad? I did. She was not a great artist by any stretch of the imagination, but I almost feel persuaded to call her the best minor performing artist I ever saw. With what, you may ask? The voice was minuscule but – note well – it was used with consummate skill, inflection, sustainment and appeal. The face was cheerful, commonplace, snub, suburban-Seine style, yet it was watched with fascination, abandonment even. By me at least, who sat open-mouthed in her presence. I was not the only one either. She married and quarrelled with Sacha Guitry but not before learning everything that stage wizard had to impart; later another star, Pierre Fresnay; many lovers on the side too I believe, naturally enough. What an artist, what a charmer. No gramophone record she made, no performance of hers I saw on stage will ever fade in my memory.

I wish she had come to England more often (but she hated the Channel crossing). She and Guitry hit us full between the eyes with Reynaldo Hahn's *Mariette* and the adorable piece about the young

Mozart in the mid-twenties; both stars came back to give an evening in Lady Ludlow's drawing-room (think of *that*, as a piece of London life, rather like having Caruso and Chaliapine round after dinner to save your guests the bother of post-prandial small talk) and then again she, on her own, came for the musical play Noël Coward fashioned for her, *Conversation Piece*, in which her hit number was 'I'll follow my secret heart' which can still be heard and makes me want to cry again.

Talking of which I must recall the first night of *Les Trois Valses* (confections of the Viennese Strauss tunes, to a sort of *Summer Manoeuvres* plot). At the Marigny or the Michodière? I was miles high in the gallery. At the first curtain, Yvonne the heroine, a cocotte loved by a handsome subaltern, had just seen him off to war, waved from the window in the dawn, stepped down to the footlights and of course did a reprise of the love duet waltz they had barely finished. The lilt and emotion were absolute perfection. With long sight in those days I saw *real* tears run over her cheeks. Ecstatic applause. I said: I'll never see anything like that again, she couldn't possibly repeat. But the French, *qui veulent en avoir pour leur argent*, insisted on a repeat. She did it and cried real tears all over again. *Comment trouvez-vous çela?*

Spectator, January 1977

Songmakers

The Songmakers' Almanack is the title for a kind of recital devised by the wonderfully alert piano accompanist Graham Johnson for a vocal quartet who will mix concert party numbers by Noël Coward with art songs by Schubert or Poulenc, and intersperse these with declaimed spoken poems delivered with assurance, even by the pianist himself as well as the four singers, who are ready to turn from Stephen Spender or Kipling to Hugo Wolf or Britten. The audience is caught guessing and highly pleased.

A danger discovered in similar programmes by the Apollo Society is that songs sometimes seem to work against speech and to diminish instead of enhancing the effect by being put together. But the danger was cleverly reduced to a minimum even where such a poem as Plomer's 'The Flying Bum' (last War joke) is used as a preface to the German Wolf's hungry Drummer Boy. It could be awkward but it runs well. This programme had a connotation for Armistice Day: poetry sung or spoken was about war and its aftermath, touching or comic.

The singers, attaining great presence in this hall, are pro fessionals at Lieder and in opera touring for Glyndebourne. Felicity Lott, riding over a cold with success, Ann Murray who is adept at anything like an Irish folksong, the baritone Richard Jackson in splendid voice who was able to get full value out of dramatizing *The Two Grenadiers* and the story of *The Parrot* after the battle of Waterloo, and the tenor Rolfe-Johnson were perfectly at home. It is obvious that the popularity of this group is going ahead.

Guardian, November 1976

Pavarotti

All the seats at Covent Garden were sold for its celebrity concert, loudly acclaiming the Italian tenor Luciano Pavarotti in a piano-accompanied programme of no very great interest in itself. The pianist Leone Magiera came out of it with distinction, if distinction can be conferred on Puccini arias in this circumstance. I would applaud him, as well as the vigorous tenor singer.

Mr Pavarotti came to this stage as a rather shy and unrehearsed substitute for a tenor of great popular favour in a *Bohème* some twelve years ago, stood like a puzzled pet dog during the first act, then let off so loud and splendid a top climax in the first act aria that the house rose at him. He smiled – and has never had to look back where London audiences are concerned.

He seemed to have put on a lot of personality, if nothing else on this occasion, spreading a white waistcoat which the great Lablache might have envied. Clutching a silk handkerchief and smiling in his beard, the very picture of the Tichbourne claimant of legend, he devoted himself to the sort of singing that the audience wanted. Dry, too dry in tone for a start, he kept a powerful penetrating line. Romantic and classic arias had little variety or dulcet modulation. But the vigour was admired.

A couple of Verdi arias were so much the right thing, artistic shading not mentioned, that we were all more or less won over – one lady leaping forward with a single rose which the stout fellow held aloft in triumph. The Tosti group had a fine fire though little delicacy. The first of several encores from Donizetti showed a strong singer at his most sensitive, which is not unfathomable. A long way to go until he gets into the Gigli or Schipa class.

Guardian, February 1976

Joan Sutherland's tour de force as Lucia

Donizetti's *Lucia di Lammermoor*, good clean fun at the lowest evaluation but capable of great tragic intensity when finely produced as now at Covent Garden, came back to the stage where it was once the greatest of tests for the Melbas and Tetrazzinis, and where it had not been on show since Toti Dal Monte gave a single showing of the old war horse in 1925. It came back as a personal triumph for the Australian soprano Joan Sutherland – a future Melba, some people would be ready to declare, on the strength of her almost flawless singing of the great scene of the third act.

Her voice, intrinsically beautiful, was under the strictest control, the ornaments evenly delivered, nothing shirked, and the entire shaping of the scene put to the most dramatic effect. The producer Zeffirelli deserves his place in the catalogue of excellence and the veteran maestro Serafin likewise, but the audience was in no two minds about where the final credit lay: namely with this lyrical coloratura soprano who on this crucial occasion, surprised her most ardent admirers. The pathos of her 'Alfin Son Tua' seized the whole house. This was exceptional operatic singing, radiant, pure, and vivid, and it won an ovation of the kind usually reserved for the favourite ballerina.

Lucia is in fact, for the light soprano, much what *Giselle* is for the ballerina. It used formerly to be given in haphazard manner with everything staked on the prima donna, absurdity rampant, and the Scottish chorus with their sporrans round their necks. This new production is full of feeling and atmosphere, with splendid sets, entirely successful costumes, and the most logical and intelligent movement. It looks like a contemporary print of the 1840s. The tenor had been laid abed with influenza and many in the audience should have been likewise kept at home. But Kenneth Neate obliged at short notice and sang with complete assurance. But it was Joan Sutherland's evening and she was acclaimed in all parts of the house and by many notable singers present: Mme Schwarzkopf applauded enthusiastically from the former royal box. Mme Callas, all sweetness at Tuesday's rehearsal, had unfortunately had to leave betimes.

Guardian, February 1959

Joan Sutherland in *I Puritani*

Joan Sutherland, who had not until last night sung the role of Bellini's Elvira in *I Puritani* at Covent Garden (though she has sung it in Edinburgh and at Glyndebourne) returned to the Royal Opera House in triumph with a dazzling, touching and above all beautifully toned performance of the part.

Her first high D was enough to set the house in a roar of excitement. No use saying the high note school of opera has died out (and there is nothing like a climactic note taken in this kind of way; long, strong, pure and slap in the middle). The big scena of madness in the second act with the refrain of 'Qui la voce sua soave', a lovely elegaic melody, brought out her most affecting and colourful tone. With her husband Richard Bonynge in charge of the orchestra, Miss Sutherland was able to take the aria exactly as she wished, taking plenty of time over it (as I bet Grisi did originally), with a pretty strong use of rubato but a good forward impulse all the same.

The ensuing caballetta 'Vien diletto' in its second appearance was ornamented in a manner which could properly be called stunning: decorations, trills and ornaments were darted into the hopping tune with a bravura to take away our breath (though not, amazingly, the diva's). In this kind of bravura singing Miss Sutherland has no peer and if it is not Tetrazzini rediviva, it is something you still would know was due to become a legend. And with it all the voice sounds mellow and sweet.

Has she improved as an actress? Is this really much different from her Mad Scene as Lucia? Enough to say (while the audience is probably still howling for her to take yet another call) that the scene was affectingly done, with grace. The question can anyhow wait. If she couldn't act at all, it would still be Bellini's Elvira to the life.

May it be the moment to ask if Mr Zeffirelli's immensely lavish scenery (the whole production comes from Palermo) is really right or necessary for this gentle pallid old *bel canto* piece with its exceptionally silly story?

Elvira, daughter of the governor of Plymouth Castle where Charles I's relict Henrietta Maria is in gaol, goes mad on her wedding eve (and stays that way till the last duet) when she learns that her bridegroom Arthur, a cavalier, has led away the unknown lady under cover of her (Elvira's) own bridal veil: cavalier behaviour provoking collapse of reason in tall party.

The music varies from the exquisitely plaintive to the kind of rum-tum (as in 'Suoni la tromba') which might make a Salvation Army bandmaster blench. However Mr Rouleau as Sir George and the Parisian baritone Gabriel Bacquier did it with panache and brought down such pieces of the house as hadn't already fallen in for Miss Sutherland.

Charles Craig, not perhaps nature's choice for a *tenore di grazia*, nevertheless by shutting his eyes and transposing it down a semitone managed to bring off the formidable 'A te, o cara', which was intended to exhibit Rubini's C sharps.

The splendour of the scenery and the numbers of staircases involved us in an extra interval. The stage pictures were striking if perhaps a bit too colourful for such puritan surroundings, but long after all that has been forgotten it is the leading lady's blithesome roulades which will linger in the mind. *I Puritani* compared to *Norma* is small beer and it does not at any point pack the dramatic punch of Donizetti's *Lucia*, but last night the audience loved it and hung upon Miss Sutherland's singing with doting but justifiable relish.

Guardian, March 1964

'The Most Beautiful Woman I Know': Ljuba Welitsch

The critic of the *Daily Telegraph* at first described her as 'an opulent Viennese type'; with perhaps a faint air of condescension, perhaps not himself being one who, like Tosca, lived both for art and love. She was certainly no diaphanous wraith as once in those pre-*Hair* days her Salome over-enthusiastically disclosed, nor was she Viennese, except by adoption. Some distant Bulgarian or Sephardic origin gave her that red gold hair, that princely, feline stride, that *strahlende sopran*. I speak of Ljuba Welitsch in the past, and *passée* she must now be in a sense, though vivid still I'll bet, and married to the handsome Viennese copper she bumped into with her car and retired with.

But incontrovertibly beautiful, if in a very individual way, she most certainly was when first she bounded on stage in that Vienna Opera visit which showed that the war had not killed quite everything in life. She was a tigerish Donna Anna to Frau Schwarzkopf's delicate Elvira. I met Frau Welitsch some time later in the foyer at Covent Garden. 'I know you, I know you,' she said advancing. 'Yes, we met once at Walter Legge's office,' I rejoined. She went backwards at a run. 'I don't know you. I don't know you,' she said.

Ljuba Welitsch sang on her nerves – clear stream of tone like Rethberg, a diamond, top C like the evening star ('like a saw-mill,' said Boyd Neel, not so tender).

I took a trip to Vienna with another music critic at a time when the Russians were still able to cut off all the petrol at a moment's notice. It wasn't a good trip, but 'the Welitsch' was a golden hostess. First night: a box at the Volksoper where a rival diva sang

'Die tote Stadt' (Korngold). 'I love her leedle face,' said Ljuba, but when the lady sang, she pressed back into the shadows of the box, and raising a minatory finger said *Falsch* (out of tune). Applause however brought her forward opulently, her advantageous profile drawing many an eye away from the stage. She applauded generously. It was not in her nature to do anything otherwise.

Afterwards, we went to a restaurant and I witnessed something I have only read about in Baroness Orczy. The Diva turned all heads and was at once approached by a crone with a basket of violets. Ljuba took the lot and turned her purse upside down into the old party's apron, notes, coins, powder, and all. What, you may wonder, were the gallant Englishmen doing? But we hadn't a schilling between us. Besides, you can't compete with generosity on that scale. She was fantastically generous, even to ungenerous criticism. '*Mein liebling, was haben Sie ueber mich im* "Manchester Guardian" *geschrieben?*' I had said she raced through Aida like a scalded cat, and wished at the moment I hadn't. 'It is so long, I can't wait,' she sighed.

Lunch on Sunday; up flights of stone stairs and one of those doors which open themselves when pressed to do so. Somewhere – not a voice was calling, but a goose was cooking. We stepped into something not unlike Nathan's costumiers; corridors no, marshalling yards, avenues of costumes, Turandot's clobber weighing down the picture rails. Beyond was a salon, hung with the names of the famous on gorgeously framed photographs – name-dropping on a cosmic scale. On a huge bed, sideways, sat Ljuba, beside her a portable gramophone of the humblest description, even more sideways than its owner, so that the turntable revolved like the rings round Saturn – playing records of herself.

Every time the record reproduced a high note, she would fling up her arms in triumph: '*geschossen*' (Bull's eye). That's it in a word: beauty.

Guardian, February 1969

Dietrich Fischer-Dieskau – I

Schumann's setting of Heine touches the miraculous and great lieder singing can be an indefinable miracle of communication. When presence, dramatic sense and the ultimate in vocal control are brought to bear, the result transcends painstaking analysis. As Fischer-Dieskau asked the question in the last song of Die Dichterliebe cycle at the Festival Hall last night 'Know you wherefore the coffin must be so large in weight?' and sent the three words 'schwer mag sein' out on a perfectly sustained rising *pianissimo portamento*, one was conscious of a dozen critical points to be made but somehow all otiose: the control, the immense dignity and sympathy which totally exonerates the poet from any mawkish overemphasis, the fact that the whole cycle was being, *had* been, accomplished without a false emotional accent at any single point. Yet uppermost in one's gratitude for Fischer-Dieskau's incomparable artistry is the way these so long familiar songs seem to come fresh minted, unlaboured, to new life each time we hear him sing them.

The mechanics are so unobtrusive one has to force oneself even to notice the feats of breathing, e.g., the placing of the second verse of 'Ich hab im Traum geweinet' in relation to the more positive first and third verses strikes you, but you are left no time for technical marvelling, so urgent is the dramatic modulation into the next, urgent mood. I think I never heard 'Am leuchtenden Sommermorgen' more ravishingly sung, nor would change one iota in its presentation, *ralentando* and all. In that matter anyhow the Japanese pianist Michio Kobayashi likewise carried total conviction as an artist. Here was a most eloquent partner to a giant of the world of lieder singing – taking their bows together made a picture which seemed to ask the brush not of Landseer but of someone like 'Max' – German giant and oriental pearl fisher clasping hands. The pianist's postludes were a poetry of their own.

Three songs made an initial group and included 'A frost fell over night' Schumann's last Heine setting, sinking to a final 'gestorben, verdorben' – which sounded a note of chilling sadness. Thereafter came the Liederkreis with a specially beautiful rendering of 'Ich wandelte' and a very stealthy, unshowy entry into 'Mit Myrten und Rosen' which seemed the absolutely logical step from the proud 'Anfangs wollt ich fast verzagen'. A night to remember, with a great singer in the rose and perfection of his maturity.

Guardian, October 1971

Dietrich Fischer-Dieskau – II

It might sound mad to select the huge Albert Hall for a Wolf recital with piano by the rightly famous Fischer-Dieskau, serious Goethe songs needing strong definition in projection.

The hall was not full but the audience was rapt and hung on every word, each clear and true, an exemplary feat of enunciation, remarkable even in this prince of lieder singers. At first I felt I was too far away from him, merely in visual terms (he is upstanding, totally calm, and grand in presence, thinner than of late).

The voice came over the distance full and generous, even the smallest tones carrying on the air perfectly; as they can well, in this auditorium, where we used to hear Kreisler and Tetrazzini without thinking about 'volume'. The great German singer and his pianist with him quickly got the measure of the house, throwing out lovely sounds in such songs as 'Anakreon' and the powerful 'Prometheus'.

The woe of 'Wer nie sein Brot' (from Wilhelm Meister) had already established the rapport with the audience. Wolfgang

Sawallisch backed the artistry of the singer to perfection in his energetic accompaniment.

The evening had many minutes of Goethe through Hugo Wolf, at the most searching level. Above all, what a firm, flexible and true scale of baritone range there was to admire.

Guardian, February 1977

Hermann Prey

Hi-fi Hermann Prey: the Schumann recital in Covent Garden last night was a sound to treasure. The German baritone is in quite exceptionally good voice just now. An old wound, a tendency to pitch slightly under the note, has been completely cured. The timbre, as always, was very beautiful, pushing critics into describing his voice as the most beautiful of its kind to be heard today. And there were things in the Dichterliebe cycle – 'Am leuchtenden Sommermorgen' which I think I have never heard more exquisitely voiced.

But of course a singer does not always hit form at first. Nor can you ask a singer who has just done the Liederkreis and the Dichterliebe to choke us with a cream of encores. All the same 'Dein Angesicht' was an extra to savour, whereas in the first half of the recital, you knew that the singer did not quite feel his way into full expression: 'Waldesgespräch' for instance was dull. He is not an artist to cut corners or make meretricious dramatic effects.

The trouble must be that the Royal Opera, where of course he is at home when he comes to sing Rossini and Mozart on stage, may seem rather daunting when arranged as a concert hall, with a platform built out over the orchestra pit and a wall of plush curtain behind you. The pianist too, Leonard Hokanson, ideal in later stages of Dichterliebe, hung back in the first songs of the opening half.

But his unobtrusive style goes very happily with this master singer, who strikes no attitudes, goes to the very heart of the business of singing lieder. 'Ich hab in Traum geweinet' on a thread of perfectly sustained tone and the rueful irony and acceptance of Die alten, bösen Lieder (the last song) with an exact selection of bold and withdrawn nuances right through the registers were the essence of great interpretation in this field.

Guardian, May 1975

Boris Christoff

Boris Christoff, the Bulgarian bass, came back to Covent Garden last night to give a deeply moving performance as Boris Godunov and to receive a tremendous welcome. This great artist has been very ill and it did seem in the prologue as if his voice, in certain stretches, had not yet regained its former amplitude.

But all misgiving was swept aside in the first scene of the second act when the volume of the voice, let alone its historic impact and unsurpassed expressive inflection, seemed actually more imposing than ever. An exceptional volume of personality Christoff has always been able to exploit not to mention 'an eye like Mars to threaten and command'.

The scene in which the shifty counsellor breaks the news that the supposedly dead child Dmitri may still be alive and the usurping Tsar is tortured with guilt and horror was terrible in its intensity – as Salvini, Kean or Olivier might make Shakespearean remorse terrible. The house was gripped, then roared its tribute.

Guardian, December 1965

Jon Vickers in *Otello*

Jon Vickers the Canadian tenor sang an exciting and vivid Otello at Covent Garden last night, his first here. It marks a milestone in a career in which he has held his place with remarkable talent and seems a far cry from that Don José, about fifteen years ago, at which point I think I even urged him to stick, since he was so good in such a role. But Otello and of course Tristan beckon irresistibly. His Otello has magnificent enunciation, vivid histrionic appeal and an intelligence and animal strength which immediately catch at the audience.

If one could ask simply for more weight of voice, more volume, one is not likely to hear the role better managed on a purely artistic level. In short he knows what Verdi wanted, even if he cannot at all points, or could not last night, quite drive the point home in purely vocal terms.

The conductor was Colin Davis (also a first at this great opera). Fine detail, sympathetic approach, but that inexorable turning of the screw in such things as the great ironical exchanges between the Moor and his wife in act three and the forward march of the orchestral comment on the great monologue (at 'Spento') are still to be developed fully.

Great strength came from the cruel and highly-coloured Iago of the Greek baritone Paskalis, not quite a Gobbi but an artist to reckon with and thank. Other newcomers were Ryland Davies (Cassio), Heather Begg, Paul Hudson and Howell, all making their mark, but Joan Carlyle's Desdemona, experienced, dignified and often very touching, was at first too pale, muffled and cautious to measure up to my memories of her best performances in this supremely grateful part. The whole production speaks of an artistic and sensitive approach and after seventeen years the stage pictures still look good.

Guardian, June 1972

Carlo Bergonzi

Commendatore Carlo Bergonzi is a paragon, a *primo tenore* in the most obvious sense of having a lovely voice and a perfect command of the refinements of *bel canto*, but is also a phenomenon in putting his talent to most rare and delightful musical good sense. He is also very 'outgoing', as the phrase is, and can throw himself into Neapolitan songs with an infectious glee which has an audience even in a hall as big as this begging for more – even if it is F minor again with a climax top C, just as before. It is in the singing of such things as Tosti's 'A vucchella' (a posy) that the art which can turn – well, not a pig's ear but something rather banal on paper – into a silk purse is demonstrated to the full.

I love Tosti sung like this and make no apologies, in company of a few thousand others. The singer even had the wisdom to warm up with this composer, a piece called 'Tormento' which might seem an odd invocation for the start of a programme but one which was to be fine singing all the way. Bergonzi started as a baritone (Rossini's Figaro) and there is a certain tug in the timbre of his lower notes which is very satisfying (just as with Caruso). His full volume has splendour, the climax of 'tu m'appartienni' in the aria from *L'africaine* and the line of 'Quando le sere' from *Luisa Miller* – this is surely our best Verdi tenor – were irreproachable. As for the dropping legato curves of the Mignon aria they were as delicate as Tito Schipa's, as full but better shaped than Gigli's. He must come back and will soon to Covent Garden. Meanwhile this first recital in England made a fine effect. The pianist was Enrico Pessina.

Guardian, April 1972

Elisabeth Schumann

To say one feels Elisabeth Schumann's death as a personal loss can mean nothing to people who do not so feel it. Yet what thousands of people must have stopped for a moment when they heard that news and searched the echoes of their hearts – a deathless artist if ever there was one. If you met her in private or on the platform your first and abiding impression was the true one; she was that rarest combination: wit *and* goodness. A supreme artist, she had the demure simplicity of a child with the radiant wit of the most highly civilized society. The voice was a perfect expression of herself, in a way not all voices are. It was small but flawless; mercurial, yet limpid; Mozart's voice or a thrush, at will; perfectly pitched, perfectly controlled, used with a perfect sense of style, fitness and poetry.

In certain *lieder* she could make you cry with sheer happiness. I think of 'Aufträge', but everyone will have his own favourite; the stilled passion of 'Nacht und Träume', the serene ecstasy of Strauss's 'Morgen' or 'Freundliche Vision'; the laughing grace of so many minor miracles of art. In opera her Adèle in *Die Fledermaus* was no less perfect a thing than her Zerlina or her wonderful Sophie (*Rosenkavalier*), and those who heard her as the Wood Bird or as Wagner's Eva can never forget the heavenly, air-born quality of the voice.

Ernest Newman said of her once, 'This is Mozart as he might be hearing himself in heaven.' I picture them meeting, now.

Time and Tide, May 1952

Paul Robeson

Paul Robeson was a great figure in the late 1920s and early 1930s. American Negro artists, as we were allowed to call them then, were rare birds on the London scene, especially those of such high calibre.

His huge frame, sonorous basso voice, his big noble smile and gleeful look were greatly in demand. He was in *Sanders of the River*; in *Show Boat* he was the 'fraid-of-dying stevedore who captured the town with 'Old Man River', who just kept rolling along.

When he sang 'Swing Low, Sweet Chariot' the Albert Hall audience was awash. But he couldn't manage the more intricate Schubert songs. The quality of the voice, black velvet, was the thing. The line was not so strong.

He did two Othellos in England, one before the war at the Savoy with Peggy Ashcroft, which had a pristine force not found in his later, after-the-war Othello at Stratford.

I remember him best in O'Neill's *All God's Chillun* with Dame Flora Robson, a miscegenation modern tragedy of black scholar and white schoolmarm which I saw standing back of the gallery in NW8.

The players produced, at one moment, such fire power that a woman standing near me fainted clean away. Robeson was in every way a big fellow, used as a willing stalking horse by left-wingers on whom he wasted a lot of talent and time.

Guardian, January 1976

Beniamino Gigli

The people who complained that Gigli had no taste missed the point like those who will call an orchid 'vulgar' or the Alps 'sentimental'. They must have been deaf to the sensuous, animal appeal of a voice in itself without compare. Its peasant possessor was innocent of intellectual taste and he was only unlike some other singers in never bothering to acquire any: so that he was always capable of finishing off some lovely piece of singing with a gulp or a spurt of tone merely for the fun of it. He saw no incongruity in capping Handel with 'Ritorna a Sorrento' or dealing out three repeats of 'E Lucevan le Stelle', each more lachrymose. But his voice was a thing of such beauty that all was forgiven.

It developed out of a contralto choirboy's voice which never, in the conventional sense, 'broke'. A high lyrical tenor, it was seamless, perfect from top to bottom, and, in the vague terms we employ to describe sound, it was golden, melifluous, liquid, and so perfectly placed that it never needed forcing. No brass was in it, no dark animal passion: it was dulcet, smooth as a lovely complexion, yes, even a little effeminate. It was perfectly 'on the breath', which made it odder than ever when Gigli would flex its elasticity with much use of intrusive aspirates. But it was utterly unlike Caruso. There was little of the pressure or 'spinto' quality of a Martinelli. I heard Gigli sing his first Radames in Rome, but he was never a real 'robusto'. He suffered in the early stage of his career (paradoxically pioneered by the gramophone which Caruso had 'made' as a mass entertainer) from unjust comparisons with the great Neapolitan.

He was born for the lyrical roles, for the heroics of Puccini and Gounod. Andrea Chenier and Massenet's the Chevalier des Grieux were his loves. Because he never had to spin out a little voice, he only latterly came to phrase 'The Dream' in *Manon* with the art of a Tito Schipa (he of the small voice). But the ease with which he soared to the famous *Ut de Poitrine*, the high C of the Cavatina in *Faust* was one of the world's wonders. I think the most magical high note I ever heard was the C in the aria of Gigli's Rudolfo in his first *Bohème* here – right at the back of the gallery, it enveloped you in its beauty, as if the tiny frog-shaped figure on the stage had reached up and stroked your ear.

He had a mild talent for comedy and audiences loved his simplicity. When he sang Rudolfo to his daughter's Mimi after the war, he dropped all pretence of acting in the love duet and held her forward to the footlights as one who should say 'Gentlemen, this is my girl, see why I am proud.' It was affectingly done, being so spontaneous. His voice lost wonderfully little of its resilience as the years went on; and he never lost a certain peasant glee or his Italian sense of devotion. He was always at heart the little Benjamin of the sad-eyed adoring mother – Esther, the cobbler's wife at Recanati.

Guardian, December 1957

The voice was a natural wonder and a Gigli recital was like a diet of hot-house fruit, each note from that seamless, effortlessly placed, flawless compass to be savoured like a grape full, rich, with a bloom on it and a temperature neither hot nor cold. For anyone who cared for the magic of a perfectly produced tenor voice, Gigli spun a spell of pure enchantment.

Opera, February 1958

Christa Ludwig

The Wigmore Hall on Saturday was crammed with a wildly enthusiastic audience applauding the esteemed mezzo-soprano Christa Ludwig, probably and rightly thought the best of her kind today, although she is better known on records than from her rare visits in person. We do not see her often enough, more is the pity, for she has an excellent platform manner.

She uses a rich voice with heart and great skill. The vowel sounds are especially magnificent, the vocal scale is smooth and under flexible control, capable of a light and silvery top as well as a powerful thrust, and low tones deep without hollowness. The dramatic interpretation in Wolf's *Mignon* songs was extremely telling, especially the first and the last of them. The voice was lightened and dimmed for the three Mahler songs of 1905 and from the expected staples of Schubert and Strauss came lieder singing as fine as you may hear today.

The climax of Schumann's 'Silent Tears.', the way the voice moved like a cello in the 'Sapphic Ode' of Brahms were unforgettable feats – the singer is often at her best in slow but not too exhaustingly extended phrasing. But the dialogue of the unhappy young couple in Brahms's 'Eternal Love' was much less secure. Geoffrey Parsons was the accompanying artist at the piano and did everything to admiration.

Guardian, July 1978

Teresa Berganza

I have never heard Teresa Berganza in better form or more clamorously applauded than last night in the Queen Elizabeth Hall (one which exactly suits her beautifully centred Spanish mezzo soprano, sounding clean, strong, full but with a tiny touch of metallic ring in it, a wonderfully live and colourful instrument). She is of course an actress too as we know from her Rosina and Cherubino and it would be absurd to underrate the adventitious charm of such merry eye-work in some of the songs. Dress of black with a few vivid ornations embroidered on the shoulders; silver nails; a quick modest but clearly delighted platform manner and a range and artistry which takes in the solemnities of Haydn's abandoned Ariadne, an exquisite sixteenth-century song of courtly amorous grief ('Alma sintamos' by one Esteve) and the childish high spirits of Mussorgsky's Nursery Songs, with the doll's lullaby and the hobby horse on the hop.

Even among the encores she showed us what a delicate lieder singer she can turn herself into at will. But it must be admitted that what set the huge audience in a roar – house crowded to the doors – were the Spanish songs of Granados: the timid Majo contrasted with the passionate Maja Dolorosa and then the knock-out success of the six popular songs of Falla. To these she brings perhaps less of brass and salt than some of the most famous interpreters of the past. The voice never brays or barks (as voices sometimes can, not without effect, here). The tone was golden and flexibility marvellous. I cannot imagine the Jota sung more 'speakingly'. Her husband, Felix Lavilla, was the perfect accompanist.

Guardian, January 1973

Helga Dernesch in
Die Frau ohne Schatten

An exceptionally grand and moving performance of *Die Frau ohne Schatten* at Covent Garden elicited a huge swell of applause for what came over more certainly than ever before in my experience, as one of the supreme masterpieces of the Richard Strauss and Hugo von Hofmannsthal collaboration. Sir Georg Solti returning as a guest conductor to the Royal Opera got the huge orchestral forces to play for him, with magisterial authority and eloquence and on stage the whole company seemed magicked.

Chief honours – and I insist that discrimination is necessary here – go to Helga Dernesch who, once again, seems to be in the very plenitude of her power as a singing artist. I never heard Lehmann in the role of the Dyer's Wife but I cannot think it would have surpassed the warmth and psychological truth of this interpretation. Paired with it, Donald McIntyre was very fine as Barak – drawing tears of pleasure from one listener at least at the start of the third act. New to me, and very striking, was the cunning Amme (Nurse) by Ruth Hesse; real strength and personality here. The latter requirement is less easily found in the interpreters of the Empress (she who is shadowless, i.e. sterile) and her consort, the Emperor in danger of petrification.

Heather Harper sang nobly, often catching the gleam that was surely written into the music with a view to Jeritza singing it. Many beautiful minutes. But James King, the Emperor, remained as perhaps the role must, slightly shadowy (if that is the word in this opera). Too many fine lesser contributors for space here. But shortly I must say how I have come round to admiring the production by Dr Hartmann who came back to bring it up to its present vividness, and the sets by Svoboda which once struck me as too paper-flower shop, with those huge dappled staircases, are now lit by William Bundy and executed by Bill McGee to weave a spell worth casting over Dernesch's soaring, soprano ecstacy.

Guardian, June 1975

Mme Yvette Guilbert

Even if one had never seen Lautrec's 'Yvette Guilbert Saluant', the manner in which the greatest of *chansonnières* acknowledges applause would always remain etched on the mind. She has this in common with a few other artists, that not the main outlines only but every smallest detail of her performance holds attention. The catalogue of these nods, shruggings, and quick asides cannot be made, but one such, from Friday's entertainment, may be mentioned. Speaking of the cinema (and be it recalled that some of us first saw Mme Guilbert on the screen as Martha in the silent film *Faust*), she had occasion to deplore the lack of interest in *la chanson* shown by the *cinéastes*. What a relish of scorn did she spread on that pretentious noun!

Her programme, once again of 'favourite songs', ranged from one of those dramatized Nativities to Paul de Kock's ditty of the scandalous Mme Arthur. A lesser artist might have made either of these pieces an uncomfortable experience. That one was anxious, and indeed able, to remember every moment of Mme Guilbert's performance is a measure of her art. Which of the twelve songs was most enjoyed? Perhaps Béranger's 'Mme Bontemps' and 'Dans ma jeunesse', with its sighs for the delights of youth, were the most charming. And 'Jean Rénaud' was the most dramatic. We were told that this ballad has its counterpart in nearly all languages, yet we could not think of our own exact equivalent. It had affinities with 'Lord Ronald'. The final announcement of Rénaud's death was terrifying.

The Times, May 1939

PLAYERS AND
PERFORMANCES

Gielgud's *Hamlet* 1944

This *Hamlet* is classical – it is austere, true, satisfying. If, long-awaited, it is already old history, that is one inconvenience attendant on touring repertory. Another is that except for the Prince, the Queen (Marian Spencer), the Ophelia (Peggy Ashcroft) and the Polonius (Miles Malleson), we could all think of happier casting. The production by the Cambridge don, George Rylands, is a triumph of sanity, real taste and knowledge. No tricks, no concessions to the mode for arty costume drama (Ruth Keating's Henry VII setting has a connoisseur's 'dryness') – it will be called chilly by the fashionables who would prefer it as a Borgia ballet. All the legitimate points are made; all the exciting spurious touches eschewed. Few supers, an un-frightening court, no fearful presages of doom. Result: the storm gathers, not *around* a spotlit, musing adolescent, but grows, and grows urgently, *within the mind* of a well-liked heir-apparent, a man of parts and of mercurial temper. It is a mind into which we, the audience, can look steadily. (Complete triumph, that.) No question, for us, of mad disorder there, though (triumph again) – is there not, perhaps, growing beneath that deadly clear sanity, as it might be in your mind or mine, the real madness of the ultimate, unanswerable question?

I have never thought that Gielgud had a living peer in the part. Now I am sure. His is not 'one of the ways' (tomboy, tenor, mystic, governess, etc.). It is *the* way; a realization, now nearing perfection. Mercury of voice and gesture he always had. Now the very idea of *Hamlet* has the quicksilver quality. No facile romantic pathos dulls it. It races into every vein of the portrait. Here it is, instantly: the core of the tragedy. Man, the best possible instrument, is finally unequal to circumstance. What a piece of work is man . . . and how inadequate.

Judge how you will (but best by the soliloquies, here really what they should be for once, the heart) this portrayal continually stops the breath by its mastery, just as sometimes by its true artist's austerity it stops the tears. Never have I seen a Hamlet so rightly and rewardingly deny himself all easy, emotional solutions. The faults – any fool can pick on mannerisms – grow from the virtues. Too high-mettled he is. He needs, ideally, more animal greed.

The play's fine treatment must be crudely summed as logic and clarity before dramatic emphasis. It is for connoisseurs to judge the effect of such things as this Gertrude's guileless goodness, or Hamlet's ignorance of the spy-trap or the King's missing the dumb show – and so on through the countless minor problems here so loyally and sanely met. Absence of cuts; very good lighting; but an excess of cramping 'curtain' scenes and a negative treatment of King and Horatio must be recorded. The general verdict is strongly in favour on most counts. If something of the stress and purging anguish of the great play is missed, this version will be remembered among the many versions, by its noble quality – as of a page of finely written history.

Time and Tide, October 1944

Wars of the Roses

I have been in the wars: *The Wars of the Roses* at the Aldwych, being ten hours of Shakespeare's *Henry VI* plays edited and topped off with *Richard III*. Talk about the longest day!

We went in on Saturday morning fresh and marvelling, came out on hands and knees scarcely more than an hour from Sunday.

Of course there are rewards in seeing it all in one fell swoop. The march-of-time aspect, so to say. And that means among other things the quite marvellous, fearsome performance of Dame

Peggy Ashcroft as Margaret of Anjou, who skipped on to the stage, a lightfooted, ginger, sub-deb sub-bitch at about 11.35 a.m. and was last seen, a bedraggled crone with glittering eye, rambling and cussing with undiminished fury eleven hours later, having grown before our eyes into a vexed and contumaceous queen, a battle-axe and a maniac monster of rage and cruelty who daubs the pinioned Duke of York's face with the blood of young Rutland, taunting him the while so horribly that even the stoniest gaze was momentarily lowered from this gorgon.

Yes, Dame Peggy is marvellous and there are a dozen other performances worthy to stand with her. I will recall some of them. But I must also say that the effect is cumulatively deadening to the senses. *Richard III*, coming in the last three hours, does not lift the heart: it sickens it, leads to a cynical shrugging. For a masterpiece of this length one seems to need an ending with, if not uplift, catharsis (so it is with Wagner for instance, or the Oresteia taken on end, even endless O'Neill).

So long as sweet saintly King Henry is alive there is the continual return to beauty, sympathy, and peace – as even in the middle of the crashing broadswords, smoke, din of battle, and blood-spurting, severed limbs, the King's great lament for the responsibilities of monarchy, his thoughts turning to the carefree shepherd under his thorn hedge, make that essential contrast, that andante which even a battle symphony must have. Wonderful here, as gently spoken by the highly-sympathetic David Warner, is the triptych of grief: the King in the middle on his knees, on either hand a father who has slain his son, a son who has slain his father.

The things I preserved from the day were nearly all from the Henry plays: John Welsh's superbly rounded portrait of Duke Humphrey's days of power and terrible fall: the comedy of the false miracle at St Albans; the utterly irrelevant and delightful scene of Squire Iden's almost accidental destruction of Jack Cade: the Talbots, the scenes with La Pucelle (so odd when one knows Shaw from hindsight), the ironies at the council table which keeps mushrooming up before us.

Was it that I was simply too tired to enjoy *Richard III*? True, I agree with Karl Baedeker: 'Enjoyment ceases where Fatigue sets in.' But I have a feeling that this last play is actually much less well produced.

It has been fascinating seeing Richard Crookback emerge from boyhood, sonhood. But does he ever grow big and menacing enough? Is he ever the 'boar', so much insisted on? 'Bottled spider' certainly; as he went widdershins reeling about Bosworth Field, blindly swinging ball and mace, he looked hideous with the ferocity of a poisonous reptile. But the gloating and the glee were hardly strong enough. Ian Holm is a splendid actor; he has voice and presence. But I want more volume still for this part.

If 'My kingdom for a horse' is not to make our hair stand on end, what is it for? If it is only like a man moaning for a cigarette it serves no object. Similarly in their tents both Richard and even more Richmond played it down, conversationally. I don't agree with this. Of course we can't have Kean today (who caused people to faint in the stalls in that scene). But can this naturalism and deliberate flattening-down, even of the whole episode of haunting, really produce the proper climax?

This is carping at what is an enterprise 'of great pith and moment' which honours our theatre in this Shakespeare year most highly. You might say there has been too much dickering with the I Ienry plays, but the result in clearness is welcomed by me. I do not think enough of the civilized side of this world emerges (nearly all the classical allusions, except Icarus by Talbot senior, are lost). These contemporaries of the Borgias had some fine painting and music, after all. And Edward IV (Roy Dotrice) should not be shown as a playboy; that scene is meant to show how brave a king he was to sleep in the front line, not that he was bedded down with a camp follower.

'Think you these wars will ever have an end?' We didn't laugh (hadn't the strength). It's 'magnifique' all right, but punishing. Take it easy is my advice.

Guardian, January 1964

Peter Brook's
Midsummer Night's Dream

All went like a dream at the Aldwych for Peter Brook's circus, mod-comic production of *A Midsummer Night's Dream*; all, that is to say, except for the mutterings of veteran critic Hope-Menace ('fidgetty Phil' to the usherettes) who kept dropping things, sighing and yawning. But he was also wiping tears of laughter from his eyes – a good sign: nothing equals a good laugh in the theatre and David Waller's Bottom, in the Gordon Harker manner, up against Glynne Lewis's Tommy Trinder Flute is a real joy. Indeed the laughter is great and general. What then do I not so much like?

Critics lead lonely lives. It is horrid to feel in a minority of one. 'You must be mad,' they said, 'why, the Americans adored it, and Mr Harold Hobson said . . .' 'Americans don't know,' I cut them short. It is people who do not know and love this play who will best like a freak-out production, with fairies in swings and Chinese opera noises. Alone however I am not, in finding that there is *no* dream, *no* midsummer and only the most superficial Maskelyne and Devant sort of magic. No less a judge than jolly Jack Priestley is with me in this.

But I must hand it to Peter Brook for originality, to Sally Jacobs for her white gymnasium (or swimming pool) setting and for the daring and wit of stroke after stroke. What of the enchantment? I suppose I am (thank heavens) stuck in the Guthrie era in so far as this loveliest of plays is concerned: Mendelssohn music, muslin wings, Vivien Leigh as Titania and Helpmann (who else) as king of the fairies. The RSC fairies are all great rugger toughs who do some shockingly saucy things in miming Bottom's lubricity, besides sending the Beatles sky high in their Indian consort on trapezes. However the fairies are only a part of the play as actually I found last night. Sara Kestelman (who also doubles Hippy) spoke the stuff about the little Indian boy most touchingly; I was quite won over also to the zany Puck of John Kane and the sharp-eyed Oberon of Alan Howard.

I recall that one (now deceased) drama critic of this newspaper was summarily dismissed for saying that the lovers' quartet was 'Shakespeare at his feeblest'. That occasion must have been doleful. Done with lust and relish as at the Aldwych, it is a growing and sportive delight: Frances De La Tour's beanpole Helena, with galosh mouth and wriggle, and passionate little Mary Rutherford being especially well contrasted, and Edward Flower's flowing guitar plonking an accompaniment to these young people in a way to make the hardest old critic soften up. In fact I have quite come round to this Dream and most heartily recommend a visit. It may fidget you but it will also have you awash with tears and laughter.

Guardian, June 1971

Two Lears: Laurence Olivier 1948, John Gielgud 1950

King Lear: New

A most interesting and capable performance of *King Lear* opens the new season of the Old Vic Theatre Company at the New Theatre. Mr Laurence Olivier produces and plays the King with great ease and mastery, in a degree higher than you expect even of this attractive and steadily improving actor. He starts a most intelligent reading of the difficult role very quietly, with an almost comic old buffer of a Lear – it might be G.B.S. dismaying some priggish students' debating society; makes little or nothing of the early thunders or the pain of the first insults to majesty (calculated savings which pay later high dividends); and only begins at 'Ay, every inch a king' (spoken sitting – unique, surely?) to bear at our hearts. From this point onwards he is intensely moving and his broken old man is extraordinary for its dignity and for a pathos which has not one note of whining in it – very rare. Most Lears begin in a ferocious roar and end in a whimper, a trickle of sorrow oozing from the old cracked head. Whereas Mr Olivier's greatest moment of dignity is when he kneels to Cordelia.

But what dangers are run! It is always hard enough to 'get' Lear's majesty at the start; and it was, of course, shocking that his first entry 'mad and decked with flowers' should have made the pit laugh. But it was a sign surely that we had not been made aware enough of Lear's royalty. The poetic idea, the balance of the tragedy and logic may be better served by this kind of interpretation; but the play considered merely as a piece of theatre tends, I think, to suffer. There was nothing, not even the curse upon Goneril, to set us tingling – certainly not the operatic storm scene with full orchestra and searchlight tattoo, which never gave the effect of a real storm or yet of something happening inside Lear's head – the two possible ways of doing it surely. The early part of the play seemed flat and chilly, lacking the sweep of passion and pity which would carry us over the play's strange weaknesses. It is loyal and right perhaps to try to expose the play as lucidly as possible, in the decent, intelligent and sometimes almost conversational Shakespeare style favoured by this company. But I am not sure that *this* play repays such exposition. We ought to sweat more, and think less.

But, all in all, your reaction to the particular actor is what makes or unmakes a Lear as it does a Hamlet: for myself, I found I was able to listen to 'Howl, howl!' dry-eyed. I remembered being *interested* but not moved by 'Beat at this gate', or 'Down my heart'. This is my fault, not Mr Olivier's. Comparisons are odious, but like much that is odious very interesting. Perhaps they should only be made on the personal plane. So Mr Wolfit's Lear moved me more, but monotonously and illogically; Mr Gielgud's, though brittle and in sum a failure, had some wonderfully mercurial passages. I cannot think of another English actor who could play the part with more sustained, even, and controlled intelligence than Mr Olivier. His is a Lear without strain and a Lear who wins and holds our affection.

Time and Tide, October 1948

King Lear: Stratford on Avon

I am told the second performance of *King Lear* was immeasurably finer than the first. Very likely. Lear has to be played on the nerves. Mr John Gielgud plays on his nerves. This can produce fire but sometimes also power-cuts. There seemed to be one in the second third of the play. The opening had been thrilling, with an arrogant Lear, courting the humiliation which must purge this hubris. Again the end was fine. But in the middle one ought (ought one not?) to see Lear racked.

But from the first I had doubts about the production. Leslie Hurry illustrates the play *à la* Arthur Rackham, but theatrically this permanent set was tiresome. I also make bold to say that where you have a fine-boned rather than a broad-shouldered Lear, the load needs to be shed not multiplied by 'bringing out the inner meanings of the sub-plot', etc. Better, I think, stylization, a surround of chessmen, mere ciphers of good or evil; if Regan, for instance, is to be allowed all those Chekhovian speaking looks and *moues* we begin to be distracted by the thought that the play may be about something else, something we are missing. Is the sub-plot really redeemable, in any case, by intelligent handling?

Lear is the most intractable of tragedies. Though I am no Lambite, I never felt more strongly than here Lamb's famous contention. *Othello* is a tragedy of jealousy. *Macbeth* of ambition. What is *Lear*? A tragedy of self-pity? Or is the trouble that we are now too far democratized to feel the pain of shorn *majesty*? One is so often on the wrong side in the arguments about the servants. 'What need twenty?' What, indeed! Ingratitude and old age to be sure – but then we have really to take too much on trust.

However the earlier scenes were exciting. Gielgud is an aristocrat. On the other hand he is not Jove brought low. Lears fall roughly into three classes: Wotans, Bernard Shaws, and Don Quixotes. If two other Lears of our time have taken up the former two attitudes, Mr Gielgud comes nearer the third category. This was the immediate comparison that I used when telephoning a notice of the play at curtain fall and afterwards I feared it might seem unjust. On reflection I think it should stand. Moreover the later scenes are absolutely consistent with this conception of the aristocrat in decay, having nothing or little about them of the terrible war-father disarmed. The conception is consistent and full of beautifully-managed detail in this line. The rages are sarcastic rather than overwhelming; there is nothing in the least Promethean about the storm scene; the end is gentle, almost sainted.

One way of doing it, certainly. Only on the first night the pathos of the last scenes somehow failed to come and the rest of the production hindered rather than helped, as did also the theatre building itself, enemy of all intimate and delicate playing. Perhaps too Mr Gielgud's pathos which touches the very nerve in *Hamlet*, in *Richard II*, in Raskolnikov, misses something in old Lear's heart. And I think that is why he plays Lear as he does. Again and again the poetry had a crystal clarity. I cannot imagine a more intelligent or a more fastidious Lear. But that is not quite the whole story. In a wicked world, in the practice of the theatre, some wild Welsh bull might actually carry the play better.

Time and Tide, July 1950

Paul Scofield: An Early Hamlet

Do we ask too much of a Hamlet? Inevitably. I would myself have liked a little more striking power from Paul Scofield (the young actor from the Birmingham Repertory who is now in his third Stratford season and growing all the time). Yet this simple, touching and unintellectual Hamlet exercises a peculiar gentle hold on the imagination. He is not your German Professor Hamlet, nor one of those inexplicably irresolute athletes who bound about so much; but a good and true and very plausible likeness of the 'sweet prince' of Horatio's adieu, pensive, big-eyed and sad, with a lenitive cadence and a curious moth-like fragility. He, too, would be a ghost, one felt, and with less reluctance than his father.

Time and Tide, May 1948

Twelfth Night

Most strongly do I recommend this RSC *Twelfth Night* which we all liked at Stratford last year and which comes to London greatly enriched in all aspects. 'Daylight and champagne discovers not more' as Donald Sinden-Malvolio declares with relish as he falls into the trap and deciphers the decoy letter. This scene Mr Sinden plays with the full music hall bravura of the late Max Miller evoking the kind of squealing feminine response which shows how strong is the spell (none of your don's wife's titters, real squawks). I thought and still think this is a marvellous Malvolio though it is only one of several ways of playing the part and I could do with something less prim and more bumptious (which makes the humiliation more effective, for me at least). If you saw it before you will be happy to feel again the sheer magic of Emrys James's Feste the Clown: manly, elderly, not fey, not dreary, but catching and crystallizing the mood with every touch of his lute. The mood is sea girt: we hear the breakers on Illyria's shore.

The other lynch pin is Judi Dench's Viola, fully alive to every facet of the tender comedy and most appealing. I only wish she'd join up the pauses through which one could drive a coach and horses in 'A blank, milord, she never told her love,' etc. But it is a most taking performance as is Richard Pasco's Duke, grandly lovelorn and sleepless. A Scots Aguecheek didn't quite persuade me before but Barrie Ingham now makes him very funny and even plausible. The same with Elizabeth Sprigge's over-the-border spinster 'body': Maria as governess rather than soubrette, but again persuasive. Leslie Sands's Sir Toby is grey with a tipsy self pity which somehow makes his occasional spurts of gaiety the more touching: the midnight carouse, with the owl hooting and Malvolio roused from bed hits you between tears and helpless laughter.

Guardian, August 1970

Love's Labour's Lost

This handling of *Love's Labour's Lost* by Peter Brook is certainly the most beguiling production of the play that I have ever seen. Had it been done in Moscow, we should never have heard the last of it. For one so young Mr Brook is really a most cunning and experienced artist. In a decor suggesting Watteau – permissible surely – this performance is wonderfully fresh, gay and delicate, and does for a modern audience exactly what Shakespeare surely intended to do for his. True there are some tiresome freakish touches, but for the most part Mr Brook steadily contrives to make a play of many tedious ups and downs into a beautifully smooth pastoral episode . . .

David King-Wood's Berowne has uncommon elegance and wit and indeed the whole young company appears to great advantage in this young play. The most interesting performance comes from Paul Scofield, who here matches his greyhound Lucio and his bull-terrier Cloten in *Cymbeline* with a Don Armado faintly reminiscent of an over-bred and beautiful old borzoi – a charming rendering of a part often made needlessly grotesque.

Technically the lighting and the range of movement are extraordinarily well studied. But it is fair to say that a like degree of artificiality and over-production applied to many plays would be a most uncomfortable experience.

Guardian, September 1946

The Winter's Tale

The Winter's Tale in the high summer of festival comes most happily to remind us how lovely it is to hear Shakespearean acting of the top class. This production by Peter Brook, in decors by Sophie Fedorovitch, is the best I have ever seen.

True, the Perdita, Virginia McKenna, is better for the eye than the ear; and the Autolycus, given with immensely likeable gusto by George Rose, who is brilliantly funny in his own right, perhaps misses something of the picaresque charm of that snapper-up of unconsidered trifles. On the other hand, how wonderfully the Sicilian Court is tenanted even down to such minor figures as Camillo and the steward of Paulina, who so enormously enjoys telling a tale.

The danger of this play, which is practically two plays, is that it will fail to catch our credence at the start or will lose our interest in the middle. This time, though there were moments of doubt, it made a dramatically coherent whole. John Gielgud started Leontes lunatic jealousy on so high and exciting a note that we had no chance to cavil. It might have been *Lear* (after all, the opening of *Lear* does not stand much rational examination either). This high note was sustained by the superb, simple pathos of Diana Wynyard as the wronged Queen and by Flora Robson's ringing advocacy of her innocence.

We came to the end of the first part well under way and looking forward to the bear – which ate Sir Lewis Casson splendidly, it being Peter Brook's production. The discovery of the babe amid the mists and howling weather was delightful; so too was the snowfall which marked the passage of the years, smothering time and the whole world in silent whirling splendour – a lovely stroke. And then it was Autolycus and the sheep-shearing. And if voices were heard to whisper that the rural romps had been laid on with too large a Mummerset trowel, it was discovered also that this pastoral interlude is not after all a different play but that it is possible to carry over the mood of the first part and also join it to the last. It was triumphant. After the determined high jinks at last starlight shone down on the silence.

The statue scene was most beautifully done: by Gielgud with real tears and penitence; by Miss Wynyard radiant and lovely; and especially by Miss Flora Robson, whose delivery of Paulina's lines touched perfection and was – how shall one say? – something almost tangible, the voice hypnotizing the whole theatre with its sound and feeling, even in its lighter tones.

Time and Tide, July 1951

The Country Wife

Maggie Smith as Wycherly's Country Wife gives the most marvellously inventive and hilarious performance of the famous letter scene I have ever beheld, better even than Ruth Gordon's long ago, which was something I never expected to see outshone. In the old days at the Vic before the war this play, about a phoney-eunuch whose reputation acts as a passport to all the boudoirs in town, was thought so improper that the Charity Commissioners, who then controlled that theatre, had to be invited by Miss Baylis to witness the essential innocence of the piece.

Much water has flowed under the bridge since then. The Chichester audience last night yelled with delight at the most recondite bawdy. But if it is a play for the time, our time, it is also a difficult one to project successfully in this great circus tent of an auditorium and it is a brave producer, as Robert Chetwyn clearly is, who believes that a Wycherly plot can be followed intelligently at the pace which is deemed necessary if longueurs are not to occur. I believe he justified his confidence – once the cast had got over a frantically nervous bout of shouting in the earlier stages.

Miss Smith captured the audience totally with a performance which, for all its vivacity, seemed on the surface as juicy, wholesome and smooth as a Worcester apple, shiny and sweet but immediately whetting the appetite and delighting with the taste of its clowning and wit. She does not lack support. Gordon Gostelow's jealous husband is a splendid foil for her comedy. As Horner, the supposed castrato, Keith Baxter cuts a naughty dash and as Lady Fidget, Patricia Routledge takes her opportunities very funnily, but she seems to clip her lines too short, perhaps only because the Edith Evans drawl stays so strongly in memory. In the wildly complex embrolio, Gary Hope, Hugh Paddick and Renee

Asherson are never at a loss.

Music, dancing, lighting and handsome designs, the latter by Hutchinson Scott, are an important part of a wonderfully lively revival.

Guardian, July 1969

Goethe's *Faust Part I* at Frankfurt

It is tempting to try to draw comparisons between the supreme wisdom of this great play and the supreme unwisdom of the present hour. But perhaps for the foreigner it would be impertinent as well as unwise. In any case too much has been written already about *Faust*, as if it were only a handbook to philosophy: too much, indeed, if we remember that certain of Goethe's countrymen would see in it a 'tragedy of Freemasonry'. Such nonsense need not concern us. There are plenty of people who still see the work as it really is. But if we stare too long at Goethe the philosopher we shall see behind him the figure of Spinoza; and that, too, would be inconvenient. Of the main themes, the lesser is the problem of the co-existence of good and evil, the greater that of the insufficiency of man, who can aspire, god-like, to all understanding and all riches of existence and yet remain, when all is had, empty and unsatisfied.

Yet in Part One these themes are only exposed; what in music would be called their development comes later. For most of us Part One is, rightly, the setting of the scene followed by a poetic presentation of the tragic legend of the old man made young and of his love for Gretchen. The Gretchen episode – and in the fact that it is for Faust only an episode lies half its tragedy – is one of the few love-stories whose appeal is universal; and yet the story is peculiar in that Faust is at once a lover and a sage and that, by the very nature of the case, the tragic problem of the inequality of love is thrown into the sharpest relief.

But Goethe, unlike Shakespeare in *Othello*, does not succeed in making us see the twin tragedies of both the lovers, as it were, with the same eye. The angle of vision continually shifts. Is the reason to be found in that splitting of Faust's personality which the physical appearance of Mephisto entails? Reading the play, one may see Mephisto as an extension of Faust's mind. Seeing it on the stage, Mephisto becomes a separate being, with a tragedy of his own. Faust, especially Faust rejuvenated, becomes a curiously empty figure sometimes, 'Everyman' though he is.

However that may be, it is most clearly and steadily Gretchen's tragedy that we see and feel; which is the more remarkable if one reflects with what reticence that tragedy is told. She appears only in a few short scenes – one had almost said poems. The passion, the seduction, the madness, and the violent deaths are kept always half in the dark. Yet how dazzling are the few glimpses. Gretchen at her spinning-wheel, and on her weary journey to hear the gossip round the pump; Gretchen on her knees before the Virgin, or a writhing figure seen in outline against the brightness of the candle-lit cathedral, her voice raised in torment against the *Dies Irae*; these glimpses are enough to bring us in full knowledge to the last meeting of the lovers in the prison – a scene for which more cannot be said than that it drills as sharply on the nerve of pity as Desdemona's protests in her bedroom.

This production is fortunate in its Gretchen (Else Knott) who early strikes the right note of simplicity and holds it even through those scenes where broken pride and grief bring her to a witless fury. Only 'Neige, du Schmerzenreiche', in its position here, might have been quieter. Faust, for many reasons, one of which has been suggested, is almost too hard a part. Youth and a fine ear for the verbal music were on Herr Müsil's side. Yet sometimes a wider range of expression seemed imperative. Herr Richter's Mephisto, however, was in its way (one of several ways possible) wholly satisfying in its deadly joviality and its suggestion of painful boredom.

A place at once so haunted by the medieval spirit and by the memory of Goethe as is this Römer Square might seem to make praise for the producer's work superfluous. But the manner in which Herr Meissner exploited the *genius loci* would make long and admiring study. The cathedral, market, and wine-cellar were given the fullest possible effect. Faust's lonely cell and Gretchen's home, both harder tasks, were no less well contrived, and, hardest of all – the scene in heaven – was made possible as a vision of early German piety, in a manner to which only full description can do justice. Only the 'Witches' Kitchen' failed in its too strained and modern fantasy.

The Times, August 1939

Red Roses for Me

The little Embassy Theatre has the honour to present an Irish company in Sean O'Casey's new play *Red Roses for Me*, thus exposing London to a full gale of passion and poetry and the rare experience of making contact with modern genius – though it is a 'tattered sort of genius, bejabbers'. Early on, one of the Dublin characters who has been rehearsing Shakespeare says, 'Let me put off this cloak now or it'll be giving me gorgeous notions.' The garment of splendid verbiage which O'Casey throws about his slum-dwellers gives us all gorgeous notions, though to describe them is like exposing an actor's fustian to the sunlight.

The play has some of the hilarious, seedy humanity of *Juno* and much of the apocalyptic afflatus and expressionistic method of *Within the Gates*. It is an affair of strikes and funerals, self-deluding verbosity, and religious clap-trap, of passion and poverty and futile heroism, and it is all swept along by language which on the stage, if not in print, goes to the heart and the head in a way which makes the tritest matter liable to seem the very stuff of the universe. What could be triter than the motto theme: '. . . shatter the vase if you will; the scent of the roses will hang around it still'? But the sublime and the banal seem to join in the Irish jig without the faintest touch of incongruity. The vase, one supposes, is the young railway worker who values the ideal gesture and the hope of a better world highly enough to fling away the red roses of life and love (for his girl and his mother) in some futile Dublin strike. And O'Casey is right in thinking that we do not need to have the incidents more fully explained or contrived (though the play would certainly gain thereby). It is enough that we see the young romantic alive and then dead and laid to rest in a tragi-comic funeral scene impermissible perhaps to any other dramatist but Chekhov. And between whiles we see him share with the Liffeyside loafers a vision of splendour in which beggars are suddenly transfigured with the glory which they know is still in their hearts and the Dublin murk turns radiant with hope. It would be hard to exaggerate the poetic grandeur of this interlude or to describe the peculiar daring of the fusion attempted and achieved. But the down-to-earth comedy of the first and last acts – such incidents as the bashful tenor's unwanted rehearsal – is what makes the play's success. This brave and presentable production had neither the range nor the power such stuff demands, but it had two sizeable performances (Kieron O'Hanrahan as the sturdy hero and Eddie Byrne as a vagabond fiddler) and it greatly excited its audience.

Guardian, February 1946

Uncle Vanya

The magnificent *Uncle Vanya* from the Chichester Festival, one of the finest pieces of creative acting to be seen in the English theatre these thirty years, has rightly arrived in the repertory of the National Theatre, in the framework of the more conventional Old Vic stage. There are slight modifications, as a result of compressing the action into this stage which is not, like Chichester's, open on three sides; but in its essence it is the same production, an extraordinarily beautiful and moving and delicate assumption of Chekhov's tragic comedy, which hits us between wind and water, sets us marvelling at the absurdity of human pathos, holds us enchanted by the sadness of human self-pity, at the play's intransigent morality, as exemplified by Sonya's 'faith' and belief in patience, at Chekhov's sense of the impermanence of it all, as in that scene of Astrov's would-be light-hearted farewell to Ilyena: 'We have become good friends and now suddenly we are never going to see each other again . . . it is like so much in life . . .'

Wynne Clark replaces Dame Sybil as the old nurse and Keith Marsh is the new Telyegin. Enid Lorimer replaces Fay Compton as the pamphlet-reading 'Maman'. Otherwise the cast is unchanged from last year except – and it is surely a big exception – Sir Michael Redgrave's characterization of the name part is even richer and subtler. The disappointments of the third act and the dawning sense of uselessness were finer than ever in this superb performance, the endearing buffoonish good nature shines out far more simply and tellingly in the second act.

As for the other piece of masculine character-acting Sir Laurence Olivier's Doctor Astrov, the appropriate superlative eludes me. It beggars description. His sobering-up scene, with the watchful Sonya in the second act, is sheer perfection. Nor can I imagine the scene of the 'pass' made at Ilyena in the third act better done. Redgrave and Olivier, always greatest as *character* actors (never at their best as 'leads') are here at the very apogee of their talent. Nothing finer has graced our stage that I can recall.

Rosemary Harris's Ilyena is not quite on this level, nor Max Adrian's selfish old Professor, though both rise to their big moments with superb effect. The shooting was better in the arena circumstance of Chichester but it is wonderfully managed here also – farce and tragedy contending in unresolved combat; one of the great moments of the theatre, where one knows one *may* laugh, yet is almost ashamed to do so.

Towards the start of the last act there is a scene where Doctor Astrov at last has to show some professional sternness, demanding back from Vanya (Redgrave) the morphia he has palmed; and appeals to Sonya to reason with her uncle. Redgrave turning his face away, Joan Plowright places her hands on his shoulders. 'It is possible that I am even more unhappy than you are . . .' It was quite heart-breakingly well done, without the slightest tremor of self-indulgence. And the efforts at consolation at the end somehow grew out of that moment as if there had been none of the intervening comedy of the townees' departure and the re-establishment of the country silence, like ripples settling outwards over a deep dark pool. A wonderful occasion.

Guardian, November 1963

The Wild Duck

The Wild Duck was written in 1884, after *A Doll's House* and *An Enemy of the People*. Perhaps Ibsen first intended a satirical social comedy (not unlike the latter play) but in Gregers Werle, the self-appointed moral reformer, we see, if not a self-portrait, at least a forerunner of the tragic human Ibsen was more and more to study;

the self-appointed superman, such as Masterbuilder Solness. Ibsen here is moving away from his position as a social moralist, he is becoming a humanist; he is, not merely technically, growing greater. This is a great play, but rightly seen here as a great ironical comedy shifting at the last on to the highest tragic plane. Hjalmar, the egotist, happy in a *bourgeois* contentment founded on a lie, is a magnificent comic study; and even at the end, with our eyes full of tears, we can almost (*almost* is the operative word) laugh at him; with his dead child, not in fact his child, in his arms, he is King Lear, but he is also a windbag deflated. It takes the drink-degraded Dr Relling to point that out. Ibsen makes his point three times; right, left and then, with Relling's piercing 'He'll get over it', makes it dead-centre.

It is a brilliant and intensely-shocking comedy; people who tell you that Ibsen is gloomy must surely be very stupid? But many of us can remember when Chekhov was thought 'gloomy and queer, my dear'. True, some of the *Wild Ducks* we have seen in London have flown very wide of the mark; it is fairly evident neither Archer nor Shaw really got to the bottom of what Ibsen was after.

This very good production by Michael Benthall gets the emphasis just right. Gregers Werle is, for instance, treated with the utmost sincerity, as surely he must be. If the play is not to fall to the ground, we must feel *with* Gregers to a large extent. I thought Robert Harris entirely right; wrong-headed, but in his idealism perhaps righter than the wrongness of the wordly wise; he was just the child of the unhappy marriage of such a worldling as old Werle; he is a type, creed-ridden, doctrinaire, working today as in Ibsen's day ruthlessly, faithfully and without a clue to what life is really about.

With these main characters so justly played (and Anton Walbrook has never to my knowledge done anything half so good as this handsome tragi-comic Hjalmar) it may be guessed that a play exposed with such consummate technical mastery as was already Ibsen's by this date could not go wrong. There remain two stumbling blocks. One is the language; Ibsen was a great poet and his prose here is said – by those fit to tell us – to have the 'inevitable' quality of language greatly used; perhaps it is untranslatable, that essential poetic quality, though we get hints of it. This adaptation by Max Faber seems to me to get close to the heart of the matter.

The other difficulty is the naturalism which for various reasons the poet Ibsen considered a better vehicle for his huge moral and metaphysical dilemmas than the patently poetic fantasy of *Peer Gynt*. He thought his ideas would be simpler if worked out in terms of homely symbols and *bourgeois* behaviour. Maybe he was right, but inescapably that naturalism has by now become not merely foreign (as it always was) but 'period'. We cannot see the play for the antimacassars and the bustles. And the symbolism sticks too. The present generation has no difficulty with Chekhov's symbols: Nina as a seagull, the cherry orchard as the fine flower of the past and so on. But Ibsen's symbols arouse incredulity and vacant confusion even in otherwise appreciative critics. It takes some time to think of Hjalmar's retouched photographs as 'dead images of life' and so on. We scale the heights, yes, but in such very 'period' bootees!

This splendid production couldn't solve that difficulty but, after a congested start, did what it could to help. The play came through clear, bitingly true and intensely moving. Walbrook and Harris I have praised already; unlooked for was the perfection of Mai Zetterling's Hedwig; this Swedish actress simply *was* Hedwig and I never expect to see it better played. Her final interviews, first with the blundering Gregers, then with her 'grandfather', were scarcely tolerable and the thought of what she must have been trying to steel herself to do out there in the outhouse made the end of the play as terrible as Greek tragedy. Everything falling into place, we come last (incredibly) to Fay Compton and Miles Malleson as Gina and Old Ekdal; it says something for the production that here two of our cleverest players were content to play to perfection two studies in uncomprehendingness; if you think how difficult that must be for an actress as aware as Miss Compton you will see what I mean.

Time and Tide, November 1948

Hedda Gabler

Taking a Hedda and coming a cropper any actress worth her salt will risk. No wonder. It is a prime hurdle. Not all overcome it – in recent years Sonia Dresdel, Jean Forbes-Robertson (in condition) and Dame Peggy Ashcroft stay in the mind. Now Maggie Smith bids fair to eclipse all others. I found the performance gripping though not moving, except in an ironic, mordant way, which is surely right. She keeps as long as possible a wonderful, bitter sense of humour half-hidden like a beautiful cat's claws. Her mockery, self-mockery and fencing (with a peculiarly fine sardonic Judge Brack from John Moffat) are a sheer theatrical pleasure moment by moment.

Should we care more for her cry on learning the truth of Ejlert's far from 'beautiful' suicide or violent death (no 'vine leaves in his hair' in this translation by Michael Meyer, so unobtrusive and good) that cry of self-disgust: 'Why is it that everything I touch turns ridiculous and nasty?' I suppose I used to think it was necessary to be moved by this, as it was difficult to be moved by 'I am burning your child' while she stokes the mislaid manuscript into the stove (Charles Morgan thought that piece of symbolic melodrama a 'cancellation of genius'). Here it seemed as ineluctable a stroke of self-dramatization as the disdainful little bobbed curtsy she makes to the Judge before escaping, by death, from the trap that her meddling with life, her effort to give it a strong turn of the wrist in her favour, to have power over the destiny of a man she admires, in fact has so wickedly, nay comically, misfired. Yes, a wry smile is not inappropriate, though what Janet Achurch would have thought of it, I do not know.

Gripping I said, but not moving. This is a production by Ingmar Bergman, who brought a similar reading from Sweden for the

World Theatre. Some would call it too bare, too abstract, almost surrealist, a red velvet, screened, acting place, not realistic at all. I am not sure I like all that eaves-dropping. Some of the hints seemed to be violent nudges. The action, like a film significantly, 'merges' Act One into Act Two in a way which would be hard to follow if one did not know the play.

And there are strange little details, for instance – Hedda sleeps on her couch with her shoes on (which struck me as unlikely), yet sheds this footwear before shooting herself in our full view, and her own, before a full-length mirror (better as Bea Lillie said, with your shoes off – but a woman I consulted said this action of Hedda seemed to her natural). What is not in question is that the flavour of the play comes over most powerfully – true flavour, I would say, blow the exaggerations here and there, unlike the tilt that Mr Bergman, a producer of genius, gave to Goethe's *Faust* which I found hard to forgive. I am sure the National Theatre was wise to invite him and the huge audience in the Cambridge Theatre (where the National Company is currently playing as well as at the Old Vic) thought so too, judging by their attention and applause. Robert Stephens (Ejlert), Jeremy Brett as George Tesman, and Sheila Reid as mousey Mrs Elvstead are fine support. Memorable.

Guardian, June 1970

The Father

Fascinated but strangely unmoved, I find myself tempted to turn away from Strindberg muttering 'the man's mad'. Certainly a bad performance of *The Father* has this effect: the sheer unfairness of his view of the sex war, the wild masculine self-pity, the pathological hatred of the opposite sex – the enemy, the destroyer – seems to invalidate the drama as if it were something to stand beside those casebook stories which are felt to be special, 'curious', untrue for the run of our own suffering humanity.

Yet a good performance of *The Father* probably comes nearer than any other of his plays, except perhaps *Easter*, to persuading us of the universal truth in Strindberg's point of view. The play is, besides, a towering part for an actor; since Robert Loraine, Michael Redgrave and Wilfrid Lawson have shown us so much. Last night Trevor Howard once again held an audience in silent horror as the wretched man, driven out of his wits by his wife's insinuation that the child he loves is not his, is manoeuvred by the old nurse into the strait-jacket and lies impotently, cursing his wife as 'Omphale', the queen who enslaved Hercules and robbed him of his club.

Pithy, short as plays of the date (1887) went, *The Father* is here presented at the Piccadilly for a short run in a patently clear, intelligent, and unstilted translation by Michael Meyer and a production by Casper Wrede which has plenty of atmosphere without any straining for effect. It is not that the melodramatic aspect is played down, but it is very carefully rationed and emerges late. The father producing the pistol in the last interview with his child is properly horrible but, more important, it is really surprising. The trapping of the rampant male, so often slightly absurd, is wonderfully convincing as Mr Howard and Gwen Nelson do it – almost hypnotic, or ritualistic.

Joyce Redman as the implacable Laura does not make the mistake of looking baleful and resolute too soon. The part is all the same preposterous: a cut-out from the dramatic world of Zola. Nigel Stock, Alfred Burke as the doctor and the pastor are good in support and the scene, designed by Malcolm Pride and lit by Richard Pilbrow, is exactly right. But of course Trevor Howard's study of pathological dissolution, so strongly and naturally conveyed that it seems inevitable, is what makes the evening memorable. The audience was not in doubt.

Guardian, January 1964

Phèdre: Comédie Française

When Mme Marie Bell brought her famous Phèdre to London
with La Comédie Française just after the war the late James Agate,
perhaps unconsciously resenting an intrusion into the corner he
had made in Sarah Bernhardt's interpretation, dismissed Mme Bell
with contempt. Further it was felt that one who had been seen as so
pretty a film star could not also be a great tragedian, and since
precise judgement of French acting is so rare in London Mme Bell
was generally misprized.

How wrongly, she demonstrated in the first of her three
Racinian heroines. (Those of us who have followed the Parisian
theatre since the war know that her Agrippine in *Britannicus* which
she played for La Comédie and her Bérénice which she played for
Barrault are no less impressive.) Since her last visit Mme Feuillere
also has given a Phèdre which was clear, intelligent, and at times
lyrical, but it had in my opinion nothing of the power of Mme
Bell's incredibly swift torrential declamatory style.

With her the great tirades are virtuoso arias taxing the
enunciatory art to its very limits; rushing forward with the majesty
of some natural catastrophe, a tidal wave of passion and grief,
spraying us with mute e's, commas, elisions, and caesuras which
whip the grammarian in us into a blush before drowning us in a
surging sea, with the beat and the roll of the Alexandrines going
over our heads (let us admit it, more than once). I call this
wonderful, the great high tradition of Racine at the Theatre
Français; full scale yet never falling into rant or bombast, and I bow
to such a force as to a force of nature, the singing of Flagstad, or the
four-minute milers. Mme Bell can also linger, magically; and she
has an instant way of shifting a mood. The solo invocation 'O toi
qui sais la honte . . .' was wonderfully detached from the dialogues.

On the other hand, I find a certain tearful note unbeguiling, and this, I thought, spoiled the great speech where Phèdre dwells on the happiness of her rival and Hippolyte, 'Tous les jours se levaient clairs et sereins pour eux'. This is acting, all the same, of magnificent line and attack. Contrived? Down to the last finger-tip. Mechanical? Never. On the contrary, the style generally of this production is both logical and even 'natural'.

The young Hippolyte was Hubert Nöel: the imposing Thésée was Jacques Dacqmine. M. Chevrier did the tremendous 'recit' of the last act boldly.

Guardian, March 1960

Le Misanthrope: Comédie Française

Not all our days are dark; for the second time since the war we welcome to London a party from the Comédie Française, oldest and best of state theatres. What a tonic! What a lesson in acting! Sheer acting, all acting, nothing but acting. No producer's name on the programme, no dam' electricians, a minimum of 'business', decor a minor consideration, but the word, the play itself, every splendid, taut, muscular syllable of it, acted for all it is worth.

The play this week is *Le Misanthrope*, Molière's greatest play, perhaps the greatest comedy in the world; the wittiest most stylish and laughable of all the tragedies of disillusioned nature. How shall one describe it? As though Hamlet had walked into Millamant's drawing-room? Opinions differ about Alceste: how far towards the pathetic may he be safely taken? How far must he remain the butt not merely of the ridicule of his fellows but of ours also? M. Pierre Dux, as he showed us at the last visit, is a comic mime of the first order. His Alceste is so naturally and easily comic that he can afford to line the ludicrous discomfiture of Alceste with a brilliant gleaming pathos. When Arsinoé spurs his jealousy and Célimène breaks his heart, he touches tragedy with a light and bitter thrust, and even when out of countenance safely takes us with him. It is a performance instinct of Molière in which sympathy and style are perfectly blended.

Time and Tide, October 1948

Mrs Warren's Profession

Here is a good occasion. Immensely enjoyable to find the National Theatre pulling out all the stops with that now unfashionable thing: the drama of the rational, the articulate, the communicative. *Mrs Warren's Profession* (respectable brothel keeper or at least owner) may seem a thousand miles away in the present age of porn and permission but the play's merit in purely theatrical terms remains splendidly and immediately arresting. I would strongly congratulate the cast and the producer Ronald Eyre for believing in the virtue of Shaw's early morality and doing it proud. Not only is it fine theatre, out and out, it leaves one gasping that such an immensely righteous sermon, so witty and light-handedly cogent would ever possibly and in any circumstances have been considered an offence against public decency and unworthy of public showing. I admit the play's premise, i.e. that girls become whores out of economic need, now seems cant. Still, Sarah Badel gives a fine unsentimental and sympathetic performance of a Vivie Warren, not afraid to call herself a reformed prig who sees that brothel-tainted money and lounging about in Surrey with an old vulgar goat (Bill Fraser, doing Crofts as one of his goldfish vulgarians to perfection) is an insufferable prospect. The moment, right at the end where, in Shaw's stage directions, Vivie throws herself into that cure for all ills, specially heart-break – into the all consoling business of 'work' (as a lady-solicitor's clerk, if you please) – was made moving and true, though I think I would have felt it more keenly if I had taken more strongly to the presentation of the renounced young Frank by Ronald Pickup which is first rate in every way except that of charm: we can't help feeling Vivie had a happy escape: but his is a loyal and deft performance laying off the easy chance for sentiment.

As for Coral Browne as what I suppose today would be called a Madam (though merely the respectable landlady of 'houses' in Ostend and elsewhere) not a chance is missed. Miss Browne is regal, harsh, blighting and as handsome as hell in velour and broderie anglaise. But might it not be better if she were a little more refined a Mrs W, only stung into vulgar reproach and loud, ugly self-pity in extremity? Perhaps overdressed too. I loved the big showdown but wished it had been rather more cautiously approached in the early scenes. Miss Badel, however, profited from so loyal and confident an actress to play up to. Paul Curran (the Rev.) and Edward Hardwicke (raisonneur, *en route* for Verona) were Shavians of high spirit. Alan Tagg a good designer.

Guardian, December 1970

Caesar and Cleopatra

I did not hope to enjoy the Shaw play so much. But intellectual high spirits streamed off the stage. It was delightful and fresh. Not at all irritating; not at all dated (in spite of being written in defiance of a style of historical drama now désuète). Michael Benthall's production has pace and colour and an impetus which does not flag. There is the very minimum of labouring the point of Caesar's character of magnanimous liberality – perhaps almost too little, I wondered if we should sufficiently have him 'placed' by the all-important fourth act. But we had. Olivier, while apparently throwing much away, slants the character just right and, incidentally, disposes completely of the only too facile notion that Shavian characters are always just ideas on legs.

The first three acts of exposition were charming; the scene on the Sphinx and the scenes where Mark Antony's name is first sounded especially so, and Sir Laurence and Miss Leigh played them delightfully and humanly, Caesar growing all the time in our minds, Cleopatra growing all the time in hers, until the famous antithesis of the fourth act brings the Shavian and the anti-Shavian face to face, with Cleopatra challenging Caesar on exactly those her new-won territories of love and power where he has really long abdicated. It is all the more thrilling for the ease (apparently) with which it has been approached.

The end, with the weary shrug, remains humorous. Olivier sounds no note of doom, nothing high or philosophical about what is in store. That is perhaps right, in the long run, but it is *chosen*; for in the earlier scene he gave the very firmest authority to the cardinal speech:

> To the end of history murder shall breed murder, always in the name of right and honour and peace until the gods are tired of blood and create a race that can understand . . .

The words of a man who will be murdered, surely?

Well, of course, it wouldn't be Shaw if one wasn't sometimes puzzled and worried. But I think you will not for an instant be bored.

Time and Tide, May 1951

The Winslow Boy

Good after twenty-four years not to have to eat your words. In a now rather breathless-seeming notice, I admired then, and find I still admire, Terence Rattigan's immense theatrical know-how, his sympathy and sheer skill in playing on an audience's emotions. The casting and the idealistic mood of the time have changed, but the effectiveness of the dramatic method has not been found to have slipped or rusted. Above all, what struck me then was the way the dramatist made the Archer Shee case, a long drawn struggle to vindicate the honour of an Osborne cadet falsely accused of stealing (a subject for a documentary film perhaps) into a sharply shaped drawing-room comedy.

His cunning took two moods: the boy himself is not the protagonist, merely a pawn who has to stand up as a target for a home cross-examination, but is thereafter phased out as an emotional factor; and the way the dramatic emphasis is transferred to the boy's sister (a new woman idealist who suffers a jilting as a result of the case's publicity) and to the tenacious loyalty of the boy's father, ready to go to all lengths in a dull decent ex-bank-manager sort of way, to support his lad once he believes him innocent. As make-weights, Mr Rattigan uses the boy's mother quite unsentimentally (a wise reticence) and has a talkative maid as chief messenger and a Dobbin of a family solicitor to take the weight off the shoulders of the great QC (or KC, I suppose in 1914) whose bewildering bullying of the boy, followed by a relentless pursuit of his acquittal, keep the evening so tense and interesting.

Kenneth More, as did Emlyn Williams, manages this effective, easily-turned part with aplomb. But it is Laurence Naismith as the father who steals the thunder, in a superbly unselfish and muted performance. (Before it was Frank Cellier, I recall, whose son Peter

Cellier this time has a charming little success with the unloved family solicitor). Annette Crosbie was a girl of that household to the date and the life: not perhaps with the great flash of indignation which her predecessor Angela Baddeley brought it, but touching in its resignation and in that old suffragette courage which was no mere Shavian invention (it really existed). Megs Jenkins and Hilda Fennimore pick up the more obvious moments. Frith Banbury produces impeccably, and the scene set by Reece Pemberton and Beatrice Dawson recreates a vanished pre-1914 home to a tee. Did we really care more in 1946 for *De minimis curat lex* and 'Let right be done'? I thought last night's audience was getting the message pretty well.

Guardian, November 1970

The Deep Blue Sea

Terence Rattigan's new play, *The Deep Blue Sea*, at the Duchess Theatre, tonight, was listened to with that unmistakable hush with which a first-night audience, though calloused by current trash, still knows how to honour a finely written and superbly acted piece of emotional drama. Mr Rattigan's heroine has a fate less harrowing but quite as pathetic as Madame Butterfly: she, too, is a woman (a barrister's wife to be precise) who has left her world and her husband for life in the uncertain undivorced wretchedness of a cheap flat, as mother-mistress to a young airman her inferior in years as in feelings, now rather softened by drink. He is no boor, but he cannot stand the emotional demands of the situation and he is, during the play, in the process of leaving the woman to try to resume his old job of test pilot.

Our heroine begins as a would-be suicide and ends as a philosopher of kinds, and in between it is an unrelieved and exquisitely true study of a woman destructively and hopelessly in love with the wrong, the impossible man. Put thus baldly it sounds like merely another Lady of the Camelias knowing how to sacrifice herself for the sake of 'Cheri'. But that is to reckon without Mr Rattigan's now consummate skill and a heart-searchingly beautiful performance by Miss Peggy Ashcroft which moved her audience more deeply than anything, even *The Heiress*, since the days when she played Juliet.

It is playing of such truth and tenderness that it wipes aside tears even as it reaches out to touch the heart: not harrowing, finally, because so courageous: and yet infinitely more pathetic for its unhysterical decency. Certainly it is a tale of unrelieved sorrow, but so much could be said against half the world's tragedies. This is no tragedy: it is a study in pity, and those who can appreciate differences will not miss the distinction. Peter Illing (a refugee doctor), Roland Culver (ex-husband), and Kenneth More (lover) share the honour of supporting this magnificent piece of acting.

Time and Tide, March 1952

Home

I greatly enjoyed David Storey's new play *Home* at the Royal Court (his fourth), far more than I did that tent play, *The Contractor*, over which some raved while others yawned. By the time we had gone twenty minutes into it, after an exquisitely acted scene of desultory, gentlemanly chat between Sir John Gielgud and Sir Ralph Richardson, as two old codgers, probably fellow guests at a boarding-house it seemed (and I can't think who else could have played the scene at all so perfectly) it was too late to start feeling compunction that we were about to laugh at, as well as sympathize with people who had been, as they say, 'put away'.

The Home is a Home from Home, an asylum. Presently this genteel pair, bragging and feinting, indulging in fantasies, spinning boring but polite yarns about non-existent feats and relatives, is joined by a couple of old trouts, rather like the 'ladies' whom the *Punch* artist Belcher used to draw: Mona Washbourne, all raucous saucy laughs, with foot troubles and some not-to-be-guessed-at secret connected with strangling or nymphomania or both; and as her sparring partner, Dandy Nichols, full of malice and baleful admonitory glares.

The gents keep them company, as far as the lack of a fourth chair makes this possible. The talk goes in circles but in a pattern of rosalia. 'By Jove', say the chappies or 'My word'. The ladies use broader idioms. There are sulks, bouts of direct curiosity ('Wot you in here for then?'), idle tears, local gossip and uncertainties about the weather (they are in a very bare garden). By way of an interval after fifty minutes, they go in to lunch.

After this we meet another inmate (Warren Clarke), a childish giant wrong in the head. The men are a little scared of him. The women scornful and unkind. 'Done your remedials then?' they ask. 'What were they? Baskets, I might have known.' The harridans depart, the giant carries in the chairs, evening begins to fall. It seems as if one ought now to be picking up an allegory about the whole of our country and society being a lunatic asylum but this did not in fact come very clear to me, at least, who had been content to take the short two acts in Lindsay Anderson's delicate direction as a perfectly straight study of a day among the 'abnormal'.

With the fading light a great sadness is diffused between the elderly males, hanging in the air like a dusk which will not settle. There is a long time ahead for these inmates. I wished I hadn't laughed at them so much, but wasn't quite sorry after all. It is that sort of play, rare and beautifully done.

Guardian, June 1970

Serjeant Musgrave's Dance

Serjeant Musgrave's Dance by John Arden, who wrote *Live Like Pigs*, is a long and challenging play. Even now, at curtain-fall, some of its import escapes me, but for the best part of three hours it has worked on my curiosity and often put that ill-definable theatrical spell on my imagination. I think it is something short of a great play. But wild horses wouldn't have dragged me from my seat before the end.

The first two-thirds is like an eerie Victorian melodrama (the sounds which supervene on the slow, silent, strike-bound colliery town in the 1880s made me think of *The Bells*). A party of Redcoats, three odd sorts and a fiercely religious serjeant, come to the town on what at first seems like a recruiting drive, though the surly strikers and their pastors and masters assume for different reasons that the soldiers are there to be 'used'. They are billeted in the ale house and it gradually becomes clear that they are deserters, led by a maniac, driven out of his mind – or the prison of his sense of duty – by appalling memories of a massacre in some Colony.

Serjeant Musgrave's mission is a reversal of all soldierly values, violent, coercive pacifism, which is to be preached like the word of Jehovah at the point of a gun. He duly has his great inside-out recruiting jamboree, but already his great, revealed, heaven-sent plan has gone agley. The brand of Cain is on the lot of them. Fighting breaks out among the missionary party. Musgrave ends behind bars.

Pacifism, the author seems to say, which is only militarism written backwards, is futile. Better and safer the human anarchy of a strike-bound colliery township in all its hypocrisy and rancour.

The play is written with an acute sense of language, which somehow fits the period without conscious archaism. There are occasional deviations into the jingles of folk ballad, but in the main the writing is remarkably strong, yet unpretentious. It gives the actors every chance, and Ian Bannen, in particular, as the fanatical Serjeant, gives a magnificent performance. Werner Krauss, whose death was reported this week, would have given just such a fine fierce heavy mould to the role.

Donal Donnelly, Frank Finlay, and notably Alan Dobie bring great conviction to the three other ranks, and Freda Jackson as the ale-wife and Patsy Byrne as the barmaid could hardly be better. The rest are mostly illustrative types – priest and mayor, such as O'Casey or Buechner might have drawn them. But they have their places in the rather confused climax in the market place.

Lindsay Anderson produces with strength and economy in the earlier scenes, which are beautifully set and lighted (decor by Jocelyn Herbert). I wish I could think that the production brought the audience the maximum help in the last act. But that this is a highly original and challenging experiment in drama is not in doubt; and it seems to me worth a dozen of the slices of slum life, didactics, and comedies we have endured at this theatre, including one by this same author.

Guardian, October 1959

Mourning Becomes Electra

Since we last saw *Mourning Becomes Electra* we have seen the two great works which after an abstention of twelve years marked Eugene O'Neill's return to the stage, namely *The Iceman* and *Long Day's Journey into Night*. I had expected *Mourning* to have lost some of its power and found my guess was right. We have also at the Old Vic been given the Oresteia of Aeschylus, the myth as seen by a contemporary as it were, whereas *Mourning* is O'Neill's retelling of the tale in terms of American puritanism, and times of the Civil (instead of the Trojan) War, of New England in the 1860s.

The original had the shock novelty of a modern-dress *Hamlet*. Now the shock has worn off a little. The French, who have always been nearer the classical legends than we, have constantly refurbished them and now the mood, via Giraudoux *et al* has long established itself in London. It is still a powerful play; a powerful recreation. Aeschylus never has Electra meet Clytemnestra (as an O'Neill character might put it), Euripides does. So the comparison is not solely with the Aeschylus trilogy.

But the parallel is interesting; like seeing two Crucifixions by artists of wholly differing schools hanging side by side – anyone may make his own suggestions for comparisons from Giotto to Dali. But one is struck by how much O'Neill depends on the effect of the two actresses *confronting* one another. This is what one recalls when the rest has slightly dimmed; Laura Cowie versus Beatrix Lehmann, Mary Ellis versus Mary Morris, and this time Sonia Dresdel, red in tooth and claw, confronting Barbara Jefford, white with exultant grief. At these moments, of silence rather than speech be it noted, *Mourning* becomes electrifying.

Yes, I am back at it. Words and music. For what do we not lack in O'Neill if it is not the words which soar and sweep? I found the Volanakis translation of the Oresteia deficient not merely in words but a quality which I can only liken to the ritual of Wagnerian music drama and which creates in itself the tragic dimension. And so it is with this play: it fails, as for instance Richard Strauss's opera *Elektra* does not fail, to express itself mightily or memorably.

It was O'Neill's misfortune as an artist to live at a moment of the theatre's history when the language a Coriolanus could use to a Volumnia would be unthinkable, an impossible heightening of what in fact American sons do say to mothers in moments of stress, to wit 'Aw Mother . . .' O'Neill hasn't a tragic language to work in.

Guardian, November 1961

The Finest Ham

I have never been one for fashions, feeling I knew my own mind best (Mr Hope-Wallace's clothes by Gamages, said a sharp-eyed critic). This goes for the theatre, too, but I must say I was a bit taken aback by the howl of derision which greeted my plan to 'collect' Sir Henry Arthur Jones's *Mrs Dane's Defence* at Leatherhead recently. Some of my colleagues had never heard of him, let alone *her*. Which is all very well for the younger generation who imagine that apart from Shakes and Shaw, the drama in this country sprang like Minerva, but rather less well armed or wise, from the brain of John Osborne in 1956.

Why may not I admire Henry Arthur Jones (d. 1929, the year I went to college)? Musicians – and I have a foot in the opera camp, if that word is still permitted – would never jib at going down to, say, Fulham to collect Charpentier's *Louise* which, though still great box office in France, is even obscurer than poor old *Mrs D.*

We British playgoers – or perhaps I had better say we critics – are fools so to neglect our heritage, to assume that apart from received classics, only new or modern plays are acceptable or are what the public wants. The evidence is strong that the public does not want an unbroken diet of classics and novelties.

Obviously there is room for so-called boulevard theatre on our so-called main streets. The theatre of Henri Bataille, Sudermann. Pinero still has an appeal. I know that the National Theatre now does Ostrovosky's *The Storm* and that in European eyes we are not as provincial as we used to be or as Broadway certainly now is. But I seriously think that there are plays by Granville Barker and Galsworthy which are now likely to seem actually *less* dated than Osborne's earlier invective and belly-aching or Pinter's teasing doodles. Not that it is social significance in theatre that I would stress: *that* at least was not invented by Osborne. We had, to the incredulity of some present pundits, quite a lot of it even in the 1930s: *Love on the Dole, Idiot's Delight, Musical Chairs* and so on.

What I am sure of is that now derided and 'old-fashioned' Edwardian plays were often excellent occasions for the art of acting and that there is an audience that likes the art of acting for *itself*. May I draw a comparison with the ballet? Anyone who likes classical ballet as I do will go again and again to *Giselle*. Why, for the music? For the scenery and spectacle? For the story? Surely not any of those elements. But because it gives the art of the ballerina incomparable scope and opportunity.

I ask for a play that 'works' the audience so that it cares what is happening and I say that Pinero and Jones were better than Mr Mercer in *Belcher's Luck* in providing for these requirements. How feeble is many a modern playwright's 'curtain' even if he has one and doesn't end his play with a whimper, a whisper, and a fade out. How little did I either understand or care when Belcher shot the mare which had been his pet. I was not even sure he liked her or that 'mare' might not have been a symbol for his mother (Fr. *mère*. Shades of *Black Beauty*!) If you do get a horse on the stage nowadays, it's only a lot of electronic whinnying and kicking. Is there nothing to be said for 'ham' which is unequivocal, as 'the rest is silence' or 'the lights burn blue' or 'You never can tell, sir' are ham at the finest? If so, why disclaim inferior cuts (madam)?

The £400,000 I am winning on the pools next week is to be spent on a revival of *The Notorious Mrs Ebbsmith*, for whom I hope to engage the Irish actress Eithne Dunne to star and we shall see again the grand moment when Mrs E., chidden for her social sin by a talkative clergyman, slams the door on him, takes her New Testament and flings it into the roaring stove; then, alone by the footlights, repents and is *seen* to repent of her blasphemy; runs to the grate, plunges her fair white arm into the blazing stove, retrieves the sacred book and falls in a faint mid-stage. How about that for a curtain?

Guardian Bedside Book 1966–67

The Confidential Clerk

T. S. Eliot's new play, *The Confidential Clerk*, was an enormous success here in Edinburgh. It honours not only the Festival but, comic though it looks on the surface, I think it also honours the English-speaking theatre in a larger sense. It is both wise and witty. And since there is no shifting of mood or hocus-pocus of any kind, it is never more puzzling than a drawing-room comedy, which is more than you can say for some of Mr Eliot's other plays, with their ghostly asides.

The simplest way to describe it to a person who has not just now experienced its frivolous profundity is to ask him to imagine *The Importance of Being Earnest* rewritten by an Oscar Wilde who uses the problem of John Worthing's paternity to start running some very lively metaphysical hares about the problem of identity: and from this problem of identity to the kindred question of heredity, and hence to the subject which also lay at the heart of *The Cocktail Party*: that is to say, the question of salvation through finding your own true vocation. If you imagine, as this hero did, that he was the illegitimate son of a financier and could find his true self by replacing his father's retiring clerk you will have to come to a very different decision if you are at last shown to be the son of an entirely different kind of man.

The hero of this play is saved from trying to be someone he is not and sees where his true bent lies, making it a true comedy, just as the end of John Worthing, embracing Miss Prism, is the perfect end of a farce. Yet serious though Mr Eliot is beneath the surface his farce is almost wilder than Wilde's. There comes a moment in the second act when almost everybody on the stage is proved to have an ambiguous, if not an illegitimate provenance which is pure Labiche.

The audience in the second act was laughing as it laughs at Lady

Bracknell when Isabel Jeans, as the erring mother in search of a lost son, is thumbing through her memory. The audience had forgotten that it was watching the least funny of things in the general way: a verse play with strong religious overtones. But this only proves how triumphantly Mr Eliot has now elaborated a theatrical language which needs no Greek chorus or slides into the portentous or cathedral echoes to express his idea. Yet the audience attends even to the most serious discussions of the nature of identity, vocation, and the discovery that what one thinks is a change in one's personality is only a deeper awareness of one's self and that this awareness comes only from knowing another person.

You might not know, any more than we did in *The Cocktail Party*, that the play is in verse or at least regularly stressed prose of a poetic kind, but the cumulative effect of listening to this language is wholly different from listening even to the most elaborate prose. It imposes a lightly-felt rhythm which holds the audience. 'It's strange, isn't it, that a man should have a consuming passion for something for which he had no capacity?' is a line which is fairly typical.

The play is perfectly cast and produced by Martin Browne as the author intends, with the appearance of a smart comedy with smart clothes and charming sets. It is beautifully acted so as to bring out without forcing the very clear studies of character caught in a wise farce of paternity problems. Margaret Leighton and Denholm Elliot, as a couple who are attracted only to find themselves as they think brother and sister, carry the serious implications of the problem of the true self most persuasively. Peter Jones bounces about as the real man of mystery. Isabel Jeans is uniquely funny as the smart woman in search of a lost son. Paul Rogers is finally most moving as the man who wrongly thinks that he has a son. And Alison Leggat makes a late appearance and a telling one as the woman who can bring to these people the curing of the secret wishes of their heart, while Alan Webb as the retiring confidential clerk makes a perfect and modest master of these most civilized ceremonies.

Guardian, August 1953

Flaubert on Television

It is not too soon to say that BBC2 is making a success of *Madame Bovary*, for already we are half-way through it with last night's second episode lifting us speedily to the move to Yonville and the meeting with Léon Dupuis. And before you say 'How can they compress a novel so rich and fruity, so slow to be read?' (as it was slow to be written), please remember that in 1933 Jean Renoir in his film had even less time to put it on the screen than Richard Beynon with his four twenty-five-minute instalments.

Nice to be able to mention Renoir's film with Valentine Tessier, in the same breath. So screening Emma Bovary *can* be done and make good entertainment, plausible, authentic looking, when not too smart – provincial Normandy was scarcely the epitome of French elegance even in that day, but a slice of dull life, marvellously spiced.

Spiced by what? By Flaubert's pen? There's the rub. The pleasure given will be wide but strongest to those who have not relished or re-read the book itself. For those who have not, it might come out vivid enough, a period tale of a demoralized marriage and wasted life, like a tale by whom? Maupassant, Arnold Bennett?

But fatally one misses the pungent tone of voice of this unique narrator. It is like Dickens or Jane Austen put on stage. The events are there, the social irony, the verbal repartee. But the narrator's commentary – *le style c'est l'homme* – is particularly true in Flaubert's case. Thackeray's voice could do the same. When Flaubert thunders: 'In adultery Emma found the same boredom as in marriage' we get a blow from off the printed page right between the eyes. How compensate for loss of that with a visual grimace or gesture?

Then Flaubert's own 'visuals' – the footmen climbing on each other's shoulders to break the windows with a broom when the ballroom grew suffocating (no sash windows, then), the shadow of the night-rider thrown up on a street wall when a night-baker flings wide his oven doors: the screen catches a lot of such magic. Francesca Annis springs the right sort of response as Emma. Brave effort.

Guardian, January 1974

Glorious Performances: Peggy Ashcroft

'The paths of glory lead but to the grave.' Too true, adds the cynic, sometimes none too soon. All the same there are ways and ways of treading such paths (especially on the stage) sidestepping the larger incongruities. Take legendary Melba now: last seen at the incredible age of sixty in the circumstances of singing, in a white nightgown, the sweet Gounodisms of Juliette on a cardboard balcony to a Romeo half her age. 'Ah, *ne fuis pas*' indeed! Of course there are wiser ways, though in a sense that event was a marvel in more ways than one: to the ear, not just the ear of faith, if not to the eye, Time's Revenge had been parried.

On the other hand last time we saw Kchessinskaya dance she was well into her sixties for the occasion was a Royal Gala at Covent Garden in the mid-nineteen thirties and the archducal ballerina who had been the last Tsar's mistress (and from whose sacked villa balcony Lenin addressed the mob in that outstanding photograph) died last month in Paris at the age of ninety-nine. *Her* dance was, if I could recover my programme, simply described, I think, as Old Lady's Dance, and we saw a delightful old person in peasant frock, with much arms akimbo, head nodding, and wreathed becks and smiles, treading *moujik* measures with a vitality I have also noted in elderly Highland postmistresses who think nothing of dancing reels by the solid hour.

Vitality, that's the secret of the great career as of the great performance. Nine-tenths, said Maggie Teyte, the other tenth being technique. *And* surprise: the ingredient, the power, the trick if you like that informed all the greatest performances I've ever seen from Werner Krauss to Fischer Dieskau (never take a breath where they expect you to, said Jean de Reszke). 'Great,' you may be saying, 'for whom?' Myself when young? For of course nobody ever quite beats your first Isolde, your first Beatrice, your first Viola, even if she *was* Lady Ben Greet!

But back to Juliet, Shakes's this time. Compare my favourite, pristine unforgettable and yardstick of a Juliet with old Melba-pots. I refer to Peggy Ashcroft, Dame understood, but she wasn't then: she was just the Juliet of my generation, honoured the OUDS with it and joined in that – yes – great *Romeo and Juliet* in which it was to Edith Evans as the cynical nurse ('slow as a cart-horse, earthy as a potato' in Darlington's fine phrase) that she, Peggy, unbelieving Juliet, betrayed, said 'Speakest thou from thy heart?'

Now that was heartbreak, that was glamour: or was I young and easily bewitched? I don't believe I was. It was intrinsically good, great even, all round. Gielgud (only later surpassing himself with his second Hamlet and incomparable Leontes) was a Romeo whose 'If I profane with my unworthiest hand . . .' simply stopped the heart, hushed the house like a sacrament elevated before the pious. He alternated, do you remember, with Olivier's swaggering, mischievous Mercutio – and whose 'Tis not so deep as a well . . . but tis enough: why the devil came you between us?' was the first intimation I ever had that here was an actor who was going in time to move me so deeply (in Strindberg, forsooth). At that time I found *his* Hamlet and his Romeo, though visually superb and memorable, audibly too much inferior to Gielgud's flawless Shakespeare speaking, so intelligible that a turn of speed was possible that today is almost unknown. (Yet gramophone records show Ellen Terry, his aunt, doing Portia *andante*.)

But I wander from the Ashcroft and must leave memorializing her 'It is an honour that I dreamed not of' – to point out that unlike some Honoured Artists of the Republic one could name, she no longer plays Juliet in – what is it? must be *her* sixties too, dammit. How perfectly she has paced her career; how instead of one great performance continued in rude battle against time, she has acted just what suited her, moving from Juliet to the youngest of the Three Sisters with an 'It is not in my power to love you' to Baron Tusenback (then Mr Redgrave), to Helpless Hester's heartbreak for worthless Freddie (Ken More) in Rattigan, to Ibsen's femme fatale of the fjords, yes even to an infinitely touching Catherine of Aragon fading into death at Kimbolton.

And think of that termagant Queen in the Wars of the Roses. You could say of her, as Enorbarbus does of that 'lass incomparable' that 'Age cannot wither . . . etc'. because of course age has not somehow ever entered into it. Never did 'A bit past it now . . .' whisper like a snake in memory. It has all made a career which is cumulatively deserving of the Great epithet. I dare say I am as liable to dwell on glory and the rewards of not always comfortless memory on other isolated splendours: how's Frida Leider's Isolde, Bette Davies as Regina kicking her brother's coffee cup in *The Little Foxes*, Sybil herself tearing up Joan's recantation? But my list would just fill columns, so much have stage, screen, and opera house meant to me. But in one case at least I do see a path of glory which, telescoped in perspective, does at least seem great and brightly shines. Shall I end by seeing my best Juliet end as Juliet's nurse, full circle? Ripeness is all.

Guardian, January 1972

Sybil Thorndike

Sybil Thorndike, who has died at the age of ninety-three, had long wrestled with the Angel of Death and one began to suspect that he would not vanquish this indomitable woman, felt to be heroic if not immortal to some extraordinary degree. With immense physical courage and will-power and an unflagging vitality she disguised, save from her closest friends and family, that shattering heart attacks of the most painful kind were increasingly weakening her. To the public she was up and about, spry, 'words' all perfect, attending services, reading on platforms, being in fact, though to a less terrifying energetic degree, the kind of generous public figure that she had so long become. 'If not reading Bunyan to lonely Nigerian nurses,' I once wrote, 'she and Lewis [Casson] would be doing one-night Shakespeare stands in Dunedin.'

Agate once described her as having a heart as big as a railway station and, changing the metaphor, as like a fire engine which answered every call. Indeed there were those less prodigal of unselfish action who thought she espoused too many causes, even dubious ones, because they seemed to need her help. This, with an effortless drawing to herself of the limelight, her marvellous 'projection' of sincerity and emotion perhaps irritated lesser mortals who might not have espoused the same cause. But what volume of personality did she command!

As an actress she may be said to have had scarcely any failures. I did not like her Imogen in *Cymbeline*, which seemed to me kittenish: her comedy however grew with age. In plays such as *The Corn is Green* (with Emlyn Williams) or *The Linden Tree* by J. B. Priestley, or again as a quiet foil to the show-off character played by Edith Evans in *Waters of the Moon*, she was a sensitive comedienne. The little part of the old nurse in the wonderful Chichester *Uncle Vanya* was quite unmatchable. Her enormous sense of adventure and appetite for struggle made her take on indeed some odd roles – one remembers, in a composite way, her terrifying deportment as a big-game huntress walling up a rival; and her glee and gusto in playing the absurdest Grand Guignol was on a par with the tingling energy and relish she put into her readings from the New English Bible.

But it was in the heroic roles – from Ancient Greek Hecuba and Medea down to the peerless Saint Joan (which Shaw wrote for her) – that the spell put on the audience was total. Nor was it only the spell of the play. I find that I can never see another Mrs Alving in Ibsen's *Ghosts* without recalling the power and thrust of her scenes of greatest emotion: it was like a physical blow between the eyes. I recall her Lady Macbeth trying to rally her distracted king at the banquet, her Queen Katharine of Aragon rounding on Cardinal Wolsey. Lastly the sheer sweep and gaiety of her reciting, at a recent Royal Opera Gala, Browning's *Up at the Villa*, waving her stick at us to acknowledge applause, reluctant to leave the scene. 'There's a great spirit gone.'

Guardian, June 1976

Edith Evans

This is a most enjoyable and well-written life by Bryan Forbes of a specially wonderful actress. The cover shows a little Victorian miss, with a sly, witty, enigmatic look. Children's eyes don't change; go with them all through their strenuous lives; with no difference to show. The face, the voice and personality – those have a different fate.

This is a just, perceptive and penetrating account of the great

Dame who was said to be inimitable but was imitated by all and sundry, so individual a timbre and cast of phrase did she employ.

With autobiography, any fool can do some sort of a masterpiece. But biography, especially of recently-defunct stars, is often sorry stuff. This, by Bryan Forbes, is a shining example of the good. A view not unintimate, since he knew her off stage, her spartan ways, her shyness and being-at-a-loss with people, especially young people, her doubts and childlessness and inner self-respect, not fawning on the bitch-goddess success whom she had never invoked or expected to answer her prayers.

It's a careful, true unvulgar summation of her unusual personality and her art. Most biographies of actresses are either dotty hagiography (the star could do no wrong, the critics raved, etc., etc.) or a cheap sub Lytton Strachey style: the goddess had feet of clay and a dubious love life. Forbes gets it right, dead-centre focus.

He supplies a lot of his own which we did not know and doesn't disdain the many Edith-isms so beloved of theatre gossips: the *quod libets*, the delicate snubs, the suggestion of imperiousness which was merely a shield for the shy heart.

She had no theatrical background, did not have to prove anything. She was a milliner in South London who liked reciting and taking little parts in amateur productions by women's institutes and that sort of thing. Then she caught William Poel's eye, or ear.

Poel did more for Shakespeare than anyone in our century. Edith once talked to me about him. 'Do you require great volume?' she asked. 'He did not; he said it was all music, *whey wee whop whoop twoo lar* – singing in effect; accent all important and rhythm, of course. But the sound picture had to be right. I cottoned on,' she added, drawling slightly.

Presently Herbert Farjeon, the best Shakespeare critic of the century, was talking about 'the queen of the English theatre'. So she was; but did not much like rich food or effusive parties.

Her Shakespeare was indeed memorable, in the strongest sense of the word. Her Rosalind (which she repeated when too old, with

Redgrave, but was still 'inimitable'), her Nurse in *Romeo* of course. Even her Cleopatra, 'O withered is the garland of the war' just out of this world, though the audience laughed when she said: 'I'll give thee bloody teeth' because they thought she was Lady Bracknell, a role she grew to hate from her facility in it.

She had a protean scope. Wilde apart, Restoration comedy was her heaven. I must have seen her Millament a dozen times, listened to her Mrs Sullen – 'I loathe the country, I nauseate walking': I can hear it now. Too late for Shaw really, non-intellectual, her great modern performances were apt to come in plays like Enid Bagnold's *The Chalk Garden*, or N. C. Hunter's *Waters of the Moon*, with Dame Sybil as foil.

Her comedian's art was beautifully and swiftly summarized by Gielgud, who said that when invited, in a play, to take a seat, she would embrace the audience in a sly complicity as much as to say: Is it wise? look at the armchair mistrustfully as if it were a crocodile and compose herself in it, with the audience enraptured and not a sound heard. Bryan Forbes tells the story truly and without lurid glamour calls up the great one in her true likeness.

Guardian, October 1977

Some Cleopatras

I am not a camera but an accumulator willy-nilly. I'll throw away all fond and trivial records, says Hamlet, but at my age and job one has clocked up forty Hamlets or so. How about Cleopatras? Precious few: few and precious. The oddest I ever saw was the conflation which Tairov made for Alice Koonen, his wife, using Shaw, Shakespeare, and Pushkin's *Egyptian Nights*. I remember from the middle 1930s gorgeous tableaux and a puppet queen declaiming in Russian and ecstasy.

Two of the best Cleos were American, Claire Luce and Mary
Newcombe, the latter to Wilfred Lawson. There was Vivien
Leigh, but she hadn't the voice: 'I am dying, Egypt, dying to hear
you in row H,' wrote a nasty American critic. There was Dame
Edith Evans who voiced the threnody gorgeously, unlike Miss
Leontovich, whom Morgan mocked as 'O wee-di-dee de garland
of de war,' but when our own Edith told Charmian 'I'll give thee
bloody teeth' it was so like Lady Bracknell scolding a housemaid
that we all laughed the wrong way.

And of course, Dame Peggy Ashcroft, too, with her keenness
and respect for the poetry.

I wish I could have seen legendary ones, such as Constance
Collier. But Mrs Siddons wouldn't touch the role, fearing that
if she played as she believed she must, she would be 'unsuitable', unequal to that forty-paces hop or what the priests call
'riggish' (a word which often appears in print as priggish, its
opposite).

Ellen Terry thought the queen shallow and shocked Henry
James, brought up on French theatre, by touching Antony so
often. I don't know what he would make of Chichester's
canoodling, which if not very sexy, is explicit enough for an 'X'
film.

What was not by any means predictable: Chichester brings off a
fine and moving performance of this rarest and most difficult of
tragedies with Sir John Clements in noble vein as Antony and that
intrinsically grand actress, Margaret Leighton, so often wasted in
minor things, rising to the challenge of the great role of Cleopatra
in a way I have not seen bettered for many years. Hers is the real
triumph of the occasion. Her speaking, like his, is noble, full and
passionate but without rant or false emphasis. The threnody for the
hero's death and her welcoming of death for herself were voiced
with a spaciousness and ease and on a long span which arched across
the wide spaces of this open stage.

I had expected she would do justice to the elegiac qualities. What
surprised was the way in which she achieved not only full regal
status but also caught many facets of the part which might have

seemed outside her grasp; the temper, the raillery, and the humour of the scenes of dalliance and yearning. It is an assumption which will be long remembered.

John Clements, using his voice magnificently, is very much the Roman – I thought of his Coriolanus and he is perhaps more a Brutus than ideally an Antony, a little stiff and not as sympathetic in his degradation as some interpreters we have seen. But he gives a truly heroic dimension to this crumbling statue and is perhaps all the more moving in the scene of suicide for his unbending portrayal of the earlier scenes – an oak that crashes since it cannot bend.

But this tragedy is not really a love story: it is a story of war lost through lust. There is really hardly a scene, a *love* scene which Hollywood might accept as such. Shaw thought that the play didn't bite because it was inconsistent and that Shakespeare 'strains the huge command of rhetoric and stage pathos to give a theatrical sublimity to the wretched end of the business and persuade foolish spectators that the world is well lost for love', thus displeasing Puritan and healthy citizen alike.

I find Margaret Leighton berated in some quarters for not being sexy enough, not Eastern enough and so on. But is this to the point? Which is rather that the role was written for a boy, with an explicit reference thereto in the text (Act 5). I don't believe it is necessary for Cleopatra to exude 'sexiness' as it is lamentably called. The descriptions of her charms are in other mouths.

Yearning, loyalty, heartbreak, temper, and feminine caprice and guile are all there, but somehow within the compass of the female impersonator, the boy actor, or the actor of female roles in the oriental theatre, with the sexuality suggested elliptically. I think it's a mistake to put *seductiveness* first in Shakespeare's Cleopatra, a role set like a jewel in such a way that all around conspires to 'set it off'.

I should say that the very first requirement was a voice and one which obeys an ear which hears the beat of the poetry. Even Shaw said in so many words that the only way to do it is to sing it, since the very threnody is 'not even grammar'.

One must not be 'operatic' of course, the dirtiest word in the language after avant garde, where this implies patently false emotions, though why opera singers should be thought guilty of this I cannot imagine. But you have to speak big. The voice of Mrs Dale just won't do for 'Give me my robe, put on my crown . . .'

Miss Leighton looks sumptuous, even if not voluptuous (we and others supply that in imagination). But above all she sounds beautiful. Line after great line is in my memory locked, and thanks to Peter Dews, the producer, we get the detail of the play often very cleverly dug out. Yet there seems to be plenty of space and air round the crucial central performances. And Miss Leighton misses no point of the comedy inside the tragedy. I'm glad I caught this serpent of old Nile.

Guardian, July 1969

Edwige Feuillère

With her second programme Mme Edwige Feuillère brings us two comedies and reveals facets of her talents which will dazzle those who know only her gentle *Dame au Camelias*. The second comedy, it is true, is no great affair; Merimée's tale is about Perichole, the governor's favourite who takes a fancy to ride to church in *le carosse du saint sacrament* as that vehicle becomes when, in an access of generosity, she presents it to the Cathedral of Lima. This is no *Carmen*, but it allows the dignified Mme Feuillère to shout, to flaunt a lovely skirt, display red stockings, eat an apple, and flounce about in a whole repertory of sulks and sudden recoveries. It is of course delightfully done, and if it was at first rather rushed it may well be that the lovely French actress was a little nervous. To sink a personality like hers into a gamine with a Peruvian accent must be like drowning a beautiful swan and fetching up a quacking duck.

But it came off, more or less successfully, with support largely from M. Mazzotti as the gouty governor.

The first play is an altogether subtler thing. Henri Becque's *La Parisienne* of the 1880s was for its day a surprisingly mordant study of a coquette who keeps her husband and two lovers so deftly under her hand that everyone is more or less delighted, ignorant of the real situation.

This little masterpiece of irony (which we have not seen in London since Sonia Dresdel played it in the war) studies a woman's hypocrisy with a witty but loveless eye. It is a perfect Réjane part and though I imagine Mme Feuillère to be more stately, her tacking about the large stage in a series of superb bustles, her nose tipping under a sequence of delicious bonnets, transported us to a forgotten world of high comedy, of 'asides', 'sells', and bold soliloquy – all of which Mme Feuillère, looking like an album of Tissot paintings, presented with a lightness of touch and, above all, a variety of expression which never staled or repeated itself or grew mechanical.

To see this Clotilde sitting on a sofa, bringing a recalcitrant lover to heel with eyes lowered, a glove to be taken off slowly as a tortoise-race, to hear her sigh '*ah, que vous êtes exigeant*' is to recapture something like Dame Edith Evans's Millamant.

Guardian, March 1957

Vanessa Redgrave in
The Taming of the Shrew

How George Du Maurier would have delighted to make a drawin' of Vanessa Redgrave which would have come out as one of those tall fringed goddesses in bustles who raise pained eyebrows above the long captions of *Punch* jokes in the 1890s. I was tempted tonight to suggest how amusing it might be to have a Du Maurier setting of 'The Shrew', with Petruchio of course as one of the bohemians out of *Trilby*. Better not. Shakespeare producers are up to enough devilry as it is.

But Miss Redgrave's height and hauteur are great natural assets for the part – for many parts. She must be a formidable obstacle at one of these sit down and go limp affairs: yet when she plays Rosalind at Stratford-on-Avon, it is Mr Levin who is carried away!

The present production, in Elizabethan dress, is much what we saw last year by the Avon where Dame Peggy Ashcroft and Peter O'Toole played termagent and tamer to splendid effect. Myself I always like a production of this particular play which slightly veils or evades the very thing which no doubt makes it popular – especially in Germany where 'Widerspenstigenzaehmung' is often on the bill: namely, the unedifying spectacle of a virago put down by a cad: what might be called The Shaming of the Shrew.

The Stratford-on-Avon production aided by some special grace of Dame Peggy's was to make the whole thing seem a more pleasing tale of an overlooked, resentful, unloved girl who quickly took a liking to the unconventional husband and though keeping up the tantrums for the world to see was secretly delighted to see how Petruchio also scared everyone else, the dud suitors and her father among them.

This line Vanessa Redgrave also adopts, with some delightful variants of her own. The tall debutante might indeed be, as her sister says, a trifle 'mad' both in the American and English sense. But the kicking soon stops when she gets the hang of the situation; and not the least of her virtues as an actress, inherited if I dare say so from her father, is the precision of her expressiveness. We see the very second when the new possibility dawns on this Kate. 'Curst' Kate she may not always be: but she strikes twelve right away in the wooing, which she and Derek Godfrey make into one of the best pieces of subtle playing to be seen in London. Indeed I do not remember it better done. The scene, often so crude and common, is here exactly right in tone and temper. No wonder the audience responded.

Some of the rest of the play, which includes the whole Christopher Sly framework, is on a level which might cause a self-respecting Hottentot to ask for his money back. But this crew gets away with it, partly because they can always pretend to be overacting for the benefit of Sly who, like a dowager listening to opera sung in a foreign language at Glyndebourne, is not averse from a few broad winks. I think foreign visitors to London too will like it. After all you don't ever get much more fun out of such scenes as that where Tranio (James Bree) outbids Gremio (Ian Holm) under the rolling eye of old Baptista (Patrick Wymark); or Hortensio and Lucentio (George Murcell and Peter Jeffrey) make their disguised advances to Bianca (Diana Rigg). The ale-house set spins merrily; peasant faces hover on all sides; the horseplay is unflagging. But the virtue of the occasion lies with Miss Redgrave who most unusually but quite believably gives us of all things a *charming* shrew.

Guardian, September 1961

Tyrone Guthrie

'A prophet is not without honour save in his own country . . .' Tyrone, or more usually Tony, Guthrie was a genius, like Beecham, more appreciated it seems by others than by his own countrymen. Ask Americans who named a theatre after him. Ask Canadians who had a most refreshing dose of his originality.

He was as tall or taller than General de Gaulle and could sometimes be pretty difficult to get on with, though most people loved him and responded to his direction with joy. He could be perverse and irreverent, too, and made old fogies, even fairly-young fogies like myself, raise their eyebrows and say tut-tut. But when he got his hands on a play like *Peer Gynt* with Ralph Richardson just after the war he showed the great measure of his imagination as a producer. *Troilus* in the manner of Lehar, *The Dream* in the manner of Queen Victoria's favourite composer, Mendelssohn, those umbrellas at Ophelia's funeral in the first Guinness *Hamlet* are among the things which have become part of the legend.

Guthrie should surely have had far more power and position. But the last years have had to be a quieter life for him. About ten years ago as we stood in Baker Street at a bus stop he told me he had had a bad fright about the condition of his heart and felt the sound of time's chariot passing near. I said :'Go into the Planetarium, you will be at home among stars.' 'Don't go and say that in my obituary,' he said. 'I could not abide them'; but he certainly' made' a few. I thought his opera productions mostly rather tiresome but I seldom see a play today which is hailed for the originality of its production without thinking, 'Guthrie did all that years ago.'

Guardian, May 1971

Emlyn Williams: Dickens

Emlyn Williams is back with his Dickens readings, which are dull words to describe a superlative performance of passages from the great dramatist *manqué* of our heritage. They are in truth acted in a spell-binding bravura style, such as you might have to go back to Lloyd George, catching an audience in its most vulnerable state, to rival.

I used to think that no one could do the opening chapter of *A Tale of Two Cities* as well as my own father, but have to give this actor with this author a higher rating. Mr Williams appears in costume, gradually intensifies the delivery, and ends up with a horror story which fairly makes us gasp.

He begins, as before, with the Veneerings and the Podsnaps preening in society, with their guests looking like their own reflections in the backs of silver spoons, and the lady who raps her hand with her fan – 'a hand particularly rich in knuckles.'

Thence to the death of the boy Paul Dombey, which can also be found on record – I once played it on the BBC, thereby reducing the technical staff and myself to tears. This again came up astonishingly fine and moving. The parade was splendidly well-timed, full of skill, neat and secure. Miss Tox and Mr Toots came before us for just the right number of minutes. Phrase after phrase of description combined to make strong and often very comic dramatic poetry.

If this is not 'theatre' – solo recitation though of course it is in essence – I must go to school again. I shall go again, for sheer pleasure.

Guardian, February 1975

Bette Davis

Where can I find a tear-jerker? I urgently need one on medical grounds. But there don't seem any around any more. Perhaps I should say that as a *malade imaginaire* who believes in homeopathy and hydrotherapy (and not hydro only, let's admit) I am thought to resort to fanciful therapeutics. For an acid stomach for instance I drink raw lemon juice, unsweetened of course, which causes my friends to blench and avert their pained gaze. So perhaps you won't be entirely surprised that *my* cure for a certain form of depression (such as I have had recently after a long course of penicillin and water) is a jolly good cry.

Through art, of course. I don't want to go blubbing to any old funeral. But a good Hollywood tear-jerker, before lunch: that was the ticket. Come out red-eyed at 12.50 into bright sunshine and down a quick one to restore your nerve. Depression dispersed.

I wish right now I could see a film called *Dark Victory*. A simple film but it made us weep like Niagara. It starred Bette Davis who as usual acted a treat from start to finish. Bette was a tearaway rich gal who nearly fell for a handsome stable lad but instead, under his spell, took to steeplechasing and fell much harder – took a header, came a cropper on her napper. Concussion? No. Worse! The specialist shone a pencil light into her eyes, asked her to shut them (no one shut an eye as well as Bette) and identify an object placed in her palm. No reaction.

Now, here the doctor is called away. Alone in his consulting room with Tchaikovsky's Suite in C Bette takes a dekko at his (the doctor's) notes. In comes tactless Nurse O'Reilley. 'What does prognosis negative mean?' asks Bette. 'Not too good for the party,' says Nurse. 'It means there's no future.' Big chord of F minor diminished seventh on the sound track.

When the doctor comes back Bette demands the truth. 'I have a brain tumour,' she says, 'and am going to die.' Says he: 'We all gotta die one day. We all have a date stamp on us. Don't worry, you are going to have a swell life like anyone else. Dancing the charleston, getting married, jumping hedgerows . . . well, dancing anyway.'

'But what will happen eventually?' she asks. 'One day mebbe you'll feel darkness closing in a bit: then that may be it.' Well, Bette (unless I have forgotten this part) now starts to live a whale of a life. Dancing, that's nothing. Boy-friends. Happiness. Marriage to a rising business exec. Old-world house in Vermont. The only fly in the ointment is that hubby fears he won't be asked to the big convention – don't ask me of what – but in Philadelphia.

He is nervous and waiting. Bette and a pretty young girl-friend are in the spring sunshine planting bulbs. Suddenly Bette looks skywards. 'We gonna have a storm? The sky's very ominous.' 'Why it's clear as a bell,' says the friend. But Bette knows. *We* know. The sound track, back in F minor, knows beyond a peradventure. This is it.

A window flies up above the kneeling women. It is hubby. The long-awaited telegram from Philadelphia has come and landsakes can he make the airport in time? Come on in and help him pack (those eighty white shirts which big American execs. take along with them). Bette staggers to her feet. She is fast going blind.

Clutching the banisters, she gropes towards her husband's grip and puts in the shirts wrong way up, as she has to do it by feel. Will he lose his temper? Too pressed for time. Briefly and clumsily they peck. Races downstairs. Bette waves to him in the driveway but in the *wrong* direction and the music surges up into C major while the words The End creep up the screen and we stagger into the sunshine shaken with sobs. Will someone put on that film again, please?

Guardian, June 1975

The Early Promise of Richard Burton

The Stratford-on-Avon company is doing the four historical plays, *Richard II, Henry IV* (parts one and two), and *Henry V* as a cycle, with a continuity of style and casting which allows us to see Shakespeare's great design as one great play, an epic of England and a study of kingship. This not only makes it easier to follow the history, from Bolingbroke's rebellion to the battle of Agincourt; it's a new revelation of Shakespeare's understanding of the human heart, of the grandeur and pitifulness and the fun of life, in town or country, in court or ale-house. There have been great portraits by the way; Harry Andrews as the formidable Henry IV, Michael

Redgrave as Hotspur, Anthony Quayle as Falstaff. But in the later plays another figure begins to take the centre of the stage – young Prince Hal, who grows into the Harry of England (Henry V) the hero of Agincourt. The part is played by Richard Burton.

Keep your eye on Richard Burton. You won't find that difficult. This twenty-five-year-old Welshman with the wide strong gaze is not a great actor yet. He may never be. But he has something which no actor is ever truly great without; though as yet it's a God-given gift, not fully exploited. He is, in a striking degree, *visible*. (Not, like some of our cleverest actors, nearly invisible at fifty feet.) Your eye picks him out and refuses to leave him. You can call it magnetism, but it may be less a matter of personality than of proportion, lucky inches. He's taller off the stage than he looks on, rather dwarfed by an exceptionally tall company (Redgrave for instance). But he gives an impression of solid strength, a firm-standing figure who has yet to learn to move to the best advantage – he is quite frank about how much he still has to learn – but a figure who can stand (blessedly) still, and yet hold your eye. In poetic drama where so many young leads tend to be restless, not to say waspish, this down-to-earth, sturdy calm is immensely impressive. The set of the eyes, grey and wide apart, has much to do with it too; and the set of the head and its modelling which recalls (as so much else does) the young Olivier. Also – why underrate it? – there's the sex appeal; the scene of his wooing of the French princess has great charm of the kind you can't invent. All through, though he's better in the earlier part, this sturdy, likeable young actor is a hearth on which imagination kindles and burns.

A more experienced actor would have made more of the rare opportunity to suggest the growth of the character; but Richard Burton manages an excellent continuity and consistency, and it is hardly fair to go to *Henry V* expecting tremendous bravura delivery of the famous tirades as well as that. It is here, however, that you notice how immature his speaking still is – he has a good (after all Welsh) ear, and a superb vocal range, potentially; but the half-shades are not there yet, and his delivery is still unpredictable; there are places where a hundred less-naturally-gifted actors could give him points; Shakespeare is merciless to those with an uncertain vocal technique. But he commands attention. You can hear the whole theatre listening, just as the whole theatre watches him.

As Henry V, Richard Burton falls short, measured by the highest standards and by the superlative playing of some of the cast. But he is in command of our sympathy; he has many fine moments besides the wooing scene and the prayer before Agincourt, which triumphs by sincerity, mostly. I recall specially the moment where Bardolph's name crops up and you can see this Harry thinking about the old days in Eastcheap – one of the many good touches which unite the plays in imagination. As young Prince Hal in the two Henry IV plays he is at his best; the alterations of boyish high spirits and a growing responsibility; the manner with the riff-raff of the tavern contrasting with his manner at home, face to face with his formidable father, bring the character 'into the round' in a likeable and unforced way. Above all he is good in the scene where he tries on the crown of the dying monarch – one of the greatest father-and-son scenes ever written, and extremely moving – and in the scene where he repudiates Falstaff without, somehow, losing all our sympathy.

Richard Burton would be the first to admit his debt to his colleagues and his producer, but a success for him, too, it remains. His performance is something to watch.

Picture Post, August 1951

Kabuki Players

Wonderful Kabuki players are at Sadler's Wells for a fortnight: not to be missed. We have had no Kabuki in London for seventeen years and that was only an anthology of highlights at the Royal

Opera. This is far more authentic though one must warn that the major work is a classic. It's stately as Corneille and with the laconic restraint of the seventeenth century separating those scenes of realistic, ritual and long-drawn insult of self-destruction which in Tokyo set the house in an uproar of grief, just as might a barnstormer at Drury Lane of old have sent them sobbing with the death of Shakespeare's Antony. Of course one misses the Japanese audience reaction: one of the things that surprised me most in my long visits to the Kabuki the only time I was in Japan was this tremendous response, not unlike that of children to a Punch and Judy show, Jacobeans (one imagines) to *The Duchess of Malfi* and most of all – since this is nearer the domain of opera than anything else, being continuously accompanied by drum, string, flute or percussion and wailing narration – like the enthusiasm of an Italian audience for Cav. and Pag.

It was in fact the late nineteenth-century Kabukis which most excited me, with their long-drawn and mounting hysterical tension and violence of rant and sword-play. The 'Kanadehon Chushingura', about the forty-seven Ronin who in four acts come to avenge the death thrust upon their master because of the disgrace inflicted on his wife, has comparatively few of these scenes of bridling indignation and aching despair: when they come, they are riveting. The suicide of the master, no less than the grief of the lady, were marvellously projected by Nakamura Shikan, like a sort of white-faced Alec Guinness, and by the celebrated female-impersonator Nakamura Utaemon. 'She' it was who took the part of the bereaved mother in the riverside dance play *Sumidagawa*, a Noh play originally, which gave Britten the idea of *Curlew River* and made the Kabuki repertory as late as in 1919. This piece has more simple appeal, but probably the suicide scene and the departure of the faithful friend, as done by Jitsukawa Enjaku will stay longest in memory. The house was crowded.

Films like *Throne of Blood* or *The Seven Samurai* have prepared the ground.

Guardian, June 1972

Chinese Acrobats

I could not tear myself away from these Chinese marvels (more formally The Chinese Acrobatic Theatre from Shanghai) or this would be a longer notice. But it is always the little extra detail that you would hate to have missed: the trick cyclist, pedalling his machine back to front, has already had tossed at him, and has caught on his napper, a round dozen rice-bowls, when – to finish the thing in beauty and bring tears to our eyes – he places a silver spoon on his big pedalling toe, casts it aloft, makes it spin and has it land in the topmost bowl as he streaks under its twirling fall.

Of course you've seen much of it before: at the Royal Tournament, for instance, where beefy military policemen proliferate like blooming branches of a rose tree from the stem of a single solitary toiling cyclist. But they do not do it so smilingly. Really the smile is the winning trick. The diabolo turn was wonderful, the opening lions – silky and orange – smiled too and were a match for any two-person pantomime horse of your best childish memory.

The Jolly Cooks took me back to far-off days in *The Baron Stonybroke's Kitchen* when a very-high-cheek-boned pastry-cook took three real eggs (afterwards broken to prove this) and balanced them one on the other on a drinking straw which was dancing on the bridge of his nose (a small space, actually, if I may say so without giving racial offence). One of his mates sent boomerangs round the huge auditorium and called them back like homing pigeons.

Plate spinning – you've seen it all? But not perhaps six plates in each hand on top of a mountain of light benches with a bend-over backwards to pick a rose from a bunch of flowers behind your heels? Enough said: fast, smooth, impeccable, above all smiling, with music which jangled cheerfully, threatening now and again to become the overture to *The Bartered Bride* but opting for *Chu Chin Chow* instead. The theatre was packed with smilers. Applause was almost continuous.

Guardian, June 1973

Yehudi Menuhin

A lot of water has flowed under the bridge since Yehudi Menuhin, a wonder child violinist, first entranced Albert Hall audiences playing the concertos of Elgar and Mendelssohn; a programme which brought a full house once again through streaming rain last night to acclaim a great, now no-longer-young virtuoso who has played not merely concertos most memorably but also a great role as a public animator of music and causes and idealisms.

He has changed from the seemingly-divinely-inspired child into a beneficient, wise and mature artist, practical and unfailing. The eloquence is as full as ever and in the Elgar even more affectionate, deep-toiled and impressive. I miss a certain former skimming and flawless lightness of address now in some of the rapid passage work but the 'feeling' is magnificently stirring, nostalgic and noble, a threnody, in the slow movement, for a world now fading.

The Mendelssohn had a sweet-yet-large expression in the Andante and plenty of brilliance and vigour throughout the final Allegro. The audience banked up in this huge hall was hearing the music far more surely than in far-off days when such an artist as this, or Kreisler for that matter, were only overheard rather patchily by the valiant top galleryites hanging on their railings. Acoustics are improved out of all expectation.

The conductor was David Atherton, who exerted a vital command on the New Philharmonia whose playing was firm, deft and cohesive.

Guardian, October 1974

Verdi's *Requiem*

Apocalyptic thunders shook St Paul's Cathedral last night when, to open the City of London Festival, Giulini conducted the New Philharmonia in Verdi's *Manzoni Requiem*. This (which will be repeated in another sold-out performance tonight) is one of the established wonders of our day and has been heard under the microscope (so to say) in the analytical acoustics of the Festival Hall as well as in the rolling spaces of the Albert Hall.

The first performance of all which Verdi himself conducted was in a church – that of St Mark in Milan. A long echo does not damage this mighty music in the least. Giulini seemed to have the measure of the building as an instrument to perfection. If the 'Rex tremendae majestatis' made some of us sitting near feel dizzy, the 'Sanctus' could only be called seraphic: all the choirs of heaven at once.

But it is not much use expatiating on special instances, because I feel sure that the impression given must have varied greatly from place to place in the cathedral. I can only record that sitting under the dome, within a foot of Giulini's baton arm, the effect on me was stunning, overwhelmingly powerful and affecting.

The choir sang magnificently. Orchestral detail came up sometimes, it must be said, in a way which was unexpected. But the quartet of soloists, set up on a dais behind the orchestra, rather higher than the front rows of the chorus, delivered their music with the force of the finale of the second act of *Aida*: value for money, if ever I heard it, to put it at the most secular.

Nicolai Gedda's tenor was in specially good form: his 'Hostias' was most beautifully poised, the climax of 'In parte dextra' in 'Ingemisco' full and ardent. Josephine Veasey, as she had already made plain in the 'Kyrie' launched into 'Quid sum miser tunc dicturus' with such steady vibrance of tone that we knew we were in for some special grandeur in 'Lux perpetua' (and we had it). The base Arié, a splendidly dramatic singer, was not singing quite as freely at first (in 'Mors stupebit') as one had hoped but in the later half of the work he found his form. 'Lux aeterna', so often groggy in pitch, cohered effortlessly. Gwyneth Jones was the soprano and sang with gorgeous, round, full Verdian fervour, arching up over the big phrases in the real heroic manner. Capping the great chorus plea for salvation, she outdid anything I have heard from her. The two exposed high notes were tentative. But the entry on 'Saint Michael' was perfect.

Guardian, July 1966

Britten's *War Requiem*

Celebrating its quarter-century jubilee, the Royal Festival Hall is giving twelve magnificent concerts; the first of which, most aptly – even if it may need a footnote in future histories – was a memorably beautiful performance of Britten's *War Requiem* which held the audience in awe. For a long moment at the end, it seemed unwilling to disperse with conventional applause.

But great applause was in order. Bernard Haitink, with his finest judgement, drew the very best and most eloquent playing from the LPO and LP Choir, and though not entirely seraphic, the contribution of the young people of Wandsworth School was effective.

It is extraordinary how Britten's sincerity matches with his natural sense of showmanship: how Wilfred Owen's 1914 war poems of reproof and regret blend in with the austere Latin picture of the Day of Judgement. At moments in 'Lacrimosa' and above all in the sublime closing scene in Paradise, the sound went out on great seas of emotion.

Peter Pears, one of the original singers in the first performance of the mass was in great and sympathetic voice. His singing of the poem: 'It seemed that out of battle . . .' was faultless, both as poetry and music. Galina Vishnevskaya, another early artist in this work, threw out her big soprano phrases grandly, and Thomas Hemsley the baritone carried through the sense of the poems with dignity. Altogether a great performance.

Guardian, May 1976

Early Fonteyn in *Giselle*

After a postponement last month *Giselle* was revived with great success at Sadler's Wells on Saturday. There is little new to record of this lovely old ballet save that it remains one of the most appealing in the repertory. Its keynote is simplicity. The music and *décor* are completely unsophisticated, and Coralli's choreography, apart from an occasional *tour de force*, such as Giselle's 'turns in fourth' and the *divertissement pas de deux* (splendidly danced by Mr Harold Turner and Miss Mary Honer) is, in analysis, merely a wonderfully apt assembly of comparatively simple steps. The result is enchanting, but very difficult to achieve. As in music, simplicity tests the performer highly, and it says much for the Sadler's Wells production that it brings out this essential quality most beautifully, especially in Act I.

The principal parts were allotted as before and, taken as a whole, the performance was of an excellence which these dancers have never surpassed and which is not to be met with in many other companies. The chief charm of Miss Margot Fonteyn's Giselle is precisely its simplicity. She looks the part to perfection and brings to it a gentle pathos which is really more suitable than the tragic intensity with which some ballerinas have invested it. She dances in perfect sympathy with the music and with a kind of spontaneous ease and fluidity of movement which is a far rarer quality than mere technical precision. But in that respect, too, she passed the test.

The Times, 1939

Margot Fonteyn: The Swan

The time is not yet come to speak of swan song. In *Swan Lake* last night Dame Margot Fonteyn enchanted us in the *grand adage* of the second act. Splendidly partnered by David Wall and with a conductor, Ashley Lawrence, who honours the often-abused profession of ballet conducting, she was able to use her wonderfully musical ear – always, to me, these many years her prime distinction – to give us a magical account of that swooning, archducal duo. She is much too great an artist, however, to wish me to gloss over the fact that the ensuing solo was more precarious. Balance perfect, musicianly phrasing poetic, but the flash and the incision of the footwork was not on a par with the expressive arms, the anguished face of the swan-translated princess.

In the bravura of the third act we had the character of the evil genius of the heroine, the black swan, and the drama came over strongly. I still find this act splendid 'theatre' of the sort too many so-called 'musicals' totally lack. Dame Margot did not attempt the full range of bravura: the solo went well and securely: for the finish we had a round of the stage in well-centred pirouettes, to the music of the celebrated test of the thirty-two fouettés, after which Mr Wall took over with a *rond de jambe* and Dame Margot ended the sequence with some lively *échappées*, given with such smiling assurances that they set the house in a roar. But the poetry of the part and the response to Tchaikovsky's marvellous music is what makes this Swan Queen a lesson to all cygnets. Michael Coleman, David Ashmole, and Wayne Eagling made most distinguished contributions, as did many others, especially Ann Jenner.

Guardian, November 1972

Makarova

Natalia Makarova, the Russian ballerina who 'defected to the West' in the odious phrase currently used, is not a stranger to London, but she has not before danced Giselle with the Royal Ballet and expectation was high, eyes critical, rapture cautious, but success triumphantly affirmed. She is thirty, wonderfully light, as if she had no marrow in her bones (like Alicia Markova who reset the cult of *Giselle* in this country one foggy night in Waterloo Road at the Old Vic).

I had reason to recall that predecessor in the skimming, lighter-than-air diagonal *jetés* of the moonlit hauntings. At first the unspoken thought was 'Well, she has strong competition here.' Our Royal Ballet was 'on its toes'. Dowell dancing quite magnificently, noble in style, faultless in execution, with address and rhythm to perfection. The corps in the peasant dance, the variations offered by Coleman (especially) and Jenner in the tiresomely-thickened adaptation we now use were of just such high quality (like Bergsma's Queen Sprite later on) that one tended to weigh up the ex-Soviet star rather sharply – wonderfully equipped, expressive in her shoulders and arabesque, but not strikingly neat or dazzling in beaten steps. The solo went well. What augured especially well for the second act was the evident musicality: she went along with the old sweet plaintive music to sure effect.

The Mad Scene did not touch me particularly: I think it may need a slight relaxation in timing, but others thought differently. What became intoxicatingly beautiful was the second adagio announced by the solo cello where the dancer began to drift like a sleepwalker, silent, lingering in arabesque outline, with her head inclined towards some less earthly melody.

The *pas de chat* was ease itself; more like a starling hopping on a lawn than a cat-pounce. Makarova has the small head, oval, on long shoulders that entranced Parisians in the heyday of Cleo de Mérode and she captured her audience in the wistful decline of the second act: a Giselle to remember.

Guardian, June 1972

Victor Hugo at the
Victoria and Albert Museum

Don't miss this exhibition of Victor Hugo drawings: if not the first, the best so far in this country. Perhaps, like me, you hardly knew that he channelled some of that titanic energy into pen and wash drawing of a remarkably mature and original kind, strongly stamped with his personality. The best could almost stand with Goya. Others are neo-Gothic documents from the climate of taste that, for instance, led Gautier to adapt Heine – whence sprang the ballet *Giselle*. The Gothic element is what you might well expect from the author of *Notre Dame de Paris* and *The Toilers of the Deep* (with that fight with the octopus). Faces of criminals, pompous

236

dignitaries, fatuous and cruel mouths, scenes of life's callousness which Daumier could hardly better. It is a real eye-opener on to this great man.

I knew his grandson's paintings and scenery for ballet and also learned at least one anecdote about his grandfather's virility which I hesitate from delicacy to pass on in print: but the old boy was a sexual athlete, a writer of the long distance sort to rival Balzac and also a marvellous poet, surely? André Gide's silly riposte to the question who is France's greatest poet was 'Victor Hugo, hélas' (echoed by Auden just as stupidly about Tennyson) seems to me quite unworthy criticism. But see Hugo's imaginary landscapes, castles on the Rhine (fantasies), unloved brother-in-law strutting or Strewelpeter-like amorous men proposing to beaky, elderly widows: and you may get a fresh insight into the poetry too.

Guardian, March 1974

REFLECTIONS

Suit Yourself

The Five Pound Look was nearly the title of Barrie's famous curtain-raiser, but it will serve exactly here. It's about my five pound suit. *Arma virum que cano* but dress and the man I cannot. I am a shocking dresser and do not mind admitting it. Clothes were always a low priority with me (feeling perhaps that if you have height, and can manage your head in a dignified way, spectators do not reproach you too much).

In my childhood of the 1914 war anyway it was a fashion to look a bit unEdwardian, slightly rumpled and patriotically shabby, what with our brave boys up to their knees in Flanders mud. Then, in the late twenties and thirties, it was the slump and clearly a dresser was ostentatious; Oxford bags, with the thirty-inch bottoms (i.e. bottoms of the trousers) were the only permitted luxury. Fancy dress was allowed, just: I mean an ancient riding habit ('redingote') with Leander tie.

But clothes as such never much interested me. Gramophone records, foreign travel (save up for trip to Vienna), food but no drink came first. Silly old cheap clothes came second or third.

I was last year having a pre-lunch one with a certain Clifford, a sports editor of an ailing Sunday newspaper, who dresses seven times worse than I, and we opened a paper and saw an advert for One Million SUITS at five pounds each. SHOPERTUNITIES, I read. Why, I pass that place every morning on the way to the office. 'Why not go in tomorrow?' he said.

I did. Downstairs in the basement a hundred Jamaican busmen were ripping the suits off the hangers. But I, joining in, had the edge of them. The five-pound suits were listed by *Continental measures* and unless you've ever bought a Swiss raincoat, as I often have, you don't know your Continental size. Rather big Jamaican busmen were trying on suits too small: in every way.

I got mine and had it packed in a big paper container and took it proudly down to Fleet Street. 'Look,' I said, 'only *five pounds* and that beautiful lining and those pockets and those solidly sewed buttons.'

My friends looked, markedly coldly, and said 'But it's yellow.' Too true. But yellow with a fine chocolate stripe, after all. Yet I felt the love for my bargain beginning to ebb. How can people be so unkind?

I felt it a burden heavier and heavier as I lugged it back home. There I examined it with care and insight and, though the buttons and seams and lining were indeed as I knew very splendid, the actual material of this garment seemed doubtful.

It seemed to me that if I wore it out in the rain it might suddenly disintegrate like the sort of cheap suit that Harold Lloyd used to wear but also, that if I wore it at a garden party on a *hot* day, it would almost certainly bring me out in a rash. The suit did not seem to be made of what, in my youth, would be called 'material'. It seemed as I caressed it, to be made of some kind of finely-ground camel dung rinsed and starched in a light animal glue.

I have worn it now and again in the bathroom (like the late Charles Morgan who was not allowed, to his chagrin, to wear his Academie Française uniform in the town at home). But I have never ventured out in it and it hangs there, a continual reproach.

Guardian, July 1975

Enough of water

A brush with the elements; how character-forming! Pitting yourself against the forces of nature educated you better than Latin genders, or so thought the intimidating but noble educationalist,

Kurt Hahn, though, being a German, he thought you must do Latin as well.

I was never his pupil, only once his breakfast guest, when I was so alarmed that I managed to get marmalade up my right sleeve – inside I mean – which I am at pains to avoid on calmer mornings, though it does happen, even so. But the idea that walking uphill against the wind could teach you more about life, yourself and your role in the universe was a novel one, or so it struck me at the time. It now recurs with frequency.

Nemesis, the cruellest goddess in the pantheon, may have been reading me the other week, as I drooled on about the joys of sea bathing. It contained a hint of my addiction to hydrophilia, channelled, I believe by a sojourn in late adolescence in a German health spa, Bad Nauheim, where one was lowered into teak tanks of mineral water so powerful it was said it could rob you of consciousness if you lingered beyond eight minutes (a huge Hun came back on the dot and hauled you out, weak as an infant). Whether it did what Americans call my 'condition' any good I don't know, but I learned a lot of imperfect German slang, saw the Graf Zeppelin sail over the Kurhaus, and grew increasingly familiar with selections from *Der Freischütz* by a band conducted by one Willy, to whom I looked up in awe.

Anyway, whatever gods had a hand in it, I certainly had a brush with water last week when a nimbus cloud burst over the intellectual casbah in North-west London where I live, and I came home late to the sound of gentle lapping and the eerie tap of chairs knocking awash against walls of the basement dining-room. For this I confess I did not have recourse to more water as a consolation. 'Enough of water hast thou poor Ophelia.' I quoted Laertes and called it a day. An insurance man I knew, who did not die by water either, once said: 'Water does more damage and quicker than any fire,' adding 'to property, I mean'. He may have been right.

In the heyday of the drip-dry revolution when we bought shirts of thin rubber and washed them in the hand basin, I had just embarked on this exercise in the bathroom on the top floor when the phone rang and a long operatic argument ensued during which

I was faintly aware of clouds of steam passing me in my bedroom. When I returned to the bathroom, the shirt with the malignity of inanimate things had ballooned itself into the runaway pipe, and the floor was inches deep in hot water.

Mopping frantically, I achieved some sort of control, then wondered: would it have gone through? Raced trouserless downstairs (it was 8.30 a.m.), rushed into the L-shaped drawing-room, looked up like Harold Lloyd, just in time to receive the entire ceiling on my brow in a cloud of plaster, which penetrated every book, record or typewriter available. Out-of-work actors had to be tipped to help clear up. I couldn't find any such last week though they must exist – probably mopping their own basement flats.

Malignant inanimate things – the furniture which in the half-dark stretches out to trip you, the thread which will not pass through the eye of the needle like that Biblical camel, the aforementioned marmalade, and I can hardly speak of it, the new typewriter ribbon to be inserted – I begin to think these enemies are ganging up on me progressively. Or am I simply growing clumsier, with loss of power?

Do you remember how you first realized you'd have to wear glasses, aged forty-eight: it was when even by propping the phone book on the mantelpiece and walking backwards you still couldn't tell a nine from a nothing. One's eye muscles age, but I do believe the printing was better in the 'old days'. A lesson to be learned somewhere in that.

Guardian, August 1975

Lamp Blight

The lamp still burns. A fine phrase but wait a moment. It is emptier than you think. The lamp is a street light outside my bedroom window. I am therefore, as good journalists say, 'in an almost unique position' to report on this public servant for which you and I pay that it may lighten our darkness and scare off the footpads.

Very bright and obliging of it. But for many weeks, indeed months now, I have noticed that it starts eagerly to shine around midday, beams all through the autumn afternoon and goes out for good just as the last flush of sunset dies in the West.

As a matter of fact I do not much mind about this on a selfish and emotional level. The beam it used to cast on my ceiling by night needed careful positioning of the curtains, always anxious for an excuse to escape from their pelmets and bring down a rod of iron on my poor head. But rationally the sight of that lamp glowing away all through the day and darkening counsel by night irks me and I make periodic attempts to ring up what looks like a hopeful number to complain.

The number is engaged, is unobtainable, the operator appealed to at the local exchange says she will check and ring me back and does so just as I have stepped into the bath to say the line is no longer in service. I shrug like a comic French caricature. Life is too short. I have lived too long. Let us think of higher things. But every time I go out of the front door the silly symbol gripes me. A symbol of a whole hateful revolt of initially helpful robots set to frustrate and foil us.

Consider the twin lifts in a building I and my colleagues have cause to know well. Do these heavenly machines work complementarily? They do not. Just when one or other of them is wanted and has been summoned on the ground floor they embark in unison on an upward course, each stopping at each floor to usher in non-existent passengers. Their conduct is a stupidity which in a mule would lead to instant banishment, possibly to being put down. Surely the liftman was a good thing: not a job, I think, to lose a man his self-respect. Down with stultifying automation is my cry.

It is the same in the bathroom (euphemism which caused apoplexy in Gilbert Harding who heard a tot at a gymkhana say that her pony had gone to the bathroom right in front of the mayor); when I first came to the house we had a Victorian contraption, an iron tank pressed up against the ceiling and a trusty chain was hauled on and down came gallons of water.

Later we had a novelty installed, made of fragile Bakelite, with a silly little handle protruding; it progressively grew stiffer and stiffer, until finally it refused to deliver the goods at all, and the long housebinding siege of 'waiting for the plumber' began its Wagnerian cycle.

Recently I broke (no reason they should ever be breakable) the so-called radiants in my gas fire. To one who worked for the Gas Light and Coke Co. in tender years, the amount of frustration and delay in getting replacements for these friable plaster biscuits seemed nightmarish. I began to feel like Bernard Levin's mama in a similar case. I am compassed about with a whole host of inanimate enemies; stopped watches, jammed typewriters, cantilever bottle screws which will assume almost any position save one that draws a cork. It is the wisdom of Providence that I am no motorist.

The more I think about it the more I like animate helpers, and if I give it honest thought I must consider that the one positive improvement in this field has been the descent upon my neighbourhood of Uganda Asian shopkeepers whose courtesy, charm of manner and willingness seem, as indeed they are, of another world.

Like thousands of others all over the country I have been suffering from the squeezing out of the small obliging local shop (driven out by age, rents and rates). Instead we have had dozens of tax-loss boutiques selling clothes that no one in sanity of mind could wish to buy. And as for a piece of fish, a tintack, a ball of string – you could walk miles empty-handed.

Admittedly, it wasn't always easy. I used grudgingly to patronize shops which, although open for an hour on Sunday morning, refused to sell you soap or lavatory paper on that holy day (only perishable goods). I always thought the Lord would have a sharp word to say about that. At least that's gone and to gleaming Asian smiles of welcome, I find I can buy an electric light bulb (another thing that could be made unwilling to let you down) not to mention yoghurt, liver salts and cod at eleven at night, which is just when you want them, of course.

Now, bring back Leary the Lamplighter, please.

Guardian, October 1975

Travel Gent

There have always been travellers who were unhappy. Even travellers alone, a form of progress recommended by Kipling: 'Down to Gehenna or up to the Throne, He travels the fastest who travels alone' – though he'd be hard put to it in these emancipated days. It's each for himself or herself scrambling out of the caged horror of the airport lounge into the air-conditioned nightmare of the bus with steamed-up windows.

Unhappy travellers abound. I can think of few more deserving of our prayers than the hijacked or the stateless person turned back at passport control. Yet the general idea is I believe now firmly inculcated that travelling is for *pleasure*.

Recreations, one reads in a reference book, 'music and travel'. I believe also that in these godless days one child in two would suppose that the Flight into Egypt, an unhappy journey if ever there was one, might be some kind of fly-drive-cruise-up-the-Nile package.

Yet one still sees the happy lone hitch-hiker, bed on back and guitar in hand, doing it the way we did it before 'packages' were general, and alas, with the pound a pauper's pledge, so much more economical as to be practically necessary.

I have in this connection been recalling with pleasure, from my own first days of exploratory single travel on tuppence and a rucksack, the works of one now forgotten or at least much out of date if not print. The Reverend Frank Tatchell wrote a book called *The Happy Traveller* in which he had garnered a lifetime of tips and wrinkles (met. and lit. as the dic. says) during a lifetime of wanderlust.

What his parishioners thought of him as an incumbent is hard to imagine; he must always have been away walking the earth from Interlaken to Tokyo just when they needed him to bury them. But me he delighted.

Each country had a few useful phrases in the imitated pronunciation, then a novelty now a commonplace, as when Americans are coached to order *ung vare der bo-joll-lay*. Wild generalizations about national and racial characteristics, unthinkable today when we must all pretend that everybody is exactly like everybody else. Yet often very shrewd about how not to offend your host country, as it would be called now.

Not just little things about hands in pockets or not pointing your foot at a Siamese (sorry, Thai), or touching matily the arm of such and such; which is wrongly to be interpreted. What foods to avoid. The multiple uses of potassium manganate. How red wine was wiser than white, 'which fettered the feet', so he said. How to rest quickest (strange pose).

How a light aluminium bowl with a piece of oilcloth secured across it with a rubber band made a sponge bag dispensable and could be put to a dozen services besides. Above all a hat, if only because, said the Rev., you will find that your arm's length plus your hat is the same length as your leg and so, if attacked by a mad dog in Borneo or Naples, you doff your headgear, offer it to the brute which snaps at it, exposing its throat; which then accurately and smartly you kick. And the cur slinks away.

Same with troublesome 'natives' who may mob you. Strike one of them fast with your stout umbrella (another 'must' in the panoply of this righteous traveller). Strike him hard on the collar bone. 'The others' will gather around his wailing, avers this optimist, and one can get quietly away.

Also, in hot climates before air conditioning, the coolest siesta would be naked, but with your umbrella open for decency's sake: housemaids failed in Paris, he noted, to knock before entering. He patronized hotels which had male staff when possible. Fending off beggars too is a rich vein to be mined. 'Nothing for you, worthless one' is a phrase worth learning in several languages. Rather out of date?

Many other things one has learned from other sources, Baden-Powell or John Hillaby, such as pushing lying cows aside to find a warm dry bed, going down hill (streams) *not* up when lost; and nourishing yourself with the essential candle-end or pieces of your boots well masticated like the old American ladies who believed themselves lost for ever in the catacombs of Rome and did these things, only to be rejoined by the tour which they had lagged behind, after a mere forty minutes.

Rev. Frank tells us nothing of the mystery: I mean Time in relation to the novelty and happiness or otherwise of travel. It needs J. B. Priestley to explain that.

But what is it makes one day alone on a sub-alp seem timeless as heaven whereas a week of one-night stands in a coach (*car* in French confusingly) seems an eternity, crawling through beautiful scenery invisible through misted, rain-spattered glass, humping eighty bags into forty bedrooms with the certain knowledge that the former must be repacked and stand before the door six hours later?

What I believe you *cannot* do happily is to travel in other people's time-span, only in your own. Whether it be going round China or round a picture gallery you must be the captain if not of your soul then of your Time. Tourists of the world disunite: you have nothing to lose but your trains!

Guardian, October 1975

For the Record

Ring out wild bells . . . ring out the old, ring in the new. But it is not that sort of bell; rather the burglar alarm at the furriers who have closed their shop and gone on holiday to the coast and left us with the new year's gift of a row of sleepless nights: a personal present. Others, least of all the police, seem not to notice, as if like Concorde, the Loch Ness monster and, a while back, astronauts could be endured by turning a deaf ear.

Still it alerted me to the duty of 'changing over my diary', a process leading to minor social mishaps, if one postpones it. One might risk going about without written evidence of one's size in hats or policy number, let alone failing to mark up such future delights as 'Tuesday, dental extraction' or 'Wednesday, lunch with the Creeps'. For there is much in the theory of Freudian forgetfulness, I think. Just as the body forgets its pain when it has passed, the social memory sweeps over the unwelcome assignation. Good, one thinks, I have all morning free. I will read, cook a chop, drink a sherry, which enjoying – the telephone impinges. 'Creep here, aren't you coming?' Mouth full of mutton, I lie. 'My watch must have stopped, be with you as soon as I can get a taxi.' Then we begin all over again; shrimp cocktail, the mutton taste still on the lips – ugh!

I refer to one of those little pocket books full of illegible phone numbers and not really a diary at all, more correctly described by the French, who do not seem to mind Latin words contaminating their tongue, as *un agenda*. The real diary is something I have always been too lazy to keep, except for a few weeks when on an exotic or indeed an erotic trip which it seemed worth recording for future study.

But I find on re-reading such things a time later that what I have jotted down does not spring *present* memory. It seems often like the doings of someone other than oneself, the overtones of thought of the bright, living moment of the day do not come back from a note: 'rain before lunch. V brought book.' Who was V, what book?

It may be that as with photography I have no aptitude for it – all my shots of the gorgeous East seem to me hopeless, the last two-thirds of the noble elephant, the pagoda with the top out of view. I just haven't got that kind of memory and skill and usually find my unassisted memory summons up past experience better.

All the same I wish I had been a diarist if only as one who might (intentionally or not) give pleasure to others, like the intense pleasure I myself derive from diaries kept by others, where total strangers rise like ghosts in your dreams and come vividly to life as though the grave had no dominion at all. Here is Arnold Bennett going into a haberdasher's and remarking the dejection of a salesgirl and speculating on its cause and having his day penetrated by the unexplained disturbance of sympathy.

Same with André Gide. The death of a cook's favourite, a cat, the loss of a drawer key, these things come up with a disturbing immediacy which stirs a whole new life years after their occurrence. There is a mystery about what makes a good, i.e., lastingly effective and arousing diary, quite distinct from an important or revelatory diary. And who are the almost inadvertent masters of the art: the poor dear Rev. Kilvert would for me stand higher than say Harold Nicolson or Denton Welch and far above Richard Crossman.

You might think that one who like myself has been writing for years about performers: Pavlova, Lily Morris, Billy (as opposed to Arnold) Bennett, 'almost a gentleman' was *his* subtitle, that I could summon up remembrance of such unforgettables more brightly from one's own 'fond and trivial records', yellowing notices cut and boxed. But it is not so. I can get Billy Bennett and his Chinese uncle, 'Hoo Flung Dung', exactly into focus by going through the words of his best songs, the 'dickie' (useful, fake clean shirt with tie attached) jumping out unseemly, even the sound of the boots . . .

Not just low comedians but great artists of the drama come alive in my memory without the jog of re-reading what I said about them in print. Memory is immortal it seems but is it accurate? Or do we falsify it? We live in a dangerous age when 're-recording' often seems true proof – Gielgud's post-war Hamlet re-broadcast years after *proved* just as I had first thought: incomparable. But film snippets of Pavlova . . . ? Doubt creeps in. But I suppose we vary very much in these matters. I have even met people who say that they recall nothing that happened to them before the age of ten. Whereas *I* say I can remember my christening . . . you *never*, they say. Let me go on, in error if need be. It's more fun.

Guardian, January 1976

Quaker Notes

Goethe maintained that he had a strong need to feel awe and reverence: a saying dismissed with a grin by many of us English (though not by me) as priggishly Teutonic, the attitude which leads to putting up *Verboten* signs everywhere and positively taking pleasure in being fined for walking on the grass or dropping litter, an attitude of civic obedience much derided by the Rupert Brooke generation.

But Goethe often speaks for me. I used to get the necessary dose of awe in church-going childhood and I still get it at the opera from time to time. But I find it is to news of an earthquake that my reaction of the acknowledged kind is at its very strongest and – here is the curious thing – different in kind as well as degree from my reaction to news of other disasters. African massacres or famines, Indian floods, IRA bombs in the rush hour. Not indifferent of course, much weighed down.

But the news of an earthquake somehow excites me in a, no

doubt, morbid way. Not that I have ever been in one, or only one which, like the vicar's kitchen-maid's illegitimate baby, was 'only a very-little one, your reverence'. Some time in about 1936 those in upper storeys in central London at noon felt a sudden subterranean kick. But I remember it being a 'thrill' and I have been trying to trace it back because, like the flood of controversy about Divine Retribution after Lisbon was destroyed in 1755, any shaking of the earth causes man to ponder deeply, as I suggest high tides and gales do not. Is God's hand there or not? Is it in other words – a 'quake' as the prints will call it – an 'act of God'? Crucial question.

Then I recall that I may have special conditioning in this matter. My mother who would be over a hundred now was in an earthquake in Italy as a little girl and always spoke of it with such vivacity, even gaiety that I may have been led to feel that to 'take part in' an earthquake, and (if possible) survive it, was one of life's prizes and an important part of life's rich tapestry, etc.

The family for economy and, like the Brownings, for artistic reasons lived in Italy while the father was soldiering in Madras where gentlefolk of the female sex did not usually then go. The first shock at night brought down the roof of the villa on the hated German governess and an extra bonus was to sleep next night in the garden seeing a sunset of incomparable splendour, due to particles of dust flung miles up.

The second and worse shock came at church-time, Sunday. The English Protestant colony in their tin tabernacle were being preached to from the pulpit (hands up those who have never longed for an earthquake during the sermon). My grandmother was sitting at the harmonium and this inspired matriarch immediately pulled out all stops and stopped the sermon, and any panic, with the 'Hallelujah Chorus' from *Messiah*, which brought the congregation in lusty voice to their feet. They 'raised the roof' which did not fall in on them, however. While, down the road, the Italian or Roman Catholics with their plaster saints and marble arches suffered much calamity. Whence no doubt certain conclusions were drawn!

Also there is something about the sheer unpredictability of the danger that in itself forms a strange fascination: the sudden fatality which can in no wise be averted. I like to pretend nowadays that I am losing my fear of death. But you should have me as a passenger in a car where I sit rigid with apprehension striving with clenched teeth not to issue gasps of anxiety, picturing every possible contingency from ordinary collision to homicide or spending an hour suspended upside down in a safety belt in a darkened, ploughed field.

I am a non-driver and people say I should be less nervous if I *were* driving. I won't be put or put myself to the test. One does acquire some self-knowledge eventually and I know what a road hazard I should be. I always think that what makes a critic is a sense of anticipation – in a play: 'I knew that was likely to happen'; in music: 'this chord will be resolved . . . just so'. Thus, in a car, any *potential* disaster I visualize.

Yet in the days when you could get a licence by return of post simply by asking, I did possess one and – under the contemptuous eye of the red-haired Geordie gardener-instructor, who saw how untalented I was in the matter – drove my aunt's car into the Tyne.

Guardian, February 1976

Don't look now

Long ago when parents still dared to admonish their young, 'Don't stare, dear, it's rude' was a favourite piece of advice. Last week I read that in China staring, especially at foreigners, is to be officially reprobated: rude, politically damaging, and all the rest of the priggish rigmarole. It made me reach for the poet-tramp W. H. Davies and that often quoted line:

'What is this life if, full of care, We have no time to stand and stare' (unlike wiser sheep and cows).

But it seems to me that millions of us do a great deal of staring, if not necessarily at others, fellow travellers and the like. There are all those evening hours of staring at the telly or in the coin-operated swirl of suds, where the only people I see reading while they wait are representatives of the US Marine Corps (*A life in the Launderette* rather than in Sousa's *Ocean Wave*) and they read books which consist entirely of pictures! It seems tough on the Chinese at whom I know I have often stared myself, at home or abroad.

I suppose it is all in the difference between staring with disapproval and staring with interest, with awe indeed (why not?), with love. Certainly I wouldn't want to abrogate my right to stare, or expectancy of being stared *at* – in foreign parts especially. Foreign parts? Shall I ever see those again? W. H. Davies once more: 'Sweet stay at Home, Sweet well content'. Later 'Sweet Seventeen' I see, so I mustn't nobble that for myself. Anyhow Sweet Seventeen nowadays will be bathing topless in Saint Tropez or hitch-hiking to the hippie heaven of Katmandu. More young people travel more widely than ever they did in the days of the Children's Crusade. I sometimes wonder whether it being so commonplace and easily available (analogy with music, on tap all day) they get as much out of it; whether they stare enough, marvel sufficiently indeed! The airplane which has annihilated space, and so much else, has taken a lot out of the distilling of expectation and excitement of going off abroad (or indeed at home). Ferries, night trains that bump and shudder at places with exotic station signs . . . I expect I romanticize early travels of my own.

But the truth is I seem to have lost my *Wanderlust*, once, like other lusts, so strong in me. I am reluctant to think it is just a question of years. *Lust* in German means delight – and in much I still delight having been brought up optimistically like a good Carthusian on that psalm 'juvenis fui dum senex' ('I have been young and am now old, yet never saw I the righteous forsaken or his seed begging his bread' – it was at that moment that young Pen looked up and saw the broken old Colonel Newcombe with bowed head – one of Thackeray's many cannon-shot lines which hit you between the eyes, from right off the printed page).

No it is a wisdom perhaps, a feat certainly, of not wanting to spoil things which once gave you pleasure by trying to recapture that old enjoyment; because the circumstances if not patently different will be bound to make themselves felt to be so. Can't climb the last bit! So few francs to the pound you can't even toy with the idea of that menu in the window. Renounce.

There is something in *Dante* I never like to agree with (but guess may be horridly true) about the greatest pain being memory of happiness in time of woe. I don't want to try that out by going back and not enjoying places as I did. Which is cowardly but, like much cowardice, prudent. Not laziness, surely? One likes one's own bed more and more, of course. But travel is ridiculously easy, though the Fly To the Sun propaganda has not altered much since the Imperial Airways era. 'Luncheon in Paris, dinner in Athens', etc. (to which a wag would append 'and luggage in Frankfurt').

What is missing is that spring which marks what is called a get-up-and-go person: a kind of romantic challenge to oneself. What little me . . . in Istanbul, or little me a schoolboy dining at Foyot in Paris? Well, that great restaurant is gone anyhow. I hear that even Le Sphinx has been turned into council flats. *Plus, ça change plus c'est* a bit less of a good thing. Stay home and sit and stare.

Guardian, March 1976

March wins

Sitting at Covent Garden sniffing up the sulphur and cordite of the new Henze opera and watching nursing mothers being shot down to unfamiliar music by the counter-revolutionary soldiers – we knew they were that, only fascists shot down nursing mothers – I was suddenly visited by a longing to see once more the Royal

Tournament at Earls Court. Just as many bangs, I thought, jollier uniforms, jauntier music. Tinker, tailor . . . we used to recite, counting the prune stones left on our plates – someone was even said to have swallowed one once, to avoid the fate of being a beggarman or thief.

But soldier and sailor were much preferred to tinkers (with their little tin cans) and tailors with their pins and unpaid bills. 'Myself when young did eagerly frequent the Military Tournament,' I once wrote in lyric effusion. Nothing wrong for me in martial displays. The so-called Great War was much in mind. Soldiers and sailors were our *heroes*. I had effigies of Kitchener and Jellicoe, *lares et penates* of the nursery. My sister said: 'What are you going to be when you grow up? If you're a soldier you'll be shot, if you're a sailor you'll be drowned.' I said, feeling inadequate to such aspirations, 'I want to be a missionary and have a chapel . . . for the maids.' How long ago the circumstances in which such an exchange could have occurred!

Well, times change and if still not unresponsive to military swagger, what Germans call 'prunk', at any rate till I had seen Hitler at work, I was infected by the young people's pacifism which bedevilled the early 1930s whereby to evince any kind of admiration of the Forces (as they were not called then) made you suspected of militaristic, jingoistic heresy and probably the grandson of an armaments manufacturer, that legendary ogre who was supposed to promote wars for personal profit. So my visits to the Tournament grew infrequent and furtive.

But I still liked it and it seems odd to me that a spectacle which 'sends' so many large audiences, full of children as well as Chelsea pensioners, gets so little critical acclaim in the Press. I should think I have given it a 'notice' no more than twice in forty years. It is true that like, say, Wagner's *The Ring*, it is basically much the same every year, though there are variations of course, a pipe band from – guess where – Kuwait, of course, also a special finale celebrating the Great War alluded to before and which if not as agonizingly poignant as Joan Littlewood's musical play, is still pretty stirring. As for the basics, the high drama of that gun-carriage-handling competition, memory of the South African war by all that is ironic, it still sets the heart beating and the audience cheering.

With what incomparable dash indeed apparent reckless disregard of life and limb do the competing teams of naval giants, archetypical Billy Budds in white singlets and leggings, fling themselves and the engines of death (or defence?) over the mock-up walls; and back again. You don't get that sort of thing often from watching rugger, I told myself. And could Nureyev really outdo the gymnast team leader who somersaulted twice, over a row of twenty or more profiled team-mates? These later went through flaming hoops, running dive, head first. Had they been dogs what cries of protest from . . . well I needn't name the societies I have in mind. Wonderful riding too. The Royal Horse Artillery bumping their gleaming gun carriages on a galloping collision course in figures of eight. Blues and Lifeguards, alternate, wielding lances in a kind of inspired and ordered polo chukka.

Yet as always with me, in enjoyment of spectacle, it is the music which so inexplicably and if you like vulgarly (for I am supposed to be choosey about music) gets me. The band-going-by has always and I hope always will produce in this spectator astounding physical reactions, among which lump in the throat, scalp tightening are but a few. Awkward this – in times when pacifism was strong upon you: you just had to pretend it was the Sally Army band and not the marines, who were marginally better.

But the thrill was not one to resist. The effect works for me on stage too. I don't just mean *Aida* but I have also found that I can keep a stiff upper lip through the fourth act of Chekhov's *Three Sisters* until Irina says 'They [the visiting garrison] are going away' and the band begins to play somewhere at the end of the garden. What! Tears? It must be sentimentalism; or have I somehow missed my vocation and should have spent a life doing the goose-step on some far-flung parade-ground?

Guardian, July 1976

258

Biting Wit

What do I read? 'Lady judge bites intruder.' My first reaction was a sort of Australian cry of 'good-on-her'. Not ladylike of course but good judgement no doubt; the biter bit, Redskins biting the dust, Hitler biting the carpet, curs biting the hands that feed them, even that game, set and match dream-headline for sub-editors 'Man bites dog'. But a lady judge? One must not say judgess, still less judgette. But the sex of the biter somehow really seems of the essence in this case.

A mere male judge biting an intruder might be unusual but what sort of a world are we living in if it were unthinkable as a conceit? I decided I was going to enjoy this story and would read it properly with my specs on – not that one doubted that the intrusion was by a male, 'a lady-killer' perhaps? He had bled, he had fled? Cursory glance told me that. I put the paper down on the parapet of the bridge where I had been feeding ducks. Before I had got my specs to the bridge of my nose a horsefly, with the zip of a buzz-saw, bit me on the temple (unappetizing area to choose one might think but inflicting much pain and a swift swelling).

These creatures are swift movers but I seized the newspaper and made a futile swat on its retreating flight path, a gesture of defiant self-defence which came to me instinctively (gut reaction, it is called now I think), lost the paper to the ducks, who also got the carrier bag with the bread all in one go (but lost on *them* in its plastic shroud) and provoked the fall of my specs on to concrete surface.

Touching my wound (the worst thing to do, one of nature's antihistamines like a dock or alder leaf is the thing, according to folk-medicine men) I groaned at the loss involved and tried to reassert some philosophical pabulum to this grief.

I thought I shall never know the ins and outs of that story now. Even if I go back to the newsagent and buy another copy I shan't be able to read it. Better moralize about what I did know of the incident.

And this was encouraging, as I sought a nettle by which wonderful nature plants the desired dock leaf. Nature 'red in tooth and claw' not to say sting was entitled I suppose to intrude on me in this way but, biting irony, it was I who was the injured party, not the intruder. Then the memory came of how often I had read stories about householders who had taken a poker or uncle's ceremonial sword or even a blunderbuss to some intruder (in the last instance peppering his behind as he made off down the garden path).

In such cases, puzzlingly enough to such simple, even primitive moralists as myself, a judge or magistrate will show what is known as 'understanding' but will point to the follies and risks of taking the law into one's own hands.

But where does all that lead us – to the gun lawlessness of the Far West and how on earth does it square with the 'Have a go' exhortations which were coming along not many years ago, in the matter of street muggings and bank raids. Such drew some very disapproving comments from those, and they are many, who seem to have forgotten that there are evil intruders and indeed plain enemies. Everyone is *not* 'nice' or your friend. Foes are not all spiritual or political, as anyone who went to a boarding-school as a child would have been able to tell you.

How long since citizens gave up carrying swords (which meant your lady on your left arm)? Now not even sword-sticks are allowed, yet many of us carry kitchen knives, steel combs sharpened or, in more august circles, steel-shafted brollies, and those new slim metal dispatch cases wielded by their proud owners in such a way as slice your knee-caps off in bus or train.

But these are all weapons not of *offence* but of self-defence, are they not? Perhaps that horsefly felt about it like that: that I was intruding upon a decent busy insect's air space or stinging room. It seems a very confused area as they used to say of chaotic retreats in war communiqués. But it always seems to boil down to variations on 'Who began it, then?'

A younger generation than mine is sometimes surprised to be told that twice, it was the United Kingdom (still viable term) which declared war on wicked Germany and not *vice versa*. Meanwhile it is nice to know that lady judges still have something to get their teeth into.

Guardian, August 1976

Musical Cheers

The song is ended but the melody lingers on. True enough. You and the song are gone, but the melody . . . etc., which may be true but also tiresome. The trouble really comes when, for all that lingering, you cannot recall the words. Perhaps the song's name is something like 'The Old Grey Mare'. And all day one is teased by the failure to get the, after all, not-very-important wording. By lunch time, as they say about all important cricketing news, one is beginning to do it oneself.

Thus: 'The young au pair, she ain't what she used to be' (indeed, perhaps what she ought to be, though that's another story) and, by tea time, one has graduated into thinking the words are fitting enough for a song we all used to hum in old days: 'The boy I love is up in the gallery, up in the gallery . . . etc.' For which, in the professional music hall, you needed a lively conductor in the orchestra pit, a strong soprano voice, and a small hand mirror, which was wielded on the heliograph principle.

The house lights were down, all except one beaming 'spot' which, caught in the mirror, could be turned like a searchlight probe on some lucky youth in the front row of the amphitheatre (even the grand or Family Circle) which raised a blush, if he were bashful, and much surrounding laughter. Those were the days. Talk about audience participation! They knew about it then, without ever coming off the stage and sitting on your lap in the stalls.

True, it needed a strong voice and – as C. E. Montague alleged you must not say of a principal boy – an 'outstanding personality' to bring off the trick, and I dare say the victim, which I never was, needed a thick skin for it (something I never learned to grow in the garden of my destiny). But it 'worked', which I have always thought a good qualification in the theatre or music hall.

There is so much faint-heartedness about the new entertainments. Unless the Arts Council come across, we keep reading, they can't get the audiences. What I am asking for is something one could call 'bounce'. You had to get 'rounds' in those days, said a moribund Gilbert and Sullivan player to me on one occasion, with a those-were-the-days inflection. She meant, of course, you had to 'make your number', win acclaim.

That began to fade, with the microphone and the close-up, as a special theatrical skill. On the wide screen a raised eyebrow, on the radio a dim distant vocal attack can be made as powerful as one of Edmund Kean's frantic fits on the stage of Drury Lane. Do not, in fact, over-exert yourself. Audiences don't call for it, as they say in shops where some reasonable article is not stocked because 'there is no demand, sir', or 'major' or 'governor', according to your social standing (still 'love' in Manchester, I am pleased to note, from a recent visit to that city).

Do you always demand great volume of personality and voice, was what the late Edith Evans once asked me, as shyly I stood first on one leg and then the other, waiting for some artistic jamboree to get started. After a pause – one had to try to 'time' any reply to such a marvellously space-conscious artist, of whom I stood anyhow in awe – I said feebly, 'Yes.' I spoke truth. Old-fashioned of course, but where the performing arts are concerned I think 'volume' is still a desirable attribute. Expected at least.

I find it impossible to conceive of Miss Florrie Forde singing 'O, O Antonio! Left me alone on my own-io' in a little crooning whisper blown up by a microphone (which ought to be called a megaphone, unless my Greek is rusty), or Jack Jackley in the pantomime begging us to alert him, a giant-killer, if we saw the giant actually stalk up behind him. Trumpeter sound. Shout, sergeant-major. For that matter, sing out, good Tristan or Manrico. Little voices (translation for microphones much magnified) don't affect some of us as much as the real right undoctored sound, or presence.

I'm not denying one can be fooled. When a Japanese musical-comedy troupe came to a London music hall and I first experienced the art of using a chest-microphone which apparently gave these neat little fellows stentorian voices, I was wholly deceived. So were the taxi drivers, radio cabs picking the sound up at full volume, they knew not whence. In short, 'speak natural' and sing so too, if possible, even in this age of acoustic engineering. As with real, not powdered, soup, more effort may be incurred. But the genuine article may be worth the extra trouble.

Guardian, January 1977

Prophet Honours

Open your Bible. It seems that this once general and normal piece of advice is now startling and unusual. I was tut-tutting to myself over this news: that fewer people than ever study their Good Book; when the cloud of self-deception hanging above me cleared to show that it must be ages since I myself consulted the scriptures.

I've got them on the shelf to be sure, unlike the vulgar people in some Noël Coward play who wanted the Bible to swear on, or refer to, and had to send to borrow the cook's (an easy laugh even some years ago). But it is not now my bedside book; except in those transatlantic hotels where you find a copy along with the local telephone book, a copy sometimes scored with exclamation marks or graffiti on the lusher pages of the Song of Solomon, such as 'If interested in pursuing this line, ring this number and ask for Flo.'

I confess that the fun of reading the Bible was always one very important element. Such gorgeous, even lurid and improper stories. It made the popular Sunday Press look very tame when it came to mayhem and all that. Much more fun than another doing-over of Crippen could be dredged up, succinctly written too, in the two Books of Kings.

As naughty schoolboys of nine or ten, we derived much malicious joy from asking the lady who ran the scripture class what this and that meant. She was a delicately nurtured spinster, sister-in-law of the headmaster, and had been on a watercolour sketching holiday to what was then called the Holy Land and thus qualified to expound the sacred writ. At the end, she felt bound to ask: 'Any questions?'; whereat we would pipe up: 'Miss Baker what does it mean in Kings II, Chapter Twelve' and watch her change colour.

But the stories themselves did give such pleasure: more than the Greek myths, I always said; certainly ten times more than those inferior Arabian nights which people extolled. Samuel, Daniel, Ruth and Naomi, what a cast! I shall go back to it when I've finished Trollope.

There was also the fun of the 'sortes' where you opened the Bible at random and derived advice and enlightenment from the first words you fell on. This didn't always work, until one thought hard about the message. For instance, a sentence 'And it came to pass that he girded up his loins' (which for ages I used to read as 'his lions') did not always direct one's conduct. 'Out of the mire and clay to set my foot upon the rock, and to order my going' did the trick of steeling the will to some unwelcome task much better.

Just now I fell on: 'Better a dinner of herbs where love is than much meat and strife,' a perfect excuse to boycott the scandalously overcharging butcher this weekend. But I suppose this exercise is now sublimated by the Sunday (and indeed the daily) Press, just as in the matter of mulling over juicy old murders.

The astrology feature is, I am told, very much enjoyed. Not, I confess, by me very often, though more and more people keep saying things like 'You're a Scorpio, aren't you? Well then . . .' Well then what, I ask and find I don't know. So presently I am reading: 'No time to keep yourself shut away: a day to force yourself into communication with strangers.' I don't disdain such advice by any means. But I am sceptical, since I record that on the few occasions I have been robbed or carted off to hospital, if I then take the trouble to see what the soothsayer said, I usually find some such prophecy as 'Everything works in your favour today.'

'The Ides of March are come.' 'Aye, Caesar, but not gone.' I love that exchange in Julius Caesar almost as much as the earlier 'Not in our stars, dear Brutus, but in ourselves that we are underlings.' And Barrie, who used the interlocution for the title of his best play, showing how, given a second chance, we still fail to correct our course, touches a closely-guarded sentimental spot in my heart. You can't be prophesied to, any more than you can really bow to little superstitions ('over-belief' in German).

Yet I count magpies nervously on a car journey; how many, right or left? I don't ever walk under ladders (practical, I think). Sweeps? Sailors' collars? Black cats underfoot? If I am honest, I admit to more in all this than I like.

Guardian, November 1977

Box of Tricks

Old and cold, sitting in the dark I clutch my best friend, a portable transistor, made in Japan. Deprived, on a sudden, of light to read by, right in the middle of a story headed 'Britain angry about cod', I seek the philosophy of the silver-lining kind. The lights will go up again as they did for Vera Lynn, or some songstress, at the end of the war. One knows as much. It is like the promise of eternal life which, I dare say, I don't give enough thought to. Lux eterna . . . etc. Not after all necessarily soapflakes which, alas, do not last for ever.

So I sit resignedly twiddling the tuning knob: might catch Alfred Brendel playing some Schubert. But no. Thrillingly I land instead on a French programme for those learning English by radio. It is exhilarating, invigorating: perhaps I could even use the word – my least favourite – 'hilarious'. The questions that the pupils send in! A lady in the Pas de Calais asks for an explanation about the difference between being 'cut' and 'half-cut' (she has certainly come to the right shop at this moment); also the difference between 'dying hard' and 'dying fast'. Good question, as we say. Difference between fast woman and loose woman. Difference between chatterbox and gogglebox. And is Collette's use of pugilists' English 'I box you, I marmalade you' still good colloquial speech? And what is the difference between a fuse box and a refuse box? Quite astonishing the patience of those who undertake replies. I suppose they find it fun: as I do, to a point where I get up writhing with joy and hop around, which is dangerous in the dark and not recommended.

But it is sad to hear it finish. 'Darkling, I listen'; Keats was thinking of an immortal bird song but the quote seems handy. Thus I switch, for lack of any other useful switch, to Tennyson. 'Be near me when my light is low . . . and all the wheels of being slow.' But this is maudlin (magdalene) or even tawdry (from Saint Audrey, they say). So other bits of 'In Memoriam', one of the Tennyson pieces I think I can say to myself in the dark, pop up. 'The last red leaves are whirled away, the rooks are blown about the skies.' Splendid stuff, and at least you could say it sounds up to date. Because of course it is a memorial week. All Saints, the Lord Mayor's Show, a sort of funeral procession for the past, an anniversary or two, a Festival of Remembrance for the lives sacrificed in the many wars which seem to have been our lot.

Sentimentally and avidly I think I should find myself enjoying such thoughts, such events. But this view does not prevail. I am content now, perhaps, to think that we do best to forget the dead, honouring them more by so doing. Perhaps this, like the power cut, is only a passing mood: a sort of Swinburne gesture, 'That dead men rise up never and even the weariest river winds somewhere safe to sea.' We *do* forget the dead. Instinctively – and instincts are often the best counsellors – the young reject the piety of memorializing. 'Won't even buy a poppy. I don't know,' was the reaction of one old chap I saw, failing to make a collection. In a way I had to agree with him. But was it formerly overdone? When I was a little schoolboy we were herded to the school war memorial and had a two-minutes silence after which the history master, who had aspired to being an actor before he was gassed at the Front, as we used to say, read out Laurence Binyon's lines about how they should grow not old as we would. It never seemed very relevant, though I tried to think of relatives killed in foreign parts. We enjoyed the maroons and big bangs: 'macaroons' we called them. We sang 'O God Our Help in Ages Past', omitting the penultimate verse about 'flying forgotten as a dream' which might have given offence. It was a serious occasion. One boy, who broke the Silence by blowing his nose loudly, was later caned by the headmaster.

So it goes.

Guardian, November 1977

Parsing Time

Whatever became of parsing? Next to chanting the multiplication tables and dictation, parsing occupied a lot of my class time. Dictation was the greater fun. One learned little trivial but lastingly important things. A cultured voice of a pedagogue read slowly, little items about the wisdom of winding your watch at dawn when it had had a good rest on your bed-table rather than at night when it was agitated and jerky after a strenuous day-long activity.

We wrote neatly and tried to spell correctly. Then came parsing. The exact meanings of words, their names (subject, object, active verb, correct order and something called component parts). I am sure that, like writing Latin hexameters, it did some good but perhaps left one over-sensitive. Perhaps it still goes on. Yet when I used the word to some younger people than myself, they did not know what I meant and I cast about trying to remember some character in fiction, not Dickens but possibly Countess von Arnim, author of two lovely books, *Elizabeth and her German Garden* and *The Enchanted April*, who also gave E. M. Forster a rough ride as a young family tutor: the character was described as a woman who gave the impression of 'parsing her sentences before she uttered them'.

We were also not deflected by making up doggerel remembering tricks which I found myself doing recently and usefully when the local church staged a jumble sale which I welcome as it reduces the stooks of rubbish in my room although I usually forget about taking suitable action for delivery. However, the rhyme 'humble jumble' did the trick this year and was very accurate, too, as a description.

It may sound prissy, but the vague misuse of words seems a genuine danger to us English. Not just 'stock phrases' – shocking, blasphemous, racist, fascist, and chauvinist; worn, outmoded coins – but words simply misused. We read of Vast crowds on the beaches, but on the contrary it is the sea which is vast, the beachboys merely too numerous. Fog hits trains? By no means. It is trains which hit fog, if anything.

And so on to my favourite *bête noire* which you now have to say in French. I mean the word Criticism, and, as a superannuated critic, I don't doubt I am unduly sensitive in the matter. But criticism and the verb 'criticize' are now almost exclusively used to mean censure or scold. Mrs T. criticizing Mr C. Real criticism is eighty per cent adulation, ten per cent advertising copy and the rest most cautious disapproval still less scolding or derision (the days when Bernard Shaw could describe a concert singer coming on to sing 'Ocean, thou mighty monster', 'looking as if she had already swallowed it in the green room', are gone beyond recall, more's the pity).

A 'tragedy' describes someone cut to shreds at a level crossing – which it may or may not be. A farce is a pure pejorative, as if farce was not the most difficult of all dramatic media to do well. As for 'operatic . . .' well, words fail me because I happen to think operatic experiences such as Shakespeare through the eyes and ear of Verdi and Boito excel their original exemplars. *Comic* opera, they sometimes say, meaning unparliamentary behaviour in local councils; and here I must admit there is some substance, since in such places nature does only too often copy art. But merely to damn something as operatic this old opera critic (there I go again) thinks monstrous.

In one aspect I do see that there are extenuating circumstances. Life in opera is much better timed and paced than it is in so-called real life – as anyone who has watched some ancient, moribund old dear taking an unconscionable time a-dying will have observed. Impossible to repress the thought that Verdi would have had it all over within sixty bars or even two minutes. Deaths do take a bit longer if the singer wants to linger in a cavatina of course and there are some notable reluctances to depart in Puccini and Cilea and one must allow the lack of speed which Manrico, the Trovatore, shows in dashing to lift his old mama from the blazing pyre.

But generally speaking, and at the risk of making a fool of myself, I will confess I do not find opera half as ridiculous as 'real' life and much more fun and you can go through the mangle again and again (three hundredth *Madame Butterfly* hovering now) whereas we only get one 'real' innings. Watch your adjectives boys, parse your sentences.

Guardian, June 1978

Pint of View

How one's mind ranges about. We were having this argument about milk drinking, milk snatching, etc., because a doctor had written to the Press saying that drinking a lot of cow's milk was very unhealthy and predisposed you to asthma and eczema: a bit of a suprise to me who has these nuisances anyway, but has been through life brainwashed into the idea that milk (cow's) was a salutary as well as a refreshing beverage.

One must drink something, I pointed out, not letting my other preferences gain cogent expression. Weakly I added, one can't drink water – I am a Londoner. If you live in Edinburgh you can drink water but London's gushes, evil-smelling and horrible, even if boiled to rid it of botulism, standard practice in Normandy as I remember from childhood.

You should drink small beer like Elizabethan schoolboys, said a jeering, leering friend at this point. Why not? I riposted but knew I never would: beer is small enough in all conscience without so naming it. Or what the French call *abondance*; a contemptuous name for the watered wine served to the thirsty pupils at refectory dinners in many parts of France. Italians give their babies stale crusts and red wine and they are never bilious or afflicted with wind, or so said our late Rome correspondent, Sylvia Spriggs, I recall.

Yet the old thought persists, even in Latin countries. *Elles buvaient de lait*, said a French singing teacher's daughter, to explain that her father's harsh words to his pupils were accepted as the milk of human kindness by them, because he was so handsome, and they would rather be scolded by him than ignored. 'She brought forth butter in a lordly dish,' I remembered (that wicked Old Testament murderess Jael, for her enemy Sisera). 'Come to my woman's breasts and take my milk for gall,' said that other murderess, Lady Macbeth. Milk sop, however, was not, as I recall, a term of endearment. Is it bandied about today?

But the conversation doubled back to *Elles buvaient de lait*, because one of the party refused to believe that the French ever used the term. Which sent me, as in so many of life's crises, to that wonderbook, that paragon of dictionaries, Bellow's French-English Dictionary (Eng.-French both on the same page), with all the idioms you will ever need. Where else could you learn that the French of that phrase which is constantly on my lips – 'He would have us believe that the moon is made of green cheese' – comes out in French as *Il veut nous faire prendre des vessies* (i.e. bladders) *pour des lanternes?* Long live lexicography was the contemptuous rejoinder.

Well, what of that? I get immense fun from a dictionary and even buy them when they come out, which is more than I can afford to do for other books nowadays. Partridge my love, Brewer my patron saint. Dictionary of colloquial usage, of Australian slang, of thieves' cant, American variorum (Close those drapes, Turn off those faucets, Be still and don't dare play hookey) – what poetic *trouvailles* (back to Bellow's, if you please).

They say that Maurice Baring learned a whole Russian dictionary by heart between Harwich and St Petersburg – and that in the days before air travel when you moved apace and without let or hindrance. And do you know what a 'let' is and why it is incorporated in the strange locution French letter or loudly cried at Wimbledon? Oh what a well of ignorance is still to be filled up in my mind.

And the sheer pleasure – not the word for it. I hardly like to admit to the ache of joy I felt just now as I paced down a gloomy side street near the station. A private hotel or boarding-house named Limborne had suffered so much damage from the long summer monsoon we have been experiencing that the last three letters surmounting its portals had fallen off. Limbo Mansions, it was now called, a resting place for me, thought I – 'Safe into the haven guide; a wordless, silent ecstasy provide.'

But stay . . . had the rain been to blame, or was it a proprietorial dyslexia? A card in the front window, I suddenly noted, said 'Bed and . . . fast.' Many a true word is spoken in jest, said a voice somewhere above my head.

Guardian, August 1978

Out of Phrase

The fair unknown, a candid friend though not a friend, writes: 'We never read beyond your first paragraph, even if that far. You write Latin which we do not understand or in French without any accents.' Huffy, I long to reply that if she never reads me why does she know this? All I protest is that she should not think it pharisaical showing off.

I like the sounds of things in French and I find that there are some phrases I can use with comfort which would embarrass me in English – take anything at random, say 'La voix meme du silence.' Deplorable but somehow human, like some music-hall joke which needs a droll accent – e.g. 'Let me take down your particulars.'

As for Latin, I use it out of nostalgia, largely, in the spirit in which I might go to church, even if not very believing now, in the same mood as I might go to an office party or a regimental dinner. Can the leopard change his spots? No; and being fuzzy-minded I am likely to add to that, quite otiose and pointless, the qualification 'too late now' as if *young* leopards stood a good chance of accomplishing this.

The fancy certainly leads me to say things I don't really mean, just for the fun of it. For instance the seasonal question which everyone asks, without much hope of being given a stimulating answer is 'What are you doing for Christmas?' To which I reply 'I am going to hibernate,' though I know full well that is not what I shall do. The idea appeals, none the less.

It would mean taking the phone off the hook, buying a bottle of rum, wrapping two Italian army blankets round me, and snoozing for three days. This, instead of stumbling through the rain to catch ghost-trains which don't run, over-eating with loved ones far away, or fairly loved ones perhaps, and singing Hark the Herald – which I do enjoy, as it shakes up the liver wonderfully.

But I say 'hibernate' because I love the word. Since eight years old, when I got it by guesswork. 'Construe,' said the beak. It always seemed to be the same sentence and went *At Caesar hibernavit*. What did that mean? 'Use your sense, boy.' 'Went into winter quarters,' I said, pretending I had cleverly guessed it, like a champion in the Top of the Form BBC quiz.

The one I never got was *festina lente*, confused by that most unfunny of Shakespearean clowns Feste and no doubt the season of Lent when you had to refuse sugar in tea (now I hold such lenten fare year round, if I can). I cottoned-on that it meant something like 'hasten slowly' or a sharper version of the confusing advice 'More haste, less speed' – which still irks me. How can you, I used to think, put that into practice?

This has just come up while I was ploughing through a prospectus for a reading clinic. Read faster, it said. 'In a month my capacity has risen from 290 to 550 words a minute and I am reading almost twice as many good magazines and books as before.' Much virtue in that little word 'good'.

Lionel Hale, once of this paper, could read as fast as turn the pages. So could our old editor Wadsworth, a good editor in my book (if that is the phrase), because he once said I was not to be cut – which struck me, at least, as truly wise. I understand George Bernard Shaw's annoyance at not being able to write fast, as fast as he could think or talk. But we are not all GBS.

I could be happy to type a bit faster, like a pro – journalists, even in their dotage, can often hardly type better than a thoroughly ungifted child pianist. But speed as a desideratum I can't understand in many walks of life. What shall it profit a man to fly the Atlantic in a few hours after a night unsleeping in an airport (another manifestation of seasonal goodwill) and to have two extra hours in a Canadian coffee shop as his ultimate reward?

Anyhow there is surely such a thing as your own time, your own pace, your natural speed: just as people of different heights feel that architecture is good because it is 'suitable' for *them*. Perhaps giants like canyons between skyscrapers. I am six foot one and like a wide street, with three-storeyed houses flanking me. No prospectus is going to help me to improve myself in that respect; adding a cubit, like reading 550 words a minute. '*Ombra my foot*,' as I have seen Handel's 'Largo' verbalized in print.

Guardian, December 1978

Index

INDEX

INDEX